THINKING AMERICA

Becoming Modern: New Nineteenth-Century Studies

SERIES EDITORS

Sarah Way Sherman
Department of English
University of New Hampshire

Rohan McWilliam
Anglia Ruskin University
Cambridge, England

Janet Aikins Yount
Department of English
University of New Hampshire

Janet Polasky
Department of History
University of New Hampshire

This book series maps the complexity of historical change and assesses the formation of ideas, movements, and institutions crucial to our own time by publishing books that examine the emergence of modernity in North America and Europe. Set primarily but not exclusively in the nineteenth century, the series shifts attention from modernity's twentieth-century forms to its earlier moments of uncertain and often disputed construction. Seeking books of interest to scholars on both sides of the Atlantic, it thereby encourages the expansion of nineteenth-century studies and the exploration of more global patterns of development.

For a complete list of books available in this series, see www.upne.com

THINKING AMERICA

New England Intellectuals and the
Varieties of American Identity

ANDREW TAYLOR

UNIVERSITY OF NEW HAMPSHIRE PRESS
Durham, New Hampshire

Published by University Press of New England
Hanover and London

University of New Hampshire Press
Published by University Press of New England
One Court Street, Lebanon NH 03766
www.upne.com
© 2010 University of New Hampshire
All rights reserved
Manufactured in the United States of America
Designed by Katherine B. Kimball
Typeset in Minion by Passumpsic Publishing

University Press of New England is a member of the Green Press Initiative.
The paper used in this book meets their minimum requirement for recycled paper.

For permission to reproduce any of the material in this book, contact Permissions,
University Press of New England, One Court Street, Lebanon NH 03766;
or visit www.upne.com

Library of Congress Cataloging-in-Publication Data
Taylor, Andrew, 1968–
Thinking America: New England intellectuals and the varieties
of American identity / Andrew Taylor.
p.   cm. — (Becoming modern: new nineteenth-century studies)
Includes bibliographical references and index.
ISBN 978-1-58465-862-7 (cloth: alk. paper) —
ISBN 978-1-58465-863-4 (pbk.: alk. paper)
1. American literature—New England—History and criticism. 2. Authors,
American—19th century—Political and social views. 3. New England—
Intellectual life—19th century. 4. United States—Intellectual life—19th century.
5. National characteristics, American, in literature. I. Title.
PS243.T39   2010
810.9'974—dc22   2009047983

5 4 3 2 1

CONTENTS

ACKNOWLEDGMENTS

The writing of this book has been helped by a number of people who have read portions of it, talked to me about it, or encouraged me to think about things other than it. The English Literature department at Edinburgh University represents collectively all that is good about our subject, and I continue to be grateful for its collegiality and excellent humor. I want to thank in particular Lee Spinks for our conversations on American politics and culture, Penny Fielding for her generosity of spirit, and Susan Manning for her unwavering support. Phyllis Deutsch at the University Press of New England has been an exemplary model of editorial advice and efficiency, and I'm grateful too for the support of Sarah Sherman and Rohan McWilliam, two of the Becoming Modern series editors. The book's two reviewers also provided comments and suggestions that have made this a stronger work. I would also like to acknowledge the Arts and Humanities Research Council, which granted me a sabbatical award to help complete the project.

⊰∞⊱

This book is dedicated to my wife Paula Donaghue, who means more to me than she'll ever know.

NOTE ON BRIEF TITLES

The following abbreviations are used throughout the book.

CWE Ralph Waldo Emerson, *The Complete Works of Ralph Waldo Emerson*, ed. Edward W. Emerson, 12 vols. (Boston: Houghton Mifflin, 1903–21)

EL Ralph Waldo Emerson, *The Early Lectures of Ralph Waldo Emerson*, ed. Stephen E. Whicher et al., 3 vols. (Cambridge, Mass.: Harvard University Press, 1959–72)

ET Ralph Waldo Emerson, *English Traits*, ed. Philip Nicoloff, vol. V of *The Collected Works of Ralph Waldo Emerson* (Cambridge, Mass.: Harvard University Press, 1994)

JMN Ralph Waldo Emerson, *Journals and Miscellaneous Notebooks*, ed. William H. Gilman et al., 16 vols. (Cambridge, Mass.: Harvard University Press, 1960–82)

Journal Henry David Thoreau, *The Journal of Henry David Thoreau*, ed. Bradford Torrey and Francis H. Allen, 14 vols. (Boston: Houghton Mifflin, 1906)

Letters Ralph Waldo Emerson, *The Letters of Ralph Waldo Emerson*, ed. Ralph L. Rusk et al., 8 vols. (New York: Columbia University Press, 1939–91)

LL1 Ralph Waldo Emerson, *The Later Lectures of Ralph Waldo Emerson, 1843–1871, Volume 1: 1843–1854*, ed. Ronald A. Bosco and Joel Myerson (Athens: University of Georgia Press, 2001)

LL2 Ralph Waldo Emerson, *The Later Lectures of Ralph Waldo Emerson, 1843–1871, Volume 2: 1855–1871*, ed. Ronald A. Bosco and Joel Myerson (Athens: University of Georgia Press, 2001)

PW Henry David Thoreau, *Political Writings*, ed. Nancy L. Rosenblum (Cambridge: Cambridge University Press, 1996)

W Henry David Thoreau, *A Week on the Concord and Merrimack Rivers, Walden; or Life in the Woods, The Maine Woods, Cape Cod* (New York: Library of America, 1985)

WJ1 William James, *Writings, 1878–1899* (New York: Library of America, 1992)

WJ2 William James, *Writings, 1902–1910* (New York: Library of America, 1987)

THINKING AMERICA

INTRODUCTION: THINKING
IN THE EMERSONIAN GRAIN

The constant warfare in each heart is betwixt Reason and Commodity.
—RALPH WALDO EMERSON

Intellectual man lives in perpetual victory.
—RALPH WALDO EMERSON

In a July 1861 commencement address at Tufts College in Massachusetts, Ralph
Waldo Emerson asserted a claim for the authority of the intellect in the face
of political discord and economic corruption. A mere three months after the
outbreak of the Civil War, Emerson used his speech to insist upon the centrality of the life of the mind, advising his graduating student audience to heed its
"secret of power": "Power of thought makes us men; ranks us; distributes society;
distributes the work of the world; is the prolific source of all arts, of all wealth, of
all delight, of all grandeur. Men are as they believe. Men are as they think" (*LL2*
245). With this declarative variation on the Cartesian equation, Emerson's lines
assume that the work of the mind is sovereign in its ability to structure selfhood,
society and nation: correct thinking leads to successful forms of construction.
"Celebration of Intellect," as the speech was titled by the first editor of Emerson's
collected works, is a text ripe with discursive tensions; its progression by argument, qualification and counter-argument is characteristic of an Emersonian
aesthetic that I discuss more fully in chapters 1 and 2. For now, it is enough to

point out that these tensions play along a series of fault lines that are central to the preoccupations of this book and of the writers I choose to explore here. If Emerson hymns the restorative virtues of the intellect, he is also concerned to assess the institutional frameworks in which intellectual work might take place — in this instance, the college or university. The college, he asserts, "is imperatively needed. This is just its time. It is the ark in which the law is deposited." A sacred space, furnished with knowledge "from the divine oracle" (*LL2* 242), it is also "part of the community," built into the social fabric as "the most radiating and public of agencies" (*LL2* 241). Yet without casting doubt on the quality of education offered at Tufts, a few paragraphs later Emerson is critical of the role that colleges play in the nurturing of the intellect, with his comments focused precisely on the degree to which such institutions are compromised by their surroundings:

> Colleges are tests, or they are not colleges. 'Tis because the college was false to its trust, because the scholars did not learn and teach, because they were traders and left their altars, and libraries, and worship of truth, and played the sycophant to presidents, and generals, and members of congress, and gave degrees and literary and social honors to those whom they ought to have put in fear; — then the college is suicidal; ceases to be a school; power oozes out of it just as fast as truth does; and instead of overawing the strong, and upholding the good, it is a hospital for decayed tutors, a musty shop of old books in Rotten Row. (*LL2* 242)

Emerson's construction here of a sacred mission tarnished by exposure to the corruptions of the economic and political market imagines an ideal and, as we'll see, a powerfully seductive intellectual space of retreat; the benefits of autonomy are firmly set against the dangers that accompany immersion in the inevitably fraught contingencies of the actual, where "in the class called intellectual, the men are no better than the uninstructed" (*LL2* 245). When thought becomes reduced to a matter of trade or of political partisanship, the institutions charged with protecting it lose their legitimacy, degenerating instead, in Emerson's powerful image, to hospices for the intellectually moribund. Quite daringly then, given the context of the speech, Emerson raises the difficult question of the suitability of structures for productive intellectual work. Under what conditions does the life of the mind most thrive? Moreover, is it possible to imagine a situation in which thought can remain unencumbered by networks of allegiance (institutional, national, or ideological), positively alienated from forces of containment? The "warfare" that Emerson notes "betwixt Reason and Commodity" neatly expresses the problem of reconciling the apparently incommensurate demands of the Kantian space of pure thought and the economy of the everyday.

To assert intellectual autonomy is to claim a position of cultural authority *against* that very same culture. Talking to the students at Tufts, he invests them with a holy mission; they are "a band of priests of intellect and knowledge" (*LL2* 244) with the potential to effect purposive change. Yet those blessed with legitimacy of this kind are few, an elect who possess the faculty of thought that can best serve as guide and exemplar to the masses: "The whole battle is fought in a few heads. A little finer order, a larger angle of vision, commands centuries of facts, and millions of thoughtless people. It reverses all rank" (*LL2* 245). A revolution in hierarchy is promised in these words, where the standard criteria of classification (wealth, political power, social status) are negated by the superior discriminations of an intellectual class. Both more precise (a "finer order") and more expansive (a "larger angle"), Emerson's "band of priests" evinces clearer sight—a sense so central to his writing—and an authority that masters the "thoughtless" masses. Paul Bové, in a discussion of the intellectual as genealogist, focuses on Friedrich Nietzsche's sense of his own difference as being the factor that authorized his intellectual project. Driven by opposition to established conditions (a stance that Nietzsche calls a "scruple peculiar to me"), Nietzsche describes being "so much in conflict with my environment, age, precedents, and descent that I might almost have the right to call it my '*a priori*.'"[1] This sense of the inevitability of dissent, of an intellectual's outsider position as constituting his or her inheritance, is a powerful image of self-fashioning for the cultural critic, a type who is born out of a revolt against the given—the social, the familial, the national. Yet as Bové reminds us, and as this book also considers, the status of consciously alienated intellectuals is dependent upon the socially mandated role that such figures play: "It is . . . important to realize," he suggests, "that the oppositional work done by the genealogists is itself possible only because a well-made tradition of authorized figures representing the legitimacy, importance, and attractiveness of such work exists."[2] A variation on this paradox was expressed by Randall Jarrell, who noted that in the United States the authorization accorded to the intellectual was present at the very inception of the nation. "Franklin and Jefferson and Adams were men who respected, who laboured to understand, and who made their own additions to, science and philosophy and education, the things of the mind and of the spirit." Although Jarrell judges that not one of these founding luminaries would have approved of the label "intellectual," nevertheless, the belief that they embodied what "it is natural and laudable for all men to aspire to" constituted a model of enlightened behavior that "seemed un-American" to oppose.[3] The inauguration of such a nationally sanctioned conception of the place of thinking within a wider culture and polity might suggest that the intellectual is merely a product of the social forces that legitimate his visibility. And indeed it is the case that for many of the figures discussed in these pages the tension between the impulses of opposition and compromise, individualism and institutionalization, and antisocial critique and social containment structures the shape of their writing and influences the kinds of thinking they are able to perform. Pierre Bourdieu's definition of intellectuals as "bidimensional beings," occupying spaces of autonomy and transcendence on the one hand, and thoroughly implicated in social discourses and the possibilities of public action on the other, is a helpful way of encapsulating the different geometries that intellectual work takes.[4] Bourdieu locates intellectuals as "a dominated fraction of the dominant class. They are dominant, in so far as they hold the power and privileges conferred by the possession of cultural capital . . . but writers and artists are dominated in their relations with those who hold political and economic power."[5] This somewhat precarious position — situated within the dominant field but on the margins of it, retaining cultural status but always potentially compromised by structures of social enforcement — might be thought of as representing the central dilemma for the production of intellectual work, as we will see in the pages that follow.

Thinking America is a book about the location and responsibilities of a specific strand of American intellectual life — focused in and around New England — in the nineteenth and early twentieth centuries. Its regional dimensions are deliberate, and acknowledge, in part, the role assigned to New England, and especially Boston, in the creation of an American intellectual class. In May 1861, one month after the outbreak of a civil war that would perilously endanger the prospects of national unity, Emerson would declare in a lecture: "I do not speak with any fondness, but the language of coldest history, when I say that Boston commands attention as the town which was appointed in the destiny of nations to lead the civilization of North America" (*CWE 12* 188). That New England represented metonymically a repository of fine and defining American values too important to disown has become a (literary) historical commonplace. As the birthplace of American philosophical and literary transcendentalism, New England has imagined itself as being at the vanguard of exceptionalist expressions of cultural and national independence. Paul Giles has argued that the "championing of writers such as Emerson and Thoreau" has enforced a sense of their "sacralization of their native country, and their projection of a natural affinity between an empathetic, subjective self and the wider circumference of their individual worlds."[6] Giles is rightly suspicious of what he calls an "Emersonian rhetoric of idealism" (63), and his work has been instrumental in repositioning American studies within more transnational frameworks that challenge the priority and exclusiveness of such native discourses. While not wishing to dissent from the view that there is indeed a strong strand in New England transcendentalist writing that underwrites a politics of exceptionalism, I'm concerned here to think about the ways in which figures such as Emerson, Thoreau, and Margaret Fuller inevitably find their attempts to think nationally traversed by forces of difference or comparison that unsettle such bounded configurations. As much as this book considers how the expression of thought comes to signify as cultural capital in New England—thinking as practice and as occupation—it also sets out to discuss the often complex intersection of cultural critique with the national imaginary.

As a term with a complex history—and I touch on its genealogy in chapter 1—the notion of the "intellectual" has consistently been bound to issues of expertise and authority. In his book *Legislators and Interpreters*, Zygmunt Bauman traces this idea back to the Enlightenment notion of the *philosophe*, a figure with access to knowledge and with the responsibility to use that understanding for the purpose of addressing social or cultural concerns. However, the intellectual in Bauman's configuration is never allowed the luxury of a disembodied vantage point from which his or her circumscribed materiality might be overcome. Instead Bauman is quick to locate the category "within the structure of the larger society as a 'spot,' a 'territory' within such a structure; a territory inhabited by a shifting population, and open to invasions, conquests and legal claims as all ordinary territories are."[7] This is a particularly useful formulation for the kinds of exchange—physical and discursive—that preoccupy the writers I examine here. Bauman imagines the intellect as a geographical space that is permeable to the incursions of extra-territorial influence, whereby its claims for autonomous distinction may be compromised by the demands of the "larger society" that surrounds it. Even the intellectual who feels most at home within the expansive territory of the nation, Bauman implies, is always vulnerable to the transformative infiltration of "foreign" discourse—forms of intellectual contestation or conquest that have the potential to result in radical unsettling or "deterritorialization," to cite Deleuze and Guattari's useful term.[8] Set against the figure of the "expert" or the "professional," Bauman establishes the ideal credentials of the intellectual who, even if prone to the disruptions and contingencies of context, represents the class of what he calls "'thinkers as such,' persons living for and by ideas untarnished by any preoccupation bound by function or interest," those whose impact and significance lie beyond the coterie world of specialization and who are thus able to speak "in the name of Reason and universal moral principles."[9] The intellectual, then, enters the public sphere to exploit the legitimacy that specialization might give but then speaks on a topic for which that expertise does not, in itself, offer a sufficient vocabulary.

While Bauman's definition may seem to suggest a seductive Kantianism, he is clear that this ideal of unfettered thought is always, and inevitably, placed under pressure as structures of knowledge organize and institutionalize themselves. As the chapters in this book demonstrate, such institutionalization—and the resistances to it—can take multiple forms. Central to my concerns is the way in which the articulation of a national imaginary presents the writers I address here with a series of problems and comparative frameworks. If intellectual man does, indeed, exist in a state of perpetual victory, as Emerson would have it, the struggles by which that condition can be attained are mapped out in all their hesitancies, assertions, and retractions in the pages that follow. Stefan Collini, in his magisterial history of the emergence of a British intellectual class in the twentieth century, has noted that "the question of the 'foreignness' of intellectuals" might be said to represent a constitutive aspect of the term.[10] Indeed, the significance of the Dreyfus Affair in the inauguration of the word, as I discuss in chapter 1, represents the confluence of contested national affiliation and the emergence of a specifically denominated thinking class. Bourdieu's account of the development of the French "intellectual field" during the Third Republic notes the significance of a moment of semi-autonomy, when the intellectual legitimacy offered to literary professionals was more likely to be derived from their peers rather than from the changeable political opinions of a wider (and implicitly less discerning) constituency. He locates the birth of this intellectual autonomy at the end of the nineteenth century, as the moment where scholars, poets, and writers felt able to exert, through aesthetic forms, claims for public relevance "in the name of norms belonging to the literary field."[11] One of the claims of *Thinking America* is to resituate Bourdieu's fin-de-siècle analysis both geographically and temporally: temporally, by exploring the ways in which what Ross Posnock has called the "presumption of a privileged sensibility"[12] determined the contours of intellectual culture in the United States from the earlier time of Ralph Waldo Emerson; and geographically, by situating certain examples of that sensibility in the context of transnational circulation and encounter, thereby interrogating the bounded security of the nation-state and those who would claim to speak on its behalf. "Foreignness" as state of estrangement, or as a condition of dissent, characterizes the experiences of intellectual engagement described in this book. For some figures, foreignness is a geographical reality that organizes the discursive shape of their writing. Emerson's visit to England, Fuller's account of the failed Italian Revolution, and George Santayana's self-willed permanent exile from America for the last forty years of his life, all represent possibilities for cultural work through comparative analysis that has the potential to disrupt taxonomies of knowledge that are structured around ideas of national consent. For Thoreau, the problem of affiliation would hinge exactly on this term "consent" and his felt sense of alienation from the institutionalizing forces of the body politic on the eve of the Civil War. Institutionalization of a different kind preoccupied William James at the end of the nineteenth century, where the status and viability of the university as the location for intellectual work caused him to reflect on the rapidly pluralizing nature of American culture and the direction that the country needed to take in order to align transnational hybridity with national common purpose.

Thinking America begins with Emerson's famous 1837 declaration of intellectual independence, "The American Scholar," and concludes with a discussion of Santayana, whose novel *The Last Puritan* (1935) has as its central character a figure whose death, in a post-Armistice Day accident, might be said to mark the failure of a certain kind of philosophical, Emersonian exceptionalism. The apparent optimism of "The American Scholar," in the vanguard of what, since F. O. Matthiessen, has been termed the "American Renaissance," is fatally undermined in Santayana's text, which has striven for more than seven hundred pages to find a way of reconciling modes of intellectual activity with the demands of social expectation. Emerson is central to my book for a number of reasons. He provides many of the conceptual frameworks and premises that the chapters explore and test, acting as a provocation to all of the other writers I consider here, either as an intellectual model to be emulated (although not slavishly so, as we'll see in the cases of Thoreau and Fuller), or as a problematic precursor whose modes of thought seem unsuited to the changed conditions of an advancing American modernity (James and Santayana both display aspects of this skepticism). Furthermore, Emerson's status *as* a public intellectual (perhaps America's first) has recently attracted serious critical attention. Both Lawrence Buell and Peter S. Field, in their respective accounts of his development, make the case for Emerson's status within the U.S. public sphere as, what Buell calls, "a diagnostician of the challenges of doing socially significant intellectual work in the face of social pressure and attendant self-division."[13] This characterization pays due attention to the ways in which Emerson's work has been read for its aversion to constricting frameworks of occupation, class, and nation. In particular, Buell is keen to rescue Emerson from the exceptionalist paradigm that, for much of the twentieth century, dominated the terms by and through which he was interpreted. In distinct contrast to his own earlier work (in books such as *Literary Transcendentalism* [1973] and *New England Literary Culture* [1986]), Buell's most recent revisioning presents the reader with a figure thoroughly enmeshed in the transnational flows of the modern world: Emerson is "a national icon who at the same time anticipates the globalizing age in which we increasingly live" (3), able to "thrust beyond local, provincial, national contexts toward a mode of expression that could speak across borders of place and time" (156). This, then, is an explicitly cosmopolitan configuration of the New England sage, and Buell's reading offers itself as a provocative reminder of the international contexts in which models of national self-definition occur. I address this idea most substantially in chapter 3, where Margaret Fuller's deliberately dialogic and comparative approach to intellectual work generates a cosmopolitanism that culminates in her readings of the Italian Risorgimento.

If Buell's account of Emerson seeks to internationalize conventional readings of the shape and scope of American Romanticism, Peter S. Field's book *Ralph Waldo Emerson: The Making of a Democratic Intellectual* places its subject more firmly within the religious and cultural debates of antebellum America. Field's intellectual is distinctly—and radically—national. Emerson is situated "squarely in the political and social environment that impinged on a Harvard-educated, Unitarian-trained New England minister in the early American republic, with the central concerns of his life stemming from his unique attempt to right himself with his times and with a growing nation beyond the parochial confines of Boston and Cambridge."[14] Field's sense of the parochial is more narrowly defined than we find in Buell—here, regionalism needs to be overcome to enable the emergence of Emerson's national significance; Buell's Emerson is impeded by our inability to expand beyond the parameters of an exceptionalist national imaginary that restricts his (Emerson's) global reach. Both books make seductive claims for the political and intellectual relevance of their subject, yet both accounts run the risk of forcing significances that lift Emerson out of the specific material conditions of his time. To argue for Emerson's transhistorical applicability (his "own concern," Buell writes, "was with values that stand the test of time and unite the world")[15] tends to neglect the often intellectually productive tensions between this ideal and the very tangible constraints in which he worked and which, indeed, he often embraced. Likewise, Field's concern is to present a radicalized Emerson, a figure purged of "the reflexive conservatism of Brahmin Boston" following his father's death in 1811: "The intimacy engendered by financial hardships combined with social ostracism seemed to foster at least in Ralph an elemental distrust of the Brahmin elite as well as an affinity with the millions of women and men who toiled mightily to eke out a living."[16] "Social ostracism," though, rather overplays the situation here, and in his desire to claim a figure who was unwilling to be bound by class or regional affiliations, Field underestimates the degree to which Emerson remained inevitably interpellated by the values of his social scene and caste. Certainly, Emerson was often keen to reject his father's world: in a letter to his brother William, he expresses his

embarrassment over a request he has received for a biographical sketch of his father, judging William Senior's literary relics to be a palid mirror of his age, "that
early ignorant & transitional *Month-of-March*, in our New England culture"
(*Letters 4* 179). Yet as a number of studies have shown, the Unitarianism of his
father's generation was instrumental in constructing possibilities of intellectual
life — of personal and collective development — that Emerson would then go on
to revise and redefine.[17] William Ellery Channing's version of self-improvement,
"Self-Culture" (originally the title of a lecture on Benjamin Franklin delivered in
Boston in 1838), laid out a program of moral and intellectual growth that encouraged Americans not only to examine their consciences, in the manner demanded
of Puritan self-critique, but also to realize that "We have a still nobler power, that
of acting on, determining, and forming ourselves."[18] Self-reliance of this kind
had already generated within Unitarian culture expressions of both anxiety and
encouragement over the forms of conduct to be expected from the nation's men
of letters. Joseph Buckminster, another clergyman who, along with Emerson's father, was instrumental in establishing the Boston Athenaeum, addressed the Phi
Beta Kappa Society at Harvard in 1809 on "The Dangers and Duties of the Men of
Letters," anticipating Emerson's own more famous "American Scholar" speech to
the same august body. Buckminster called for the development of an intellectual
elite, neither tarnished by "the minutiae of local politicks" nor indulging in "the
luxurious leisure of study."[19] The address negotiates the problems of thought and
action, acceptance and resistance, and co-optation and independence, warning
against the "diffusion of information widely and thinly spread, which serves to
content us, rather than to make us ambitious of more" (100). "We have yet to
form," he concludes, "systems of more effectual instruction, and to assign the
departments of literary labour, where exertion shall be encouraged by suitable
rewards" (101). While Buckminster's vision of intellectual activity is more firmly
grounded than Emerson's in a Unitarian ethics of practicality, his concern here
to imagine possible scenarios of "instruction" chimes, as we'll see in the Coda to
this book, with the Concord writer's complex pedagogics.

   Emerson's radicalism is always circumscribed by forms of limitation that
work to inaugurate a dialectic of expansion and contraction, of (using Emerson's
own polarities) freedom and fate, that refuses to synthesize. As Richard Deming
has described it, "In its crisscross structure, this perpetual dichotomy is indeed
a kind of grammatical balance and remains unresolved in that it shuttles back
and forth between its two halves, each perpetually responding to the other."[20]
Such a delicately poised tension, in which what is at stake is the possibility of
language being able to bring provisional coherence to chaos, lies at the heart of
Emerson's epistemological project and, as I suggest, offers a resonant geometry

within which it is possible to situate intellectual work more generally. Emerson's attempt "to right himself with his times" (to quote Field's phrase once more) usefully describes a situation in which nonconformity is always simultaneously compromised by imbrication. "What is the hardest task in the world?" Emerson asks in "Intellect," and his answer is unequivocal:

> To think. I would put myself in the attitude to look in the eye an abstract truth, and I cannot. I blench and withdraw on this side and on that . . . We all but apprehend, we dimly forbode the truth. We say I will walk abroad, and the truth will take form and clearness to me. We go forth, but cannot find it. It seems as if we needed only the stillness and composed attitude of the library to seize the thought. But we come in, and are as far from it as at first (*CWE* 2: 331–32).

To think about thinking, then, is also to consider the locations and contexts in which intellectual work might be possible and, for Emerson at least, to recognize the fleeting and provisional nature of successful thought. "The role of intellectual duty," for Emerson, is joined with a "moral duty" (*CWE* 2: 341) that requires us to be aware of the ways in which the tools of thinking — language systems — might both generate emancipatory potentialities and be deployed in the service of what he condemns elsewhere as "conformity and consistency" ("Self-Reliance," *CWE* 2: 60).

Chapter 1 focuses on exactly this oscillation between intellectual containment and self-fashioning in Emerson's work, especially as it comes to be articulated through the organizing rubric of transatlantic comparison. His appeal to a transcendent realm of pure thought is a familiar discursive maneuver. In an address at Dartmouth College in 1863, for example, Emerson celebrates "The Scholar" as one who "is too good for the world, is in advance of his race, his function is prophetic. He belongs to a superior society and is born one or two centuries too early for the rough and sensual population into which he is thrown" (*LL2* 304–5). In chapter 1, I explore how such a model of intellectual activity remains an influential paradigm for how and where the production of thought takes place, with Edward Said cited as a twentieth-century example where a vision of transcendent intellect is offered as essential for genuine thinking. Aligning Emerson with this model, as his own writing at times encourages us to do, has nevertheless produced a reading of the Concord seer that, I argue, streamlines the complexity of his ideas into a seductive, but misleading vision of American exceptionalism. More productive is to pursue the knotty instabilities of his style by regarding his prose as contrapuntally structured (to adopt a different paradigm from Said). Acknowledging semantic and discursive oscillations ensures that the reader is alive to the processual nature of Emerson's thought; its refusal to settle into ideological coherence is essential to the work of the intellect. In *English Traits*, Emerson's most substantial piece of cultural criticism, I suggest that contrapuntal reading reveals the shifting contours of Emerson's engagement with national traditions. Acutely aware of, and at times happy to exploit, transatlantic difference as it orchestrates itself around familiar contours of innocence and experience, *English Traits* nevertheless stops short of endorsing New World superiority. Indeed, it evinces a skeptical regard for national affiliation of all kinds, so that the book's implicitly comparative framework is allowed to retain its unresolved tensions, a quality endemic to Emerson's work, and one that ensures, for him, the continued vitality of thought itself. Skeptical thinking continually appealed to Emerson (Montaigne in *Representative Men* is praised as its exemplary practitioner), for it resists the impulse to codify and to generalize too soon. If the thinker "prematurely conclude," Emerson notes in his journal in 1845, "his conclusion will be shattered, & he will become malignant. But he must limit himself with the anticipation of law in the mutations, — flowing law" (*JMN* 9: 295).

This is a version of "double consciousness," later so influential a term for W. E. B. Du Bois, which structures Emerson's thought and prevents it from solidifying into conformity. As Anita Haya Patterson, among others, has noted, Emerson would also inflect the concept of double consciousness with the vocabulary of race in ways that further work to destabilize epistemological certainty. In "Fate," a lecture that would become the first chapter of *The Conduct of Life* (1860), he maps the twin impulses of the public and private self, of fate and freedom, in the precarious construction of national identity:

> One key, one solution to the mysteries of human conditions, one solution to the old knots of fate, freedom, and foreknowledge, exists; the propounding, namely, of the double consciousness. A man must ride alternately on the horses of his private and public nature, as the equestrians in the circus throw themselves nimbly from horse to horse, or plant one foot on the back of one and the other foot on the back of the other. . . . To offset the drag of temperament and race, which pulls down, learn this lesson, namely, that by the cunning co-presence of two elements, which is throughout nature, whatever lames or paralyzes you draw in with it the divinity, in some form, to repay. (*CWE* 6: 47–48)

The bifurcated self, attempting to maintain equilibrium between the possibilities of individual volition and the demands of race in the construction of identity, expresses what Patterson describes as "the creative tension between voluntary and involuntary aspects of political obligation."[21] Such "mutually effacing discourses on national identity" (160) generate a vision of citizenship that, for

Patterson, influences the development of the more explicitly racial politics of Du Bois, whose advocacy of both rights-based and racialized discourses (Emerson's freedom and fate), in a deliberate structure of contradiction, prevents either model from becoming reductively limited. Du Bois is, of course, one of Emerson's key interlocutors. For instance, his notion of "The Talented Tenth," an elite black "aristocracy of talent and character" providing leadership for African Americans, draws upon the Concord writer's various articulations of intellectual representation.[22] Du Bois will reappear in this book in chapter 4, where the question of what *shape* the nation should take, in the face of increasing demographic heterogeneity, comes to preoccupy William James, Du Bois's teacher at Harvard, and where the provisionality of pragmatism is tested against the necessities of containment. But in exploring these dialectical rhythms between law and flow, limit and mutation, this opening chapter brings to focus many of the polarities—and the shifting positions between them—that might be said to constitute the coordinates within which intellectual work locates itself. In the case of Emerson, the seductive possibilities of exceptionalism were always tempered by an alternative awareness that such a cultural politics could easily ossify into rigidity and thoughtlessness. Moreover, our awareness of Emerson's belief in unfettered intellectual work as powerful and transformative—"The world stands on thoughts, and not on iron nor on cotton," he declared in an address in 1863 (*LL2* 307)—also needs to recognize the manifold ways in which he was inevitably tied to highly class-bound and gendered institutions and frameworks within which his ideas could be articulated. Even "Emersonianism," as I suggest at the end of the chapter, becomes a straitjacket for the unwary reader who believes that an identifiable, paraphrasable philosophy is encapsulated by that term. Henry James Senior, father of the novelist, was more acute than perhaps he realized when he lamented that Emerson was a "man without a handle."[23]

Chapter 2 examines a central dilemma for the intellectual, namely the relationship between thought and action. The incendiary example of John Brown's response to slavery as a problem of national self-definition hinges, for Henry David Thoreau, on the ethical question of whether contemplation can be a sufficient enough stance in the face of explicit injustice. This chapter addresses what we might call "an anxiety of usefulness" tangible in Thoreau's reading of Brown, where the sense of language's failure to articulate an adequate response to rising secessionist tensions forces him to question the kinds of public utterance that are compatible with political activism. Ralph Waldo Emerson's account of Brown asserts a seamless continuity between thought and action, a continuity with which, of course, Emerson himself was never entirely comfortable, yet one that he was happy to project onto his subject, "an idealist" who "believed in his ideas to that extent that he existed to put them all into action; he said 'he did not believe in moral suasion, he believed in putting the thing through'" (*CWE* 11: 270). For Emerson and, as I discuss in the chapter, for Thoreau, John Brown becomes posthumously invested with the qualities of an ideal thinker, able to resist the empty rhetoric of conventional political discourse and to translate words into action in a form that is antinomian in its effectiveness. Translation as a rhetorical and political act is important to my argument, and I read Thoreau's depiction of Brown alongside Stanley Cavell's influential account of the ways in which thought at its highest pitch can enact a transfiguration (his word) that is self-estranging and thereby potentially emancipatory. Translating Brown into a resurrected New World Oliver Cromwell allows Thoreau to fantasize about a politics of enactment that scorns all forms of conventional structuring. However, as I seek to demonstrate, such a vision of radical masculine alienation is difficult for Thoreau to sustain, and his writing oscillates between evaluating Brown as exceptional (a figure of foreignness within the American body politic) and as representative (fit to be imitated by right-thinking citizens). The case of John Brown crystallizes for us transcendentalism's nervous uncertainty about the value of practical power, and where the limits of that power should be drawn.

John Brown performs a masculinist fusion of thought and action that, even for a sympathizer like Thoreau, raises the problematic relationship that the intellectual has to other forms of political expression that might themselves entail violence. Brown is both an instance of idealized action *and* the embodiment of its dangerous excess. In its discussion of Margaret Fuller, chapter 3 relocates the question of what constitutes intellectual work to different geographical and gendered terrains. In a lecture given in the nation's capital in 1895, the reformer and feminist Caroline Dall proposed a literary history of transcendentalism that runs counter to those in which Emerson is the dominant figure. Instead, her account begins with Anne Hutchinson's colonial antinomianism and closes with Fuller's death in 1850, two episodes that mark, she argues, the life-span of transcendentalism as a movement.[24] While not discounting Emerson's significance, he is clearly placed as one figure among many in Dall's desire to imagine a more woman-centered intellectual narrative. (Indeed her books such as *Historical Pictures Retouched* [1860] and *The College, the Market, and the Court; or, Woman's Relation to Education, Labor, and Law* [1867] represent a counternarrative to male-dominated intellectual history.) Her lecture is important less for its narrative of New England thought than for its deliberate restructuring of that thought's gendered biases. Placing Fuller as transcendentalism's culmination grants her a retrospective centrality that, as my chapter explores, she found difficult to acquire during her lifetime. The characterization of Hutchinson as antinomian places her in a tradition of American radicalism that also includes John Brown, albeit his is a more forceful incarnation. Fuller's model of intellectual engagement, though, is more usefully understood as being differently configured, and I go on to suggest the ways in which she imagines thought as the articulation of conversation, a practice that could be carried out across historical and geographical distances. Her perspective is explicitly cosmopolitan, a contested term, as my chapter acknowledges, but one that understands Fuller's consideration of American identity and its social structures from a comparative position, loosened from, if not altogether rid of, those expressions of autonomy that structure the rhetoric of New World romanticism. This is especially the case in her writing from the unsuccessful Italian Revolution of 1848–49, where the cause of republican politics generates a series of considerations about the political state of Fuller's own nation. As I describe in the chapter, her theory of culture and of reading necessitates multiple viewpoints of sympathetic attachment, whereby inhabiting a position on the borders of conventional modes of belonging enables an excavation of the languages of presence and self-evidence that dominate the structures of American exceptionalism. Fuller's is not an unaffiliated intellectual stance; she fully acknowledges her debt to Emerson, for example, and her own writing is not immune from the models of discourse already circulating in the culture. Yet she exhibits a conception of the United States that is more positively transnational than is to be found in either Emerson or Thoreau, bringing to her work an awareness of the systems of circulation that structure political and literary exchange in ways that do not expunge the nation as a category of inquiry, but rather place it within a framework of translation and potential transfiguration.

The complexities of an increasingly heterogeneous social space, in which America's contact with the globe at the end of the nineteenth century was visible on the streets of its major cities, is one of the preoccupations of William James and George Santayana, the subjects of my final two chapters. Both men were conscious of the changing status of intellectual work in an increasingly professionalized public sphere, in which the demands of institutional legitimacy and commercial success had fatally undermined the effectiveness of the unaffiliated man of letters. In 1893 William Dean Howells wrote "The Man of Letters as a Man of Business," lamenting the postbellum condition of the intellectual who is saturated by the requirements and imperatives of the market. There is an obvious irony here, given Howells's own status within the business of literary culture, yet his essay despairs of a situation in which even Emerson and Longfellow, writers from an earlier age, "submitted to the conditions which none can escape;

but that does not justify the conditions, which are nonetheless the conditions of hucksters because they are imposed upon poets."[25]

However, for Brander Matthews, among the most influential American literary and cultural critics at the turn of the century, and professor of dramatic literature at Columbia University, the emergence of a professional class of thinkers was to be celebrated. He suspects that the literary intellectual is "an impractical theorist," unfit for the responsibilities of public political office: "The fervid rhetorician who wrote the Declaration of Independence and the historian of the "Winning of the West" [Brander's close friend Theodore Roosevelt] are the only men of letters who have ever risen to the Presidency; and their interest in politics is acuter than their interest in authorship."[26] Literary men, he felt, "are wont to balloon themselves up into a rarefied atmosphere where the ordinary man cannot breathe" (529). Fortunately, conditions of colonization necessitated the cultivation of general and practical skills, and with the onset of a developing society, a "division of labor had to appear. Specialization of function is the mark of advancing civilization" (534). Emerging out of this is the category of the "expert" able to communicate his or her specialism to an uninitiated audience, and Matthews looks forward to the day when the divide between intellect and practice is no more: "it is incumbent on the 'literary fellows' and the College Professors, on the theorists and the experts, so to control their utterances and so to direct their energies that the plain people will have no excuse for resuming again the suspicious attitude of bygone days" (538).

William James's relationship to structures of intellectual affiliation, and the kinds of professionalization that they encourage, was profoundly ambivalent, and one of the ambitions of chapter 4 is to explore his sense of where, and under what conditions, the business of thought might best take place. For both James and Santayana, Harvard University provided a space in which their ideas could be articulated. James recognized the desirability of this kind of institutional housing, yet was worried about the ways in which the academicization of thinking might curtail its more ambitious and daring possibilities. The character of a Harvard scholar, formed by a pedagogy that celebrated a dilettantish approach to learning, was increasingly overtaken toward the end of the century by a model of education that emphasized the systematic organization of knowledge into specialities and discrete language protocols. Despite Matthews's optimism, the development of *expertise* as a mark of scholarly legitimacy could work against a model of intellectual activity that was structured around conversation, encounter and enthusiasm.[27] It is this tension in James's writing between an Emersonian expansiveness and a pragmatic recognition of structure that interests me. In an address in 1903 to mark the centenary of Emerson's birth, James declared: "What gave a flavour so matchless to Emerson's individuality was, even more than his rich mental gifts, their combination. Rarely had a man so known the limits of his genius or so unfailingly kept within them . . . The faultless tact with which he kept his safe limits while he so dauntlessly asserted himself within them is an example fitted to give heart to other theorists and artists the world over" (*WJ2* 1119, 1121). James is keen to contain the exuberant individualisms of Emerson's brand of romantic thought within the contours of a framework that gives that thought shape and legitimacy, and which prevents it from spilling over into disconnected shards of knowledge that fail to cohere. This insistence on Emerson's awareness of his own "limits" points to James's own inclination to marry flexibility of thought with the securities of structure, something that finds, perhaps, its clearest articulation in his notion of the pluralistic universe as both a model of philosophical inquiry and, as I argue, a way of conceiving and containing social heterogeneity within the body politic. In the same way that Harvard might, ideally, come to represent the containment of vibrant intellectual plurality within a meaningful institutional space, so the nation itself might need to locate diversity, and all its attendant benefits, within clearly defined limits of social organization. James's use of the phrase "atomistic constitution" encapsulates this doubleness perfectly.

George Santayana was less patient with Harvard University than James, resigning from his position in the philosophy department in 1911 and, indeed, leaving the United States for good a year later. His 1894 essay, "The Spirit and Ideals of Harvard University" regrets the decline of an intellectual community in which ideas (and ideals) are imparted from teacher to student. The professionalization of the academy was less about pedagogy, he thought, than the maintenance of a discipline: "There are times when light and inspiration come to him [the university academic] in the process of sifting and communicating his knowledge, times when he takes a natural delight in expressing his ideas . . . But, generally speaking, he wishes to be a scholar, and is a teacher only by accident."[28] The introduction of an elective system at Harvard in 1869 had removed required courses and opened the university up to a wider demographic than the bourgeois Bostonian elite who had historically supplied it with students. Course offerings expanded, and the result was a shift in the balance away from the Arnoldian liberal arts tradition that had, up until that point, structured transatlantic university education. These pedagogical changes transformed the concept of a coherent student body into something more disparate and specialized. As one historian of education has described it, "Whereas earlier undergraduates had moved as a class through daily recitations, under the elective system each student maintained a separate schedule of courses, and no two students had the same programme."[29]

In "The Spirit and Ideals of Harvard University" Santayana had written that "It is impossible to have any affection or loyalty for such an aggregation, however excellent the instruction supplied to its constituent parts," with the university lamentably transformed into a "very large machine serving the needs of a very complex civilization."[30] The idea of "aggregation" is one which, as I suggest in the book's final chapter, signals Santayana's preoccupation with conjoining a reading of America's political structure with a keen sense of the kind of *aesthetic* form that such a structure should visibly take. How might politics be beautiful? What kinds of aesthetic criteria need to be in place for a citizen to generate an affective response to social space? If "aggregation" suggests indiscriminate disconnection, other geometries of social belonging need to be imagined. In his 1871 text, *Democratic Vistas*, Walt Whitman had identified what he called "the new esthetics of our future" as the foundational principle of American society.[31] An aesthetic sense, he writes, had been "the main support of European chivalry, . . . forming its osseous structure, holding it together for hundreds, thousands of years, preserving its flesh and bloom, giving it form, decision, rounding it out" (933). Thus, it was incumbent upon the United States to inaugurate a cultural order that could be similarly bound — in the case of America by an aesthetics of democracy. Whitman remained a key figure for Santayana, and although, as I demonstrate, his attitude toward the poet would fluctuate over a long writing career, Santayana's reading of him remained fixated on the problem of articulating an authentic aesthetic in which social experience could be embodied.

Santayana looked at the United States from a vantage point of cosmopolitan detachment. After 1912 this stance was, of course, a biographical fact, but his disposition even before his self-willed European exile had always been one of resistance to the reigning orthodoxies of the national imaginary. In the final volume of his autobiography, *My Host the World* (1953), he would write of being

> a foreigner where I was educated; and although the new language and customs interested me and gave me no serious trouble, yet speculatively and emotionally, especially in regard to religion, the world around me was utterly undigestible . . . And as the feeling of being a stranger and an exile by nature as well as by accident grew upon me in time, it came to be almost a point of pride; some people may have thought it an affectation. It was not that; I have always admired the normal child of his age and country. My case was humanly unfortunate and involved many defects; yet it opened to me another vocation, not better (I admit no absolute standards) but more speculative, freer, juster, and for me happier.[32]

Of the writers that *Thinking America* addresses, Santayana exhibits the strongest sense of disconnection from the American national imaginary. While, as I point out, his is a reading of the United States that is not without nuance—he recognizes the energy of its modernity, for example, even as he finds himself unable to live within it—he is ultimately unable either to share in the patriotic triumphs or to lament the failed ideals of its history. Santayana's sober assessment of a country thinking itself into capitalist hegemony and imperial adventure suggests the exhaustion of Emerson's flexible, contrapuntal intellectual project. As an "inquisitor of structures," his exile from the United States enacts an interrogation of some of its most cherished values, uncompromised by the requirements of political action or social reform. It is a privileged position indeed, but, as this book explores, one that generates a conversation about the purpose and the usefulness of intellectual activity.

1

AFFILIATION AND ALIENATION

There goes in the world a notion that the scholar should be a recluse,
a valetudinarian — as unfit for any handiwork or public labor as a
penknife for an axe. The so-called "practical men" sneer at speculative
men, as if, because they speculate or *see*, they could do nothing.
—RALPH WALDO EMERSON

Ralph Waldo Emerson's taxonomy of the American Scholar, in his speech of
that name delivered at Harvard University in August 1837, performs many
of the tensions and competing impulses that continue to characterize the nature
of intellectual work. In the passage cited above, Emerson addresses the assumption that the life of the mind depends upon seclusion, that an intellectual is
defined by his (and for Emerson, the scholar *is* a gendered role) impracticality,
fit only for speculation and vision. Composed during the Panic of 1837, which
saw the failure of the U.S. banking system and record levels of unemployment,
the speech is fully aware of the vicissitudes of the marketplace and hopes for
an alternative to it. The opening paragraph aspires to a time "when the slug-
gard intellect of this continent will look from under its iron lids and fill the
postponed expectation of the world with something better than the exertions
of mechanical skill" (*CWE* 1: 81). The instrumental nature of capitalist culture,
in which roles and functions are distributed with rigid precision, has an impact
upon the scholar, society's "delegated intellect": "In the right state he is *Man*

Thinking. In the degenerate state, when the victim of society, he tends to become a mere thinker, or still worse, the parrot of other men's thinking" (*CWE* 1: 84). Yet, Emerson worries about the implications for the scholar of full withdrawal from the material concerns of the everyday. In a gendered economy, such a figure ran the risk, Emerson thought, of being emasculated within a culture whose capitalist ethos was rapidly categorizing as distinct and incompatible the spheres of thinking and doing. The "clergy," Emerson worried, "are addressed as women" (*CWE* 1: 94). To counter such an image of the intellectual as an effete character type, Emerson anatomized three "main influences" (*CWE* 1: 84) upon which the scholar could draw—"nature," "books," and "action." It is the final one of these, and its significance for the intellectual, that I want to focus on here. In "The Transcendentalist" (1842) Emerson argues that the privileges of private reflection must be converted into public utterance to counter what he regarded as the crude instrumentality of professional reformers:

> The good, the illuminated, sit apart from the rest, censuring their dullness and vices, as if they thought that by sitting very grand in their chairs, the very brokers, attorneys, and congressmen would see the error of their ways, and flock to them. But the good and wise must learn to act, and carry salvation to the combatants and demagogues in the dusty arena below. (*CWE* 1: 348)

The comforts of Olympian detachment are here deemed insufficient if private thoughts are ever to be enacted, and if the partisan rabble-rousing of philanthropy is to be countered by what Emerson regards as more considered intervention; and in a lecture first delivered the year before he suggests that "we are not permitted to stand as spectators of the pageant which the times exhibit; we are parties also, and have a responsibility which is not to be declined." Once again concerned to assert a legitimacy that is couched in gendered terms, Emerson continues: "A little while this interval of wonder and comparison is permitted us, but to the end that we shall play a manly part" ("Lecture on the Times," *CWE* 1: 266).

In "The American Scholar" the meditation on "action" is characteristically vague: "Action is with the scholar subordinate, but it is essential. Without it he is not yet man" (*CWE* 1: 94). It is both less important than the other qualities and at the same time foundational for any kind of (gendered) self-definition. In what form "action" manifests itself is equally opaque. Emerson offers one version: "The preamble of thought, the transition through which it passes from the unconscious to the conscious, is action" (*CWE* 1: 94–95). "Preamble" is a curious choice of word, suggesting something introductory or preliminary, "action" as something in advance of thought. And "action" itself here is, moreover, a certain *kind* of thought, crystallized within the "conscious" mind. "Action," then, is the catalyst for something else (perhaps further thought?) rather than the result of a thought's intervention: it is "the raw material of which the intellect moulds her splendid products" (*CWE* 1: 95–96). The "attractions [of the world] are the keys which unlock my thoughts and make me acquainted with myself," writes Emerson, in a formulation that indicates both relationship and solipsism: the impulse is one of engagement (to "take my place in the ring to suffer and to work" [*CWE* 1: 95]) so as best to "manufacture" (*CWE* 1: 96) "eloquence and wisdom" (*CWE* 1: 95). In an alternative economy of the intellect, "action" embodies an encounter with the raw material of society to produce Emerson's ideal character type.[1]

The oscillation between interaction and self-culture is, of course, problematic for those who expect or require tangible social engagement in the mould of William Lloyd Garrison or Paulina Wright Davis; the portrayal of the intellectual as dilettante recluse is never entirely banished from the Emerson persona. Indeed, Rob Wilson reads "The American Scholar" as foundational in its authorizing and instituting an intellectual tradition of "symbolic writing all too abstracted from the conflicts and engagements of social history." In a damning assessment, he argues that "Emerson remains the representative man, ironically, of our political diminishment, the originary moment (so to speak) where poetry begets its transcendental and even *gnostic* irrelevance in American society."[2] Recalling Herbert Marcuse's condemnation of an "affirmative culture" ("a world essentially different from the factual world of the daily struggle for existence, yet realizable by every individual for himself 'from within', without any transformation of the state of fact"),[3] Wilson's intellectual as absent, abstracted seer is a prevalent model, as this book shows. Yet his characterization of Emerson's political redundancy semantically streamlines a text—and indeed a writing career—that all too visibly displays its shifting contours. The difficulty that "The American Scholar" exhibits in this regard runs throughout Emerson's work, and presents a major challenge to his readers. Emerson's prose often drives toward a transcendent position alienated from historical and social contingencies (in "The Poet," for example, he valorizes this exceptional figure's ability to perceive the "divine aura" that runs through "the circuit of things" [*CWE* 3: 26]). Yet such an impulse is also countered, or qualified, by an equally powerful strand that *does* pay attention to the relationship between intellectual work and tangible circumstance, between the impact of thought on action (and *vice versa*). At the very outset of his essay on William Shakespeare in *Representative Men*, for instance, Emerson chooses to deny the romantic authority conventionally attached to notions of originality. Instead artistic power is derived from immersion in the daily forms of social and material culture:

The greatest genius is the most indebted man. A poet is no rattle-brain, saying what comes uppermost, and, because he says every thing, saying at last something good; but a heart in unison with his time and country. . . . [H]e finds himself in the river of the thoughts and events, forced onward by the ideas and necessities of his contemporaries. (*CWE* 4: 189–90)

In this instance intellectual work is not situated in a transcendent realm of purified being, but takes place amid, and is influenced by, the everyday. The authority of authorship is thus dependent upon a collective effort of material endeavor, in which the poet both participates and derives benefit: "The world has brought him thus far on his way. The human race has gone out before him, sunk the hills, filled the hollows and bridged the rivers. Men, nations, poets, artisans, women, all have worked for him, and he enters into their labours" (*CWE* 4: 190–91). Intellectual production is linked here with the work of national landscaping: tangible action and creativity are explicitly allied, to the extent that, as Paul Jay has astutely noted, poems are "like hills levelled, hollows filled, bridges built by social labor with practical ends in sight."[4] Moreover, the products of intellectual work are themselves planted with traces of earlier work. "Thus all originality is relative," Emerson asserts, "Every thinker is retrospective" (*CWE* 4: 198) — a phrase that contrasts starkly with the oft-quoted lament that comprises the first sentence of 1836's *Nature* that "Our age is retrospective."[5]

The irreducible ambivalence that structures Emerson's writing ensures that any attempt at taxonomic security is riven with alternatives, qualifications, and counterarguments. As Stanley Cavell has noted, "Contradiction, the countering of diction, is the genesis of his writing."[6] The Emerson of "The American Scholar" is keen to promote intellectual activity in the face of disparaging opinions as to its worth, but his fuzzy notion of what that activity might be, and where outside the mind it might be enacted, cannot quite banish an image of cerebral detachment and purity. The essay proposes that the figure of the intellectual should be active in the world of politics and social engagement without offering the reader a clear indication of how this might happen. Allied to this tension, and fundamental to most discussions of the intellectual, are the accompanying parameters of autonomy and institutionalization, of exile and embeddedness. What do we expect intellectuals to do? And in what contexts are they most effective?

In a series of questions posed in his book *Criticism and Social Change*, Frank Lentricchia asked what it might mean to be an academic. "Do we feel at all times," he wondered, "*as* teachers and as writers, involved in the real thing, or are we continually choking down suspicions that what we do, and where we are, is not in the real world? . . . Can a literary intellectual . . . do radical work *as a* literary intellectual?"[7] *Criticism and Social Change* is concerned with the shifting cultural significance of the university, of intellectuals, and of literary pedagogues more generally, a debate that, as I suggest in the pages that follow, first emerges in the United States in second half of the nineteenth century. Lentricchia deplores the alienation and apoliticism he sees in contemporary theory, which, he argues, celebrates ironic disengagement and fosters a form of disabling quietism: "We have let our beliefs and our discourse be invaded by the eviscerating notion that politics is something that somehow goes on somewhere else, in the 'outside' world" (7). His book establishes a polemical opposition between critical paradigms that exhibit a responsibility to the wider culture and those that promote textual self-referentiality in the mode of high deconstruction, a praxis that "has no positive content, no alternative textual work to offer to intellectuals" (51). Lentricchia's strong preference, then, is for the expansiveness of the former, rather than the perceived dead-end interiority of the latter. It is not my intention here to question this opposition, although the reading of an apolitical deconstruction appears increasingly hard to support in the context of, for example, Derrida's late work on responsibility, justice, and the ethics of cosmopolitanism. I am more concerned in this chapter, and in the next, with exploring the ways in which the *radicalism* of Emerson's intellectual work (assuming that we expect our intellectuals to be radical) is resistant to the kind of reductive pragmatics of effect and result that Lentricchia so valorizes here.

Richard Poirier has established an influential reading of Emerson that locates his intellectual currency in terms of linguistic self-consciousness. For Poirier, Emerson reveals that "[t]he proper activity envisioned from 'intellectuals' is therefore essentially a poetic one. It is to make sure that language is kept in a state of continuous troping, turning, transforming, transfiguring, even to the point of transparency."[8] While not underestimating the degree to which Emerson's writing evinces exactly this kind of suppleness (indeed this chapter will go on to address aspects of it), I want to consider the ways in which his intellectual work attaches such deconstructive virtuosity *avant la lettre* to tangible sociopolitical concerns. Poirier's claim for language's ability to attain transparency as an ultimate sign of its flexibility is contentious. It suggests that language can transfigure itself out of existence, becoming so mobile that it no longer rests recognizably attached to its signified. While admiring his acute feel for the slipperiness of Emerson's textual world, I would want to pull back from the end-point that Poirier envisages here. Emerson's challenge as a writer is to marry a deep skepticism about the settled quality of words to an impulse to define and diagnose. The effect of this, more often than not, is the production of a text that is riddled with tensions and competing impulses, one that seems to work in a dialectical fashion without the reassurances of a culminating Hegelian synthesis. The "real world," to remind us again of Frank Lentricchia's phrase, located in a text such as Emerson's 1856 book *English Traits* reflects a mind grappling with a transatlantic framework and a postcolonial anxiety. Such a configuration sits uneasily with an Emerson read simply as the avatar of an enclosed U.S. exceptionalism. "All nationality soon becomes babyish," he notes in a journal entry of 1862: "The question between egotisms can never be settled. England makes Greenwich the first meridian; France, Paris: America, Washington. Who shall decide on the world's part against these private interests?" (*JMN* 15: 248). Such skepticism about the claims for national distinctiveness have led one critic recently to argue that Emerson's affiliation should be regarded as "*American* only in caricature," for his intellectual concerns are more geographically and historically wide-ranging than the standard paradigm of cultural nationalism suggests.[9]

Writing in 1831 to his brothers Charles and Edward, both of whom were working in Puerto Rico at the time, Emerson's sense of the necessary doubleness of cultural positioning is apparent:

> The great misfortune of travelers is that the expectation & the eye gradually form themselves to the new scene—in the West Indies they become West Indians in a few days—so that they cannot if they would tell the New Englander of this moment what he wants to know. You shd. keep one eye a patriot & the other an emigrant at the same time as the seaman keeps home-time with one watch & *apparent* with the other. So put on paper, Charles, instanter your early impressions, the first contrasts & surprises however slight & shortlived. (*Letters* 1: 338)

Characteristic of Emerson here, of course, is the focus on vision as the means by which modes of cognitive possibility are realized. The "great misfortune" of which he warns his brothers is the loss of indigenous sight; the danger for the traveler lies in a process of seductive reverse colonization, by which native New England traits are assimilated into the spectacle afforded by the exoticized foreign space. The implications for communication back home are profound, Emerson asserts, for travel writing becomes unable to impart to its consumer (i.e., Emerson himself) "what he wants to know." The possibility of narrative success is endangered by the fully acclimatized eye. For readers all too familiar with Emerson's "transparent eye-ball" in *Nature*, and its capacity to cast an elucidating look over an entire field of vision, the concern here with effective seeing is unsurprising. But unlike that strange later image of paradoxically imperious and self-negating sight ("I am nothing; I see all"), this 1831 passage recommends a form of deliberate double consciousness, quite different from the tormenting bifurcation he would later characterize as the fate of the intelligent sensibility.

Whereas in the 1843 essay "The Transcendentalist" (first given as lecture the year before), the pull of competing impulses between "the understanding" and "the soul," one "all buzz and din," the other, "all infinitude and paradise," resulted in a "double consciousness" that was irreconcilable and arduous (*CWE* 1: 353), the recommendation to Emerson's brother Charles that he achieves binocular sight suggests a different, less traumatized form of dialectical thinking. While in the particular instance of Puerto Rico Emerson may seem to privilege a New England perspective as the necessary conduit through which communication is possible, more radically his words infer the potential benefit of divided vision for *any* act of interpretation, including those performed on home soil by native eyes. Double consciousness in this sense becomes the means by which comforting or seductive epistemological structures are put under interpretative pressure, a confrontation that results, of course, in the characteristically unsettled nature of Emerson's prose.

This chapter explores some of the stylistic and ideological tensions that are integral to Emerson's work as they are made manifest in *English Traits* (1856), his most extensive piece of comparative cultural criticism. Acts of comparison balancing the merits (or otherwise) of two or more vistas of interpretation call for exactly that kind of doubleness of perspective toward which Emerson had gestured in the letter to his brothers. In *English Traits* the comparison is often implicit, formed by the knowledge that we, as readers, bring to the text of Emerson's institutional authority as the voice of cultural nationalism. In an important sense, one version of the Emersonian dialectic is established through the encounter between an Emerson who admires much in the Old World and our awareness of an Emerson who hymned America as "the home of man" (*CWE* 1: 391). Within the text itself, as we will see, these kinds of competing positions jostle for the reader's attention, producing a book that at once invokes taxonomies of national distinctiveness (both British and American) and undermines them as viable categories. Institutionally enshrined as an advocate of New World potential, yet temporarily (and voluntarily) exiled to the Old, Emerson writes a travel book that reflects on the polarities of belonging and distance, of affiliation and reflection, which are at the heart of his work. As the next section suggests, this is a tension that also resonates within theorizations of the role of the intellectual as a cultural phenomenon.

Translating Transcendence

The term "intellectual" as a signifier of conscious social labeling, post-dates Emerson. The word has only recently celebrated its centenary, emerging in 1898 during the political controversy of the Dreyfus Affair (1894–99) during which the Dreyfusards identified themselves as voices ranged against the virulent anti-semitism of French nationalists, who in turn dismissed them as *les Intellectuels*. As Pierre Bourdieu has noted, this episode represented a defining moment for intellectuals as the first time they intervened politically *as* intellectuals, with a legitimacy derived from the realm of letters. The novelist Emile Zola and his fellow Dreyfusards exhibited "a specific authority grounded on their belonging to the relatively autonomous world of art, science, and literature and on all the values that are associated with this autonomy—virtue, disinterestedness, competence, and so on."[10] I will be returning to this idea of the "relatively autonomous" a little later. But it was William James, a supporter of Dreyfus, who in 1907 transplanted "intellectual" into American popular vocabulary as a label of self-identification. Turning the original defamation on its head, James embraced the word as a marker of moral and critical distinction. In "The Social Value of the College Bred," an address to the American Alumni Association, he declared: "We ought to have our own class-consciousness. 'Les intellectuels!' What prouder club-name could there be than this one, used ironically by the party . . . of every stupid prejudice and passion, during the anti-Dreyfus craze, to satirize the men in France who still retained some critical sense and judgement" (*WJ*2 1246). Recognizing its foreignness (James retains the French spelling), he nevertheless advocates the term's naturalization within the United States as a noun around which might congregate types of intellectual or cultural distinction. As Ross Posnock has noted in his account of the development of a black intellectual tradition in the United States, in 1898, the intellectual was one who dared to step outside of occupational or disciplinary boxes to pronounce on political matters.[11] Ray Nichols characterizes the noun as "a Janus term"; *les Intellectuels* faced "both toward the study and toward the street."[12] For the anti-Dreyfusards, such a widening of influence was viewed with self-protective alarm. Emile Zola, for one, was lambasted for meddling in something beyond his allotted intellectual horizon, with one critic asserting that "the intervention of a novelist—even a famous one—in a matter of military justice seems to me as out of place as the intervention, in a question concerning the origins of Romanticism, of a colonel in the police force."[13]

As we see in more detail in chapter 4, William James's sympathy for *les Intellectuels* is not hard to understand. They advocated a stance of dissent by calling into question the social and political conventions hitherto held sacred. By reaching beyond proscribed roles and socially acceptable divisions, the French intellectual, like the pragmatist, opposed rigidity and the urge to classify. In "The Ph.D. Octopus," an essay from 1903, James considered the life of the mind trapped in an institutional straitjacket, specifically "the Mandarin disease" affecting the production of university graduate students for whom intellectual status was determined by the increasingly codified model of the PhD degree. "America is thus as a nation," he writes, "rapidly drifting toward a state of things in which no man of science or letters will be accounted respectable unless some kind of badge or diploma is stamped upon him" (WJ2 1113). Alarmed at what he perceived to be the increasing institutionalization of intellectual endeavor in an era of economic and corporate standardization, James felt that individual vitality was being sacrificed for the production of homogeneous and increasingly narrow minds. He was not opposed to institutions in principle; indeed, when they operated correctly, universities remained "the jealous custodians of personal and spiritual spontaneity . . . indeed its only organized and recognized custodians in America today" (1117). Unlike "the elaborate University machine of France" and other European centers of learning, James retained a strong belief in the possibility of American education being able to foster individuality and unconventional thought. An overdependence on the "outward badge," however, served only to "divert the attention of aspiring youth from direct dealings with truth to the passing of examinations" (1114).

James reiterated these concerns in a speech entitled "The True Harvard" delivered in the same year at the Harvard Commencement Dinner. At an occasion more usually dedicated to the platitudes of collegiality, he praised what he called the institution's "solitary sons" (1128), its intellectual eccentrics, for refusing to assimilate to the club image of the "Harvard man" (1127). "Our undisciplinables," he asserted, "are our proudest product." Beneath the appearance of superficial sociability lay an "inner Harvard" that retained the capacity to cultivate individuality, acting "as a nursery for independent and lonely thinkers" where minds "can be happy in their very solitude" (1129). Paradoxically then, the institution offers an environment in which autonomy can be established; the ideal Harvard can foster an intellectual who is professional without being professionalized, engaged with rather than engulfed by the culture in which he or she participates. James recognizes the danger of conformity to social structures, yet is skeptical of our ability to transcend them. Harvey Cormier's acute analysis of the inevitable compromise that James's pragmatism makes with inherited language can be extended to the philosopher's wider acknowledgment of inescapable relational networks. Cormier notes how, for James, "there simply is no relief from the skewings and warpings of prior 'truths' or language, which must figure in the accounts of the world offered up by revolutionary political thinkers."[14] Such a model of the intellectual poised in a delicate state of contained autonomy is of a different complexion to that formulated by one of the concept's most prominent theorists, Edward Said. Said, arguably a "revolutionary political thinker" in the sense that Cormier understands that phrase, is important to the argument of this chapter as he articulates an image of the intellectual that has a seductive but, I suggest, ultimately reductive parallel with a popular version of Emerson.

In *The World, the Text, and the Critic*, Said writes, "It has often been the intellectual who has stood for values, ideas, and activities that transcend and deliberately interfere with the collective weight imposed by the nation-state and the national culture."[15] Such an image of the superior oppositional outsider dominates Said's numerous examinations on the status of the intellectual, an occupation marked by the notion of exile and the welcome distance of the unfettered mind from the prevailing edifices of society. John McGowan comments that, for Said, "the urge to belong must be fought at every step; it is the worst temptation to which the intellectual could succumb."[16] To be freed from the blinding loyalties and compromised affiliations of daily life enables a clearer vision of the grand ideals (those "ideas . . . that transcend") that everyday realities continually tarnish. From outside the parameters of contingent living, Said writes, "you can perhaps more easily feel compassion, more easily call injustice injustice, more easily speak directly and plainly of all oppression."[17] In one of his final published pieces, "The Public Role of Writers and Intellectuals" (first delivered as a lecture in 2000), Said asserts that "The intellectual's role is to present alternative narratives and other perspectives on history than those provided by combatants on behalf of official memory and national identity and mission."[18] While this might remind us of Emersonian double consciousness in its apparent desire to add competing discourses to those that are sanctioned or expected, the real impetus behind this act of definition is not one of dialectic relationship, but a model that promotes instead the superiority of unaffiliated comprehension, immune from the entanglements of belonging.

Said distilled his thoughts on the anatomy of the intellectual in his 1993 Reith lectures for the BBC, subsequently published as *Representations of the Intellectual*. The book examines various conceptions of the term—those of Julien Benda, Antonio Gramsci, Michel Foucault are all considered—before presenting its author's most concentrated manifesto for the kind of self-alienated figure that has come to characterize his definition. "The pattern that sets the course for the intellectual as outsider," he writes, "is best exemplified by the condition of exile, the state of never being fully adjusted, always feeling outside the chatty, familiar world inhabited by natives, so to speak, tending to avoid and even dislike the trappings of accommodation and national well-being."[19] This is representative of Said's position: the sensation of marginality, a resistance to the mainstream with its "chatty . . . natives," and a desire to avoid the compromises of affiliation.

However, it is worth raising the question, *pace* Said, as to whether the intellectual necessarily has to be "dissident," "oppositional," or "marginal." William James's "undisciplinables," after all, do not have the same absolute outsider status as do Said's more transcendent visionaries. Stefan Collini has recently noted that there are sound historical reasons why Said's word choices are associated with the idea of the intellectual, but, he writes, "they are precisely *associated* with it, they are not intrinsic to it." While recognizing that the intellectual's task is often to locate a particular issue, giving it a more theoretical, analytical, or comparative framework than might be possible from more tightly focused conceptions, Collini nevertheless warns that "putting it like this makes clear that the values involved do not have to be 'dissident' or 'opposition' in the familiar political sense; what is true is that by representing a realm that cannot be reduced to the instrumental they will always provide the resources for a critique of this instrumentality."[20] Said's figure of the exiled truth-teller becomes aligned with the belief in art's autonomy, with its claims to superiority in the face of sullied bourgeois commercial culture. His explicit advocacy of the "intellectual as exile" posits an uneasy equivalence between separation and a higher morality. Yet, as McGowan reminds us, the different views advocated by such high modernist aestheticists as Flaubert and T. S. Eliot "should make clear that 'distance' can produce many opinions, some of which would hardly qualify as virtuous."[21]

Early on in *Representations of the Intellectual* Said makes an impressive conceptual assertion over which we might do well to linger: "The attempt to hold to a universal and single standard as a theme plays an important role in my account of the intellectual. Universality means taking a risk in order to go beyond the easy certainties provided us by our backgrounds, language, nationality, which so often shield us from the reality of others. It also means looking for and trying to uphold a single standard for human behaviour when it comes to such matters as foreign and social policy."[22] Universalism, as Said defines it here, is clearly the articulation of an engaged citizenship, a desire to forge connections in ways that are more legitimate and satisfying than those offered by our too "easy certainties." Pierre Bourdieu has written that the claim to speak "with aspirations toward the universal" determines that intellectual practice is *intellectual* practice.[23] Elsewhere he writes of the responsibility of intellectuals to "offer a language that enables the individuals concerned to universalize their experience without thereby effectively excluding them from the expression of their own experience."[24] However, behind this claim for clear thinking and arduous intellectual effort lies a debilitating tension. As any good pragmatist would agree, "easy certainties" do indeed require guarding against because they may blind us to alternative epistemological frameworks. Yet Said's language of universality and the utopian telos of "a single standard" act against his gesture toward a pluralist universe. His text points at the notion of intellectual activity as process and adjustment (he writes of "restlessness, movement, constantly being unsettled" [39]), but the dynamic nature of such a model is finally stilled by being situated on a kind of quasitranscendental, omniscient plane, one that is released from the compromising demands of the everyday. Said's commitment to a pure notion of "exile" overlooks the manner in which the intellectual articulates concepts, loyalties, and visions that oppose *and/or* legitimate the way we choose to live.

Such is the lure of the Romantic impulse for separation that Edward Shils lamented as a "universally pervasive" characteristic of intellectual self-definition.[25] This is a familiar image too for those who read Ralph Waldo Emerson as the seer of Concord in happy possession of a self-reliant transparent eyeball; it is a less comfortable fit when placed alongside the more interesting conflicted figure operating in his historically conditioned moment where one is required to "lead a life of endless warfare by forcing your Ideal into act" (*JMN* 5: 153). Indeed, as William James recognized, the opposition between a transcendent position and a situated one is fallacious. Transcendence is a necessary fiction, a potent construct for a set of firmly grounded stances whose codification in (albeit fallible) language allows us to make sense of our world.[26] Rather than being a philosophical absolute, transcendence becomes translated into a contested term, constantly malleable and historically determined. John Michael goes so far as to argue that the resort to transcendence is an indispensable maneuver for any intellectual: "without an appeal to the transcendent—to that which does not manifest itself clearly in a given situation and which projects an improvement in or advances a solution for a pressing problem, to that which articulates *in practice* principles of justice or standards of truth on which *in theory* at least all might imagine themselves to agree—there can be no intellectuals, no politics, and no community at all."[27] The tension here between that which operates "in practice" and that which one can articulate "in theory" is fundamental to what Michael calls "the intellectual's double bind" (15). It is what, I have been suggesting, renders Emerson's writing so unsettling and, as we will see in the case of Henry David Thoreau in chapter 2 can produce a radical instability that borders on semantic incoherence. As Michael notes here, the claim to theoretical agreement can only be propositional (universal criteria *might* be available), but it is a claim nonetheless that underpins the possibility of tangible effects. His formulation acknowledges the difficulty of this double perspective: intellectuals work within and among social structures, yet for such figures to have an impact, they need simultaneously to be looking toward values beyond those structures.

In a lengthy jeremiad aimed at the decline of intellectual culture, the conservative American federal judge and legal theorist Richard Posner laments the fact that today "the typical public intellectual is a safe specialist, which is not the type of person well suited to play the public intellectual's most distinctive, though not only, role, that of critical commentator addressing a nonspecialist audience on matters of broad public concern."[28] For Posner, echoing certain aspects of James, the entrenchment of intellectuals within the institutional parameters of academia has led to an increasingly specialized vocabulary and a vastly reduced constituency. He looks back with undisguised nostalgia to an earlier era of de Tocqueville, Arnold, Thoreau, Spencer and Emerson — nonacademic intellectuals all whose audience stretched beyond Posner's imagined confines of the ivory tower. However, this is both a misrepresentation of the apparent "independence" of these very figures, and also a rather labored reading of the constrictions of academic life. Collini astutely asks why the "security and freedom enjoyed by the tenured academic" should be any more constricting than being "shackled to the relentless rhythms of journalism and the need to cater to the tastes of a particular readership" or proprietor.[29] Nevertheless, intellectual activity unfettered by institutional parameters retains its potency as a form of unrealizable fantasy, one sustained, perhaps, by an awareness of unavoidable attachment and paradoxically authorized by social forms that find such a fantasy attractive.

With that in mind, Edward Said's apparent advocacy of the purity of intellectual opposition requires a degree of qualification. In the introduction to *Representations of the Intellectual*, he acknowledges the impact upon him of radical figures from the American Civil Rights movement of the 1960s, especially Malcolm X and James Baldwin. These, he asserts in by now familiar terms, endorsed for him an image of the intellectual embodying "a spirit in opposition, rather than in accommodation." Tellingly, the appeal is as much aesthetic as it is political: "The romance, the interest, the challenge of intellectual life is to be found in dissent against the status quo."[30] In an earlier work, however, Said reshapes this notion of absolute oppositionality in ways that tone down its exceptionalist vigor. *Culture and Imperialism* expounds a methodology of reading that is "contrapuntal," an adjective derived from the musical structure of "counterpoint" which Said defines in this way: "In the counterpoint of Western classical music, various themes play off one another, with only a provisional privilege being given to any particular one."[31] The sense of opposition in "counter," where musical notations work against each other and where, for Said, hegemonic cultural traditions might be challenged by marginal ones, is still present; but reading contrapuntally suggests a textual encounter that is less adversarial, and a vantage point of interpretation that is less blasé about its claims for authority. As Jonathan Arac puts it, "Oppositional criticism is aggressive; it cuts. Contrapuntal criticism is loving; it joins."[32]

As a framework for thinking about both the cultural work of the intellectual and the location of that intellectual within culture, the contrapuntal model acknowledges exchange, dialogue, and contestation. It is a mobile form of criticism which, although bringing elements together in the way that Arac suggests, is constantly unsettled and unsettling. In place of the intellectual as transcendent, exiled visionary, Said's more nuanced position recognizes that all "cultural forms [including intellectuals] are hybrid, mixed, impure."[33] Undoubtedly, the oppositional and autonomous figure has the greater degree of romance; it is perhaps the form we might like our intellectuals to take in a secular era where the secure distinctions between clerisy and populace have been eroded. The history of American Studies as a discipline has, until fairly recently, been dominated by its own romance, the politically motivated one of the United States as a separate and exceptional entity. In the service of such national self-definition, Ralph Waldo Emerson has, with much justification, been read as providing its theoretical and rhetorical grounding. But following Edward Said, I want to consider the alternative contrapuntal Emerson, for whom transcendence and sovereignty—both personal and national—are contingent and relational states.

Reading Emerson Contrapuntally

Emerson's independence is regularly emphasized. He formally abandoned the institution of the Unitarian pulpit in 1832; his "Divinity School Address" in 1838 triggered a rupture with Harvard University; and his writing does, at times, assert social disengagement and proud solitariness. The Emerson of *Nature* and "Self-Reliance" presents an attractive, teachable language of nonconformity. Nevertheless, we should refrain from automatically taking Emerson at his biographical or rhetorical word. His career may have avoided the usual paths of institutional respectability, but the image of extra-social seer that much Emerson criticism has fostered, and that Posner implicitly valorizes in his preference for the untethered intellectual, is one that I want to contest here. Emerson is compromised, inevitably so, by a number of cultural and intellectual frameworks in which he participates. The lyceum network (Emerson's principle source of income), for example, required a keen awareness of the generic form of the public lecture, along with a knowledge of the expectations of its recipients. Emerging in the mid-1820s on the eastern seaboard and then spreading westward, the lyceum's mission to diffuse knowledge to an expanding public sphere was in part modeled on the system of Mechanics' Institutes established in Great Britain at the same time to impart practical and technical skills to working men. In an essay of 1868 for *Macmillan's Magazine*, Thomas Wentworth Higginson, himself a regular speaker on the lecture circuit, sought to explain the popularity and purpose of the lyceum to his British readership. Following on from the physical work of continental settlement—Higginson regards the crossing of America's geography by rail as "the measured footstep of advancing civilization"—the circulation of ideas and intellect is made possible as the eastern seaboard is brought into contact with the nation's westward movement:

> The village once established, the railway becomes its tributary; bears its products to the market, brings it means of comfort and of culture. . . . Gradually the New England element, which is apt to be the organizing and shaping force in a north-western town, calls loudly for some direct intellectual stimulus. It must see the men of note, must have some contact with the more cultivated Eastern mind. "Europe," says Emerson, "stretches to the Alleghanies." From beyond the Alleghanies, then, must intellectual delights be sought. Let us have the orator, the philosopher, the poet; but as we cannot go to him, he must come to us.[34]

Although the material presented in American lyceums was on the whole more speculative and discursive in nature than that found in the Mechanics' Institute, both systems, as Lawrence Buell points out, encouraged the formation of "a transatlantic Victorian sodality of cultural arbiters."[35] But spaces of this kind, involving a wide range of audiences and locations, necessitated a pragmatic ability to respond to the preoccupations of any particular constituency. As Higginson noted, intellectual activity was transformed by the institutional context of the public lecture: "It saves the philosopher from becoming a pedant, the student from being an intellectual voluptuary, and it places each in broad, healthy contact with his fellow-men."[36] The democratic potential of the lecture was central to its appeal for Higginson. "Thought must be popularized," he asserted, and even if this meant its articulation became "broader and rougher, before it can be appreciated in an instant by a thousand minds," the return of "a magnificent stimulus that solitude can never supply" more than compensated for this (56).

Emerson was acutely aware of the varied constituencies of his listeners. In a journal entry of 1856, while in Beloit, Wisconsin, he remarks that just as "Shakespeare or Franklin or Aesop coming to Illinois would say, I must give my wisdom a comic form," so he too will "know to do it; and he is no master who cannot vary his forms, & carry his own end triumphantly through the most difficult" (*JMN* 14: 28). Mary Kupiec Cayton has written on the ways in which Emerson came to adjust and modify his lectures in this way, depending on his audience. She notes how, in a lecture series in practical, boomtown Cincinnati in 1850, he dispensed with his more characteristic language of religion and philosophy to communicate instead through economic, mercantile, and domestic analogies. Emerson consciously fashioned himself as a professional public speaker within an institutional context that swiftly became appropriated by cultural and economic orthodoxies. "Often presented in the same lecture series with such pragmatic materialists as P. T. Barnum, . . . Emerson's presence and message became implicated in the expansion of the commercial culture that sponsored his visits."[37] As the lyceum network became an increasingly central element in the construction of an urban commercial order, helping to transform the very idea and meaning of culture by aligning it more strongly with "the conspicuous consumption of performances of people who were nationally and internationally defined as intellectuals" (618), so Emerson's lectures "came to be part of a canon of acquired learning that defined the parameters of knowledge and behaviour within the new international bourgeois way of life" (615). Emerson, then, is a participant in the development and consolidation of a series of cultural and economic practices. Undertaking the work of a public intellectual, he places himself in a position in which he has the potential to intervene in a series of debates; but he also runs the risk of having his contribution reductively filtered for meaning that might coincide with a prevailing ideology.

In one of his essays, Francis Bacon offered some advice for the Renaissance scholar: "Read not to contradict and confute; nor to believe and take for granted, . . . but to weigh and consider. Some books are to be tasted, others to be swallowed, and some few to be chewed and digested."[38] Bacon's image of reading here is of different kinds of ingestion: some books are lingered over, some get no further than superficial tasting, some are rapidly and entirely consumed. Steven Mailloux has examined the ways in which the nineteenth century pursued this analogy of eating and reading. Both are viewed, he writes, "as aspects of the same activity, the materially effectual ingestion of nourishment (for mind and body) . . . [T]he regulation of reading and eating becomes part of the same material disciplining of individual subjects."[39] Mailloux uncovers this trope of feeding on writing in a variety of nineteenth-century composition textbooks and anthologies of rhetoric, where the policing of intellectual stimulation is effected through the vocabulary of nourishment and vitality, or its opposites, greed and gluttony. Such a trope works on the assumption of an intimate cultural proximity between moral value, mental development, and bodily exercise. Metaphors of healthy ingestion signify social stability and the desire to "refigure the disorderly process of growing up as an orderly progression of moral development" (137).

The language of careful consumption promotes wise reading as a kind of restorative process. As a recent book by T. S. McMillin has demonstrated, the

Emerson industry has been quick to locate him within this discourse. One of Emerson's earliest biographers, Oliver Wendell Holmes, wrote in 1884 that his words are "in a high degree tonic, bracing, strengthening to the American."[40] James Russell Lowell, in 1868, consumed a version of Emerson strangely detached from his textual meaning. "We do not go to hear what Emerson says," he wrote, "so much as to hear Emerson."[41] The closest Lowell came to articulating the significance of Emerson's ideas was to commend him "not so much for any direct teachings as for that inspiring lift which only genius can give" (44). As McMillin points out, readings of this kind become "a eucharistic experiencing of the host instead of the active interpretation of a text."[42] More recently, Harold Bloom's Emerson is ingested as the essence of America. In *A Map of Misreading* he writes that Emerson's "particular relevance now is that we seem to read him merely by living here, in this place still somehow his, and not our own."[43] The potent combination of capitalism and an early twentieth-century culture of self-help relied on Emerson to provide a pseudophilosophical rationale for the acquisition of wealth. In a 1937 book bluntly titled, *Think and Grow Rich*, its author Napoleon Hill constructs a manual for aspiring capitalists. Hill's focus is on what he calls "mental energy," a quality that needs to be fostered in the face of an antagonistic society. As part of his thirteen "steps toward riches," Hill extols "a few men of outstanding achievement, each of whom was known to have been of a highly sexed nature" and therefore able to "transmit[e] sex energy."[44] Washington, Napoleon, Shakespeare, Lincoln, Jefferson, Caruso, and, most curiously, Emerson are cited as members of this priapic pantheon. Emerson's philosophy is consumed for the purpose of underwriting a version of virile economic individualism struggling to find respectability in Depression-era America.

Indeed Emerson continues to be appropriated in the service of capitalist consumption. In 1988, the Reebok Corporation ran an advertisement on American television promoting its brands of athletic footwear. The slogan for the commercial read "Reeboks Let U.B.U." as viewers were treated to scenes of a number of individuals behaving in unorthodox ways. Each sequence was accompanied by an intoned caption from Emerson's essay "Self-Reliance": "To be great is to be misunderstood"; "Whoso would be a man must be a nonconformist"; "A foolish consistency is the hobgoblin of little minds" to quote three of them.[45] This marriage of corporate consumer capitalism to the high priest of individualism might seem an arranged affair, until we remember that conformity is critical to the construction of American individuality, which, like all ideologies, can only survive by creating a broad consensus. Cyrus Patell has recently noted how individualism "enforces conformity at the very moment that it extols individuality," and Michael Sandel, a prominent critic of American liberalism and its basis in individualism, makes the further claim that "such a vision of freedom" has become "so familiar . . . that it seems a permanent feature of the American political and constitutional tradition" (xii). Consumptive readings of the kind I have mentioned smooth away the often jagged complexities of a text in preference for meaning that advocates particular economic and/or metaphysical systems. Holmes, Lowell, Bloom, Hill, and the Reebok Corporation all seize on what William James called the "cash-value" of particular aspects of a text, invalidating others contrary to it. Consequently the text becomes invested with meaning only insofar as it answers the desires of the reader. To comb Emerson's writing in this way as part of a process of deductive reasoning results in a disfiguring consistency that mutes the intellectual energy of his prose by placing ideological borders around it.

My own thinking on Emerson as a public intellectual has been provoked by a specific example of this kind of circumscription, to be found in Philip Fisher's book *Still the New World*. The animating premise of this work is that, after the Civil War, American society became structured as an economy rather than a culture. This economy was dominated by what Fisher calls a system of "creative destruction" endemic to competitive technological capitalism.[46] Thomas Jefferson's 1785 construction of a land map carving up the American west into property lines instituted a model of uniformity and transparency that would eventually ensure capitalism's easy penetration by an army of commodity salesmen. Fisher celebrates the cultural sameness of mass commodity production as the creation of what he calls "communality." So the Model-T Ford, for example, is described as the "climactic national object," serving as an instrument for supplying a precious dose of cohesion and familiarity to an otherwise unmanageably variable populace and geography (46). For Fisher, capitalism drives an economy and a national imaginary that is in a state of constant reinvention and innovation. Perhaps not surprisingly, a version of Emerson is read as a central figure in what Fisher regards as America's never finished society of democratic individualism, a society that flourishes in an economy whose market fluctuations make literal Emerson's dictum in "Circles" that life is a "series of surprises" (*CWE* 2: 320). Emersonian aphorisms such as this may indeed suggest a psychology of relentless adaptation; yet Emerson's radical skepticism of fixed identity might give us pause before assigning him as a cheerleader for any kind of system, economic or otherwise. Fisher exercises great energy in trying to convince his reader of the fruitful combination of market economics and innovative writing, to the extent that he imagines an American culture operating without the presence of dissent or opposition:

The final characteristic of a democratic social space is particularly important for literature and intellectual life. Such a . . . space provides for no observers, for no oppositional positions. There are no outsiders. . . . No one is able to reflect from an external point of view on society itself. There are, therefore, no intellectuals, no critics, no utopian imaginations. . . . [W]ithin a democratic social space there cannot be organized self-consciousness and self-criticism, that is, a recognized intellectual class, and, in America, there never has been one.[47]

Reading American literature as the manifestation of a pervasive economic system, one that in its own way can be creative and energizing, allows Fisher to dispense with the necessity of cultural irritants and marginal voices. In this way, his book has intriguing antecedents with some of the canonical texts of American literary and cultural criticism that developed in the 1940s and 1950s, when the propagation of U.S. values of "freedom" and "democracy" became a political imperative. Louis Hartz's *The Liberal Tradition in America* (1955), for example, argued that Lockean individualism constituted the philosophical bedrock of the United States, one adopted so completely that the nation "becomes as indifferent to the challenge of socialism in the later era as it was unfamiliar with the heritage of feudalism in the earlier one."[48] For Hartz, individualism, and its economic manifestation in capitalism, had ensured that America was in happy possession of a state of ideological homogeneity. Alternative, potentially dissenting points of view either could not be conceived or quickly became incorporated into the national narrative of self-reliant liberalism. F. O. Matthiessen's monumental *American Renaissance* (1941) is similarly structured around a canon exemplifying a vision of American democracy. In his introductory chapter, Matthiessen notes how the authors he discusses "felt that it was incumbent upon their generation to give fulfilment to the potentialities freed by the Revolution. . . . [W]hat emerges from the total pattern of their achievement . . . is literature for our democracy."[49] His methodology combines the formalism of New Criticism with a nationalist politics to produce a canon focused on the idea and ideal of America. Yet the specificity and variety of antebellum life is largely absent from Matthiessen's account. David Shumway, in his history of American literature as an academic discipline, points out that "the great works" discussed in *American Renaissance* "differed only in the positions they took toward perennial human(ist) concerns: innocence and experience, hope and tragedy, good and evil. Differences of region, class, race, or ethnicity could not be comprehended by this practice."[50] Matthiessen's text institutes a manifesto of aesthetic humanism that articulates a discourse blind to the particular differences of American life.

Philip Fisher's own conceptual myopia lies in his unwillingness to ponder the obvious inequities of an economic system that is as disenfranchizing as it may be inspiring and liberating. *Still the New World* claims an exceptionalist Emerson theorizing the benefits of capitalism from within its clutches. For Fisher, Emerson's literary inventiveness is the product and aesthetic correlative of uniquely American capitalist innovation. Recent critical work has emphasized the necessity of reconfiguring the perspectives from which American literature might be considered. The national (and nationalist) shibboleths of destiny and promise that re-enforce a myth of a separate New World identity have been challenged by frameworks that seek to stress the transatlantic and transnational aspects of classic texts. Paul Giles has argued for the need to unsettle any idea of American literature as an "inclusive cultural field" so that we "lose the sense of the United States as a privileged and protected space" by recognizing the permeability of borders of all kinds.[51] The cultures of the United States and Great Britain are not simply established in terms of distinct antagonism, but manifest themselves *textually* as entanglement and interplay. By contrast, Fisher's reading of Emerson offers an economically inflected variation of a very familiar exceptionalist paradigm. I am arguing instead that Emerson's work is more conflicted ideologically, and that its formal hybridity (of the kind that Richard Poirier so admires) has less to do with reflecting an economic system than with resisting straightforward consumption. His prose is marked by tensions of engagement and resistance, of embrace and repulsion. Continual movement of this kind, despite Fisher, generates its own form of friction and internal opposition.

In place of consumption, Emerson himself gestures at a methodology that might be more fruitful. In a lecture called "Powers of Laws of Thought," first delivered in 1848, he offers an image of human identity that serves equally well as a theory of Emersonian reading: "Man was made for conflict, not for rest. In action is his power; not in his goals but in his transitions man is great.... The truest state of mind rested in becomes false" (*CWE* 12: 60). Transitory reading—reading that is mobile, occurring in moments of transition across sentences—seeks to resist the false securities of consumption.[52] It implies a continual undoing, a dynamic of adjustment and readjustment that refuses to settle into comfortable fixities. "I see the law of the world to be transition," Emerson writes in his journal in 1847 (*JMN* 10: 161); and in the following year, in his lecture "The Relation of Intellect to Natural Science" (first delivered in London), Emerson imagines a transitory world in which "everything alive reproduces, and each has its progeny which fast emerge into light, or what seemed one truth, presently multiplies itself into many" (*LL1* 166). Stylistically such an endless unfolding of possibility is apparent if we accept that Emerson's prose is governed by the integrity of the sentence.

Whereas with a writer like Henry James, Gertrude Stein may have had a point in suggesting that his sentences aspire to the condition of the paragraph,[53] the force of Emerson's writing resides firmly within the smaller semantic unit. Each sentence, often an aphorism, is an assertion that does not necessarily seek coherence with what has been written or will be written. Emerson's goal is not to build a new philosophical system ("There is no Fixture in the Universe" [*LL1* 166]), but to explore fresh possibilities and to dismantle some of the pieties of his culture. In his reading of Nietzsche, Gilles Deleuze explores the force of the aphoristic in the context of his subject's wider philosophical project. Deleuze writes: "Understood formally, an aphorism is present as a *fragment*; it is the form of pluralist thought; in its content it claims to articulate and formulate a *sense*. The sense of a being, an action, a thing—these are the objects of the aphorism . . . Only the aphorism is capable of articulating sense, the aphorism is interpretation and the art of interpreting."[54] Such an account of the formal qualities of Nietzsche's prose could apply equally as well to Emerson's writing (of which, of course, Nietzsche was an adept reader), where fragmentariness works as a provocation to and participation in the construction of meaning. As Philippe Lacoue-Labarthe and Jean-Luc Nancy summarize it, "The genre of the fragment is the genre of generation."[55] Value, then, lies more in the exposure to the random incoherence of thought, even in pressing conventional thought into the unthinkable, than in the destination at which one arrives. To resort to a pre-determined taxonomy of organization would, for Emerson, tend to channel mental activity along conventional lines.

As the editors of his *Later Lectures* have argued, the lecture room provided Emerson with the perfect opportunity to marry the space of performance with the intellectual flexibility of transition. The presence of additional and interleafed manuscript sheets and of multiple sequences of page numbering, as well as the clear evidence of the palimpsestic nature of the lecture text itself, all suggest "that Emerson created lectures incrementally and by organizing them around discrete thoughts occasionally strung together with transitional prose" (*LL1* xxiv). The improvisational possibilities of the lecture were obviously foreshortened once it appeared in published essay form, "in the instant of repose" ("Self-Reliance," *CWE* 2: 69). Yet, even within the constraints of the printed text, Emerson's prose continues to resist the allure of finalized thought. The appeal of the essayist Michel de Montaigne for example, the subject of one of Emerson's *Representative Men*, is exactly couched in terms of his aversion to the hubris of systematic thinking. Montaigne's *Essays* "are an entertaining soliloquy on every random topic that comes into his head" (*CWE* 4: 167–68), and the mobility of such an aesthetic is expressed as a form of physical vitalism: "I know not anywhere the book that seems less written. It is the language of conversation transferred to a book. Cut these words, and they would bleed; they are vascular and alive" (*CWE* 4: 168). Instead of the stable edifices of respectable thought, Emerson's preference is for a mode of writing that acknowledges that we "are spinning like bubbles in a river" (*CWE* 4: 155). "The philosophy we want is one of fluxions and mobility" (*CWE* 4: 160), he asserts, anticipating Adorno's celebration of the essay form's revolt "against all the doctrine . . . that the changing and ephemeral is unworthy of philosophy; against that ancient injustice toward the transitory, by which it is once more anathematized, conceptually."[56]

Transition is explicitly linked to a form of movement in Emerson's chapter on Plato in *Representative Men*. There we read that "the experience of poetic creativeness" is "not found in staying at home, nor yet in traveling, but in transitions from one to the other, which must therefore be adroitly managed to present as much transitional surface as possible" (*CWE* 4: 55–56). The phrase "transitional surface" marks the moment where motion is inscribed, the space where the known and the unfamiliar confront each other in another variation of double-consciousness, what Emerson in a manuscript poem calls the world's "bifold essence."[57] It establishes a form of comparative criticism that continually shuttles between and across borders, unwilling to rest within a single perspective of coherence. This flexibility becomes a central feature of transatlantic Emerson, and the kind of cultural critique of nationality we find in *English Traits*, a text that represents the "transitional surface" on which he enacts the shifting process of American postcolonial identity.[58]

To consider the United States as a postcolonial nation at all is, of course, not unproblematic. The country is more often viewed as part of the colonizing world than part of the colonized; more generally, as a theoretical framework postcolonialism needs to be alive to the often very different experiences of colonization enacted in different countries. Anne McClintock, for example, views the inclusion of the United States into the postcolonial family as "historical amnesia," a dangerous generalizing of the term postcolonial itself that denudes it of its power. To label the United States postcolonial, she writes, "can only be a monumental affront to the Native American peoples currently opposing the confetti triumphalism of 1992" (the year her essay was written).[59] The nation also falls outside the parameters of postcolonialism as defined by Aijaz Ahmad, for whom the idea only has currency when applied to a specific set of historical and economic circumstances resulting in decolonization after the Second World War.[60] Clearly, the United States does not fit into this category. The country occupies an ambivalent position: it is the driving force of the global capitalist core; yet it is also a settler state and was once a British-ruled settler colony. While acknowledging the force of McClintock's remarks on the neo-imperial aspects of America's development, I want to broaden Ahmad's strict conception of the postcolonial to argue that the condition of independence is, culturally, often held in a state of creative tension with its opposite. The U.S. national imaginary at the midpoint of the nineteenth century demonstrated profound anxieties over its ties to the excolonizer. In the context of the literature of the early American Republic, Edward Watts has described the ways in which the postcolonial manifests itself "by accentuating and narrating the notion of becoming, not being, of transience and process." Decolonization "invokes an ongoing dialectic between hegemonic centrist systems and the peripheral subversion of them."[61] Such a model is also suggestive of Emerson's advocacy of transition—both as literary style and as reading practice. Emerson constructs a textual and transatlantic encounter resistant to the kind of consumption that locates him securely as a variation on the familiar nationalist tropes associated with American exceptionalism, manifest destiny, or the American Adam. Instead of reassuring completions, progressive temporal schemes, and irreversible breaks, the reader of Emerson encounters formations shaped by irregularity, reversal, and ideological inconsistency—elements that characterize Emerson's own engagement with the transatlantic relationship. One contemporary reviewer of *English Traits* was quick to seize on what Susan Castillo has accurately described as "the atomistic, scattershot nature" of the text.[62] In a thoughtful and generally positive account, the ex-Fourierist Parke Godwin nevertheless lamented the lack of system in Emerson's thought, writing in *Putman's Monthly Magazine* that the book "has no organic structure, but is a miscellany of remarks on one topic."[63] Castillo quotes a similar critique from the *Westminster Review* that labels Emerson "a lover of epigrams": "It is the characteristic of Mr. Emerson's writing, that it consists of thousands of such sentences—short, pointed, yet conceived on a large scale."[64] Both reviews attest to a characteristic experience of reading an Emerson text. Rather than settling for a stable, but misrepresentative, simplification of the experience of national identity, *English Traits* requires that we engage in a perpetual dialogue between the recently colonized and the proudly independent sides of America's historical experience. Style is combined with, and contributes to, a discursive flexibility that works to hollow out the expectations of literary and cultural nationalism.

Emerson traveled to Britain three times (in 1833, 1847, and 1872), on the second occasion embarking on a major lecture tour through the north of England and into Scotland. The majority of *English Traits* is drawn from this middle visit, in the lectures Emerson delivered (sixty-four in all) and in the journal entries made during the trip.[65] An indication of the ambivalence that structures the book is to be found in a lecture that nevertheless did not make its way into the finished volume. "The Anglo-American" (first delivered in Cincinnati, Ohio as "The Anglo-Saxon" in December 1852) is a text acutely aware of its non-New England audience west of the Alleghenies, in the manner that Cayton describes. At the outset, Emerson appears keen to establish a transatlantic contrast, with American progress calculated in terms of its inordinate speed: "Everything in America is at a rapid rate. The next moment eats the last. Whatever we do, suffer, or propose, is for the immediate entertainment of the company" (*LL1* 279). Rapidity drives technological ingenuity (while sacrificing "solidity and safety"); the English, by contrast, "are loaded with stability and reverence" (*LL1* 280) that suggests intellectual inertia and ossification: "In Merton College Library [in Oxford] I found books still chained to the shelves to which they were locked centuries ago when books were precious as gold" (*LL1* 281). The attribution of national qualities, and Emerson's valuation of them, begins to slide into ambiguity as the lecture progresses, so that the reader (and no doubt the listener too) is unable to find a secure grounding in the comforts of clear polarity. The text oscillates between a celebration of New World inventiveness ("What large brains, what forcible and persevering gentlemen: six or eight citizens have pioneered the short way to California, and the short way to Liverpool, and the short railway to the Pacific. The English slow, sure finish has changed into the irresistibility of the American" [*LL1* 282]) and scorn at its carelessness ("All is hasty, and with the penalty that speed must pay. . . . All is hasty, incomplete, cheap, much of it counterfeit" [*LL1* 283]); between acknowledging the kind of "easy self-reliance" that makes Americans feel politically "strong and irresistible" and lamenting the west's "coarseness in manners" and "meanness in politics. . . . [T]he men have not shed their canine teeth" (*LL1* 285).

It is clear from such structural inconsistency that Emerson's account of American futurity is far from an unalloyed example of national exceptionalism; the resistances and counterexamples he cites to his instances of U.S. progress interrupt the smooth teleology of an autonomous manifest destiny. Indeed the lecture offers an image of Anglo-Saxon unity that is decidedly transnational in its implications, while also uncomfortably myopic in its racial sensitivities. Rather than having to decide between the claims of the United States and Britain, Emerson chooses to picture an alliance among the "liberty-loving Saxon wherever he works":

[T]he Saxon, the colossus who bestrides the narrow Atlantic,—with one foot on England, and one on America,—at home on all land,—at home on all seas, asking no leave to be of any other,—formidable, conquering and to conquer, with his nervous and sufficient civilization weaponed already far beyond his present performing. (*LL1* 293)

The image here of an imperial people unbounded by geographical borders, "at home" in the transatlantic space, temporarily stills the competing accounts of national distinctiveness, replacing it with a vision of collective identity whose nervousness and sufficiency combine to overpowering effect. Such a marriage between American and English culture, as Reginald Horsman has shown, was key to the nineteenth-century establishment of an Anglo-Saxon type that, in the United States, could be deployed against the threat of racial diversity.[66] In Emerson, the drift of progress is inexorably westward, for no sooner does he offer this conceit of a transnational Anglo-Saxon colossus than he pulls back from its more radical implications about the dissolution of nation identity to conclude the lecture on the prospects of an Anglo-Saxon *American* future: "The Anglo-American is a pushing, versatile, victorious race . . . The Mississippi swallows the Illinois, the Missouri, Ohio, and Red Rivers, and does not widen: And this Anglo-American race absorbs into itself thousands and millions of Germans, French, Irish, Norwegians, and Swedes, and remains unchanged" (*LL1* 294). This rather complacent model of incorporation presents a static form of national taxonomy that later thinkers—William James for one—find inadequate in the context of burgeoning immigration to the United States at the end of the century. Emerson's lecture resolves itself into the kind of exceptionalist "melting-pot" paradigm that would reassure its audience; but the route that has led to this conclusion is far from straightforward. As I discuss next, Emerson's meditations on race in *English Traits* are similarly tortured between the polarities of hybridity and essentialism. Elliptical turns, alternative solutions, and contradictory estimations pepper the book, in ways that mark as radically disorienting its contrapuntal tone and argument.

The opening chapter of *English Traits* presents the reader with just such a structural anomaly, being a synthesis of journal entries made during Emerson's *initial*, 1833 trip. "First Visit to England" is a roll-call of initial meetings with the British literary establishment of Coleridge, Wordsworth, Carlyle, and Landor. "If I had sifted the reasons that led me to Europe," Emerson confesses, "it was mainly the attraction of these persons" (*ET* 1). Except for Carlyle, however, these figures are eventually dismissed as intellectually tired or obtuse. The interview with Coleridge, for example, "was rather a spectacle than a conversation, of no use beyond the satisfaction of my curiosity. He was old and preoccupied, and could not bend to a new companion and think with him" (*ET* 7). A conservative Wordsworth was similarly a disappointment: "To judge from a single conversation, he made the impression of a narrow and very English mind; of one who paid for his rare elevation by general tameness and conformity" (*ET* 12).[67] At the end of this first visit, Emerson sets sail for the United States with renewed self-belief. "[T]his is my charge plain & clear to act faithfully upon my own faith, to live by it myself, & see what a hearty obedience to it will do," he wrote in a journal entry while waiting for his ship at Liverpool (*JMN* 4: 83). The opening chapter of *English Traits* works to establish a familiar Emerson; the tenor is of a breezy dismissiveness that fits comfortably into an ideology of cultural nationalism and American manifest destiny. But there are moments in these initial pages where Emerson steps back from his youthful incarnation to register the distance between 1833 and the moment of writing. In retrospect, for example, he can theorize the sense of disappointment he felt after meeting the British literary luminaries: "The young scholar fancies it happiness enough to live with people who can give an inside to the world; without reflecting that they are prisoners, too, of their own thought, and cannot apply themselves to yours" (*ET* 2). Although far from invalidating the tone of asserted independence that marks this opening section, Emerson's more mature self coolly explains the reasons behind it, while also now being able to acknowledge the limits of intellectual sympathy from those who "can give an inside to the world." "First Visit to England" exists in a peculiar kind of dialogue with what follows. Its deliberately informal style — impressionistic jottings rather than sustained analysis — is soon countered by a more solid anthropological focus, establishing the key structural oscillation of the book between the authority of the traveler and that of the scholar. As Paryż notes, at times the text "encourages the reader to remember about the author's textual position as a traveler, while at other times it erases this very memory and elicits the reader's appreciation for hard facts, grounded in scientific or quasiscientific theories and discoveries."[68] Once the first chapter is passed, Emerson the young traveler, keen to assert American superiority, more regularly becomes Emerson the established intellectual, for whom judging the relative merits of Old World and New is not a straightforward matter. It is as if Emerson makes an assertion of national identity as an opening gambit, all too aware that it will soon become unsettled, in transit to an alternative position.

If *English Traits* begins with a version of national belonging that is subject to constant testing and refinement throughout the book, each individual chapter contains within it its own trajectory of hesitancy, qualification, and ambivalent reversal. "Voyage to England" describes Emerson's trip across the Atlantic in 1847. Approaching land, he begins to muse on the nature of English authority, and as the time to disembark draws near, Emerson and his fellow passengers become aware of the dominant culture soon to be encountered. "In every man's thought arises now a new system," he writes, "English sentiments, English loves and fears, English history and social modes." The reader is then confronted with an abrupt transition, for this litany of powerful English identity is followed by a focus on England's nearest colonial possession, Ireland. No longer having to estimate the speed of the ship by watching bubbles in the water, Emerson writes that now "we measure by Kinsale, Cork, Waterford, and Ardmore." The rapidity with which the vessel is able to reach the heart of empire is measured by the time it takes to pass one of that empire's dominions. Emerson's description of Ireland in the next sentence is striking, given the historical moment of his trip: "There lay the green shore of Ireland, like some coast of plenty." "Coast of plenty" has echoes of the kind of promotional rhetoric deployed in the sixteenth and seventeenth centuries to encourage English colonial expansion in the New World. Its use here, in the context of Ireland, is uncomfortable. Emerson is in possession of the kind of independent national identity denied Ireland's population; moreover the ongoing devastation of the Irish famine (1845–50) contextualizes the phrase in a way that does Emerson no favors.[69] He concludes his discussion of Ireland—and the chapter itself—with a two-part sentence: "We could see towns, towers, churches, harvests; but the curse of eight hundred years we could not discern" (*ET* 17). Before the semi-colon, the picture is of a bucolic land—peaceful, religious, and fertile (although, again, "harvests" strikes an uneasy note); but Emerson ends the sentence with a further change of direction. The "curse" of imperial domination may not be visible from the ship, but it is an absence that is nevertheless granted the last word. The chapter had been moving in the direction of a kind awed submission in the face of English hegemony, but such a stance is disrupted at the close. The visual markers of a harmonious Ireland may be deceptive, and the failure of discernment that Emerson admits here acknowledges the possibility of an alternative colonial construction. Indeed, in one of the later chapters, "Race," we read that "In Ireland, are the same climate and soil as in England, but less food, no right relation to the land, political dependence, small tenantry, and an inferior or misplaced race" (*ET* 29).

This judgment on the plight of the Irish has wider significance in terms of Emerson's strategy of collecting disparate classificatory markers as evidence of national types. External factors and contingent circumstance (geography, climate, agriculture) are combined with an estimation of racial taxonomy ("an inferior or misplaced race") to suggest reasons for Ireland's colonial condition. Throughout *English Traits* Emerson valorizes an Anglo-Saxon ideal of a vigorously effective self. The English "have sound bodies, and supreme endurance in war and in labor" (*ET* 25); "at the present day, [they] have great vigor of body and endurance" (*ET* 35). The effect of these attributes of physiognomy and character,

Emerson judges, is an "assimilating force . . . enlarging the dominion of their arts and liberty." More dubiously he continues that "their laws are hospitable, and slavery does not exist under them. What oppression exists is incidental and temporary; their success is not sudden or fortunate, but they have maintained constancy and self-equality for many ages" (*ET* 25). This apparently benign yet powerful imperial yoke, driven by Anglo-Saxon authority, offers an attractive model for the United States. As we saw in "The Anglo-American" lecture, written at the time Emerson was on his British tour, the transatlantic potential of this dynamic type was one that he sought to harness in a vision of extranational racial unity. At a time of rising political tension at home following the passage of the Fugitive Slave Bill in 1855, Emerson's desire to identify American citizens as essentially English enables both a comforting vision of stable racial homogeneity and a belief in the inheritance of traits that would overcome division within the United States. In *English Traits*, he claims that "the American is only the continuation of the English genius into new conditions, more or less propitious" (*ET* 19); moreover, the newly arrived New World traveler "finds himself among uncles, aunts, and grandsires. The pictures on the chimney-tiles of his nursery were pictures of these people" (*ET* 35–36). Such seamless racial continuity allows Emerson to occlude the highly visible (and visibly politicized) evidence of bodily difference within the United States. As Carolyn Soriso notes, "To Emerson, Americans had to be defined as primarily English, despite the reality of a multiracial and multiethnic population."[70]

The stability of such a redescription, derived from what Emerson praises as English "constancy and self-equality" maintained over "many ages," is nevertheless prone to change, in a characteristic maneuver of discursive unsettling. In the opening paragraphs of the "Race" chapter, Emerson refutes the claims made by the Scottish anatomist Robert Knox in his *Races of Men* (1850) that racial categories are knowable, definitive, and discrete. Instead, Emerson proposes, "each variety shades down imperceptibly into the next, and you cannot draw the line where a race begins or ends" (*ET* 24), offering a curiously "postcolonial" model of hybridity and interaction given, as we've seen, his simultaneous appraisal of Anglo-Saxon stability.[71] This seeming contradiction in Emerson's thought becomes even more apparent when we read his assertion that racial mobility is not, in fact, available to all. Racial permanence, of the kind Knox imagines, remains for some a stultifying fate that condemns them to inferiority and marginalization. "Race is a controlling influence in the Jew," he asserts, swiftly followed by "Race in the negro is of appalling importance" (*ET* 26). Emerson's conformity to the racialist stereotypes of his day, while disappointing, also helps to account for his investment in an Anglo-Saxon New World future. For it to come about, he needs to balance the dialectic of evolution and stability in ways that promote an English inheritance while at the same time ensuring an American improvement on it that avoids the danger of racial entropy. One tactic he deploys to achieve this is to suggest that the English themselves are *already* hybrid, possessing a "composite character" that "betrays a mixed origin," "a fusion of distant and antagonistic elements" (*ET* 27) within the contours of an Anglo-Saxon genus that becomes the basis, in turn, for America's own development. As the lecture "The Anglo-American" reveals, Emerson imagined the Atlantic space as a benevolent filter keeping at bay "the indiscriminate masses of Europe that are shipped hitherward." It acts as a "sieve," allowing entry only to "the liberal, bold, *America-loving* part of each city, clan, or family . . . It is mainly the light complexion, the blue eyes of Europe, that come; the black eyes, (the black drop,) the Europe of Europe is left" (*LL1* 293). The color coding in such a passage barely needs elucidation, its significance for Emerson's American readers lying in its all too easy translation as a commentary on the status of African-Americans within a U.S. national imaginary.

These conceptual shifts and transitions in Emerson's theory of race—the tensions between racial identity viewed as "fate" on the one hand and a belief in national amelioration on the other—are emphasized by the often rhetorically tentative nature of his prose. "Is [English] power due to their race, or to some other cause?" he asks (*ET* 25); "What made these delicate natures? was it the air? was it the sea? was it the parentage?" These are more than just the well-practiced rhetorical tics of a professional writer. Instead they perform the contortions of Emerson's multiple and fractured thinking to produce a mode of writing that is structured around the various possibilities being considered. Perhaps the most compressed example of this in Emerson's analysis of race is when he asks: "It is race, is it not? that puts the hundred millions of India under the dominion of a remote island in the north of Europe." The assertive clarity of the opening three words is, if not undermined, then certainly encouraged to slip out of focus by the qualification that immediately follows. The case for racial essentialism is not allowed to rest in secure possession of its claims, disrupted by an interrogative that is easy to overlook as rhetorical dressing, but which, I suggest, incorporates the dialectical oscillation between fate and resistance that marks Emerson's thinking more widely. If we broaden the scope ever so slightly from the Emerson sentence to the relationship between paragraphs, this collision of possibilities is even more starkly apparent, for the paragraph that contains the assertions of Jewish and African-American fixity is immediately followed by one that could not be more contrapuntal in its shift in argumentation. It begins: "But whilst race works immortally to keep its own, it is resisted by other forces. Civilization is a re-agent, and eats away the old traits" (*ET* 26). Again, the first two clauses enact a process of reorientation in which the permanence of immortality is undermined by other, more corrosive factors. As the paragraph progresses, these turn out to be the contingencies of a nation's social, economic, and political circumstances:

> Trades and professions carve their own lines on face and form. Certain circum-
> stances of English life are not less effective; as, personal liberty; plenty of food; good
> ale and mutton; open market, or good wages for every kind of labor; high bribes to
> talent and skill; the island life, or the million opportunities and outlets for expanding
> and misplaced talent; readiness of combination among themselves for politics or for
> business; strikes; and sense of superiority founded on habit of victory in labor and
> war; and the appetite for superiority grows by feeding. (*ET* 26–27)

The fate of racial stasis, which for Emerson, as we have seen, is different from the benefits of an inherited Anglo-Saxon stability, is countered here by the evidence of everyday life, where the features of English success — noticeably economic and imperial — inscribe themselves as markers of national development. These "counteracting forces" oppose what Emerson goes on to describe as the "weak argument for the eternity of these frail [racial] boundaries" (*ET* 27). Soriso has suggested that Emerson's strategy of balanced argument and counter-argument, what she calls his "fair deliberation," might have affinities with the structure of English legal justice, which Emerson characterizes as "a belief in the existence of two sides, and the resolution to see fair play" according to principles of "singular fairness" (*ET* 45). The effect of such careful moderation of the evidence, Soriso argues, results in a "strategy of rhetorical stasis" that blocks the articulation of a consistent political position and, furthermore, may work to undermine the possibility of radical change.[72] However, while Emerson's contrapuntal aesthetic does, indeed, often refuse to settle into discursive channels, and while such openness can defer the possibility of a streamlined position, the affect thus generated is not best characterized by turning to an analogy of legal logic and the production of juridical fairness. Instead, the prose exhibits an intellectual nimbleness that is often anxious about the grounds of its own claims, evincing an energetic reluctance to cohere that can be — in turn — anxiety-inducing for the reader. Lawrence Buell has recently championed a methodology of reading Emerson that pays close attention to what Buell calls his "elusive tonalities and implications": "[P]resume that Emerson expects and wants to gratify a quick-witted readership who doesn't want or expect him to stand still but is also demanding enough to want to be caught up short repeatedly and challenged."[73]

Emerson's writing contains its own dissent, a feature that is both a mark of its radicalism and of its inadequacy as systematic analysis — hence the contortions that must be exerted onto the text if it is to be placed in what Buell calls "an exegetical container" (35) of, for example, progressive racial politics. Meaning is offered as provisional, open to the kind of revision that is suited, in *English Traits*, to a form of comparative criticism that resists resolution. In a famous chapter describing a trip to Stonehenge near the end of the book, Emerson reports a conversation he had there with Thomas Carlyle about the national destinies of Britain and America:

> I told C. that . . . I like the [British] people . . . they have everything and can do everything; but meantime, I surely know that as soon as I return to Massachusetts I shall lapse at once into the feeling, which the geography of America inevitably inspires, that we play the game with immense advantage; that there and not here is the seat and centre of the British race . . . and that England, an old and exhausted island, must one day be contented, like other parents, to be strong only in her children. (*ET* 155)

These lines tend to be read as offering an image of natural family succession, with American youth superseding British old age. While this is certainly the case, the route taken in the passage is far from reassuring. Emerson begins by acknowledging the facts of British ability and resourcefulness. He then recalls the coordinates of his own national creed by producing for Carlyle a version of the conventional topographical fallacy. But it is introduced as a "lapse" of critical insight. It is something that is "inevitably" felt, where the ambiguity of that word might mean either "naturally" or "routinely." The phrase "I surely know" again points toward either a sense of relief or of tired inescapability. Embedded within a standard narrative of American assumption are vocabulary choices that are able to resonate in an unsettling manner; the language of exceptionalism seems to have been called upon almost as a form of reflexive ritual rather than living faith.

The subtle tensions in this passage become more explicit as the talk with Carlyle and their hosts continues. As the conversation runs on, Emerson tells us that an alternative, private vision of America's future passed through his mind. He allows us to read an unspoken response, one that serves to reverse the direction of the chapter as a whole:

> There, I thought, in America, lies nature sleeping, overgrowing, almost conscious, too much by half for man in the picture, and giving a certain *tristesse*, like the rank vegetation of swamps and forests seen at night . . . and on it man seems not able to make much impression. There, in that great sloven continent . . . hides the great mother, long since driven away from the trim hedgerows and over-cultivated garden of England. And, in England, I am quite too sensible of this . . . So I put my friends off with very inadequate details, as best I could. (*ET* 162)

"Nature" for an earlier Emerson was a central feature of American distinctiveness and spiritual potential. Here it becomes a more troubling presence — excessive ("overgrowing"), and both asleep *and* lethargic ("almost conscious"). No longer the vibrant child of the earlier passage, America reverts to a "rank" incoherence, feminized in its slovenliness to match the "great mother" that it contains. Britain may be "over-cultivated" in its excessive zeal for utilitarian order, but the alternative for Emerson here is not assured. As Buell astutely notes, "Even in affirmation, Emerson remains more the cultural critic than the advocate."[74] Whereas in 1836 nature could "answer the endless inquiry of the intellect" (*CWE* 1: 75), twelve years later her power looms over men who know that it is "too much" for them. This feeling of impotence seems to be shared by Emerson as well, for his image of an unpromising America goes unexpressed to Carlyle and the others. We read that "very inadequate details" are offered instead.

These two passages inscribe an analysis of nationhood that presents an unresolved choice between exhausted Britain and an unformed United States. In *English Traits* as a whole, neocolonialist admiration of the Old Home is often overtaken by post-independence assertions of American specialness. These in turn, as we have seen, are often entangled by an anxiety as to their legitimacy. Anglo-Saxon identity is not easily locatable. Throughout the book Emerson confesses to the slipperiness of his subject. "Mixture is a secret of the English island," he writes; and "England is the land of mixture and surprise," it "subsists by antagonisms and contradictions" (*ET* 132, 120, 152). To a great extent, these antagonisms and contradictions are as much a function of Emerson's postcolonial ambivalence — his practice of transition — as they are inherent in the English character. We are hampered in any attempt we may make to read the book as either proudly nationalistic or fawningly neocolonial. Although the tendency of *English Traits* may seem to reverse the trajectory of Charles Dickens's narrative of disillusion in his *American Notes* (1842), the prophecy of a rising American civilization in Emerson's text is nevertheless articulated in the most guarded manner. His ambivalence toward his nation is felt in a revised journal entry of 1847, written not long before his trip to England. Initially the entry reads: "The air of America seems to be loaded with imbecility, irresolution, dispersion." "Seems" creates a note of tentativeness that prepares us for Emerson's revision of this qualified impression. Deletions and additions transform the statement into a question: "Is the air of America loaded with imbecility, irresolution, dispersion?" (*JMN* 10: 77).[75] A few pages later in his journal, he addresses the idea yet again, this time having regained confidence, at least for now, in his condemnation. "Alas for America as I must often say . . . it all runs to leaves, to suckers, to tendrils, to miscellany. The air is loaded with poppy, with imbecility, with dispersion, & sloth" (*JMN* 10: 79).

The final chapter of *English Traits* contains perhaps the most striking example of this kind of transitional, oscillating style. Emerson's correspondence suggests that he struggled to finish the book; its discursive plurality had rendered it difficult for him to bring it to a definitive conclusion.[76] He resolves this dilemma by transcribing from his journal a speech made at the Annual Soiree of the Manchester Athenaeum shortly after his arrival in England in 1847.[77] Just as the opening chapter presents an anomalous, earlier Emerson, the final three paragraphs of the book offer a different persona once again. They represent the thoughts of the 1847 visitor, not the 1856 writer. As readers we are confronted with a public voice, one more formal and celebratory than that of the slippery commentator of the book proper. For the most part, the speech is a remarkable piece of flattery, a paean to an English superiority that exhibits "the moral peculiarity of the Saxon race." The "commanding sense of right and wrong" is part of what Emerson calls "the imperial trait, which arms [the English] with the sceptre of the globe" (*ET* 176). In the context of an after-dinner speech, such congratulatory language is perhaps understandable; yet, retained as part of a concluding chapter to a book written nine years later, Emerson's justification of an English imperium might strike us as curious. The impetus at the end of *English Traits* seems to be moving firmly in the direction of New World obeisance to Old, one in which the practice of empire can be regarded as benevolent. Emerson returns to a variation on the youth-age pairing we have already seen. England may be "aged," but the speech quickly moves away from the potentially deleterious implications of such a judgment to effect a vision of rejuvenation: "I see her in her old age, not decrepit, but young, and still daring to believe in her power of endurance and expansion." Again, "expansion" is a revealing choice of word, a practice endorsed here in a way that Emerson found more difficult to do when thinking about his own country's actions.[78] Freed temporarily from an American context, Emerson rises to the public occasion and exclaims that England is "truly a home to the thoughtful and generous who are born in the soil. So be it! So let it be!" The force of the repeated exclamation marks would suggest the closure of his peroration. However there is one final sentence that concludes the speech and the book:

> If it be not so, if the courage of England goes with the chances of a commercial crisis,
> I will go back to the capes of Massachusetts and my own Indian stream, and say to
> my countrymen, the old race are all gone, and the elasticity and hope of mankind
> must henceforth remain on the Alleghany ranges, or nowhere. (*ET* 177)

The two opening conditional clauses propel us in a new direction. If England fails (and it seems to be in England's hands to do so), Emerson will return to an archetypal New World landscape to preach a conventional exceptionalist credo of American flexibility and futurity. But this reversal is itself reversed, or at least questioned, in the final clause—"or nowhere." This might mean that America is the *only* place for mankind's future; or, less happily, the phrase could be read more literally. As Richard Bridgman has remarked, perhaps there is *no* place in the United States for the kind of society Emerson envisages should England let him down.[79] It may be the case, to push the argument further, that Emerson's concluding position is one where the notion of the nation-state as the convenient signifier of a set of characteristics, desirable or otherwise, has become redundant. He raises the possibility that the *idea* of America may no longer be locatable in geography, his work of comparative national analysis ending, ironically, with a suggestion of disillusionment with the very concept of nationality. Those two words, "or nowhere," left hanging on the final page, ensure that *English Traits* remains unfixed, entangled by possibilities that stay unresolved. The book presents a more complex version of the American intellectual than the popular conflation of transcendentalism with cultural nationalism allows.

In December 1863, at the height of the Civil War, Emerson delivered a lecture in Boston on the "Fortune of the Republic." In many ways it is a conventional piece of patriotic eloquence, warning the North against complacency and the dangers of a compromised settlement with its confederate enemy; Emerson's analysis of the conflict appeals to his impulse to universalize forms of historical experience: "The difference between the parties is eternal,—it is the difference of moral and immoral motive. Your action is to build, and their action is to destroy; yours to protect and establish the rights of men; and theirs to crush them, in favor of a few owners" (*LL2* 331). Framing a discussion of sectional violence in the context of an unchanging moral imperative allows Emerson to widen the scope of his analysis, for the lecture quickly moves from a concern with internal division to a consideration of the United States in a comparative, transatlantic context. "We are coming,—thanks to the war,—to a nationality," Emerson asserts, in which the failure of England to support the North's cause marks a turning point in relations: "We have seen through you. Henceforth, you have lost the benefit of the old veneration which shut out eyes to the altered facts. We shall not again give you any advantage of honor. We shall be compelled to look at the stern facts." The familiar Emersonian trope of refreshed vision is here brought to bear on international relations, where the energies of warfare ("a potent alternative, tonic, magnetizer" [*LL2* 327]) enable a vision of a United States freed from European models of polity and culture.[80] In this lecture, England stands for a culture of arrested development, for by 1848 Paris has displaced London as the place where "the idea of human freedom was purest": "the liberty of London was selfish and mixed, a liberty quite too much drenched in respect for privileges, cast-iron aristocracy, and church hierarchy" (*LL2* 324). "Fortune of the Republic" looks beyond the immediacies of the internecine crisis to project a vision of American ascension; but even amid the stirrings of exceptionalist rhetoric, Emerson pulls back from imagining an isolated patriotism, favoring instead a state of universal equilibrium toward which nations either approach or from which they fall away. The positive trajectory that Emerson plots—from the rise of Christianity via Luther's Reformation to the political revolutions in France and the United States—is set against the mechanical struggles over arbitrary and materialist aims epitomized by England's Wars of the Roses and the imperial adventures of the European powers. Because Emerson's focus is on the attainment of a universal ideal, from which local practices have diverged or departed, he is able to propose a transnational alliance of "the truly cultivated class" who are detached from the professionalized forms of social practice that determine national definition. (As an example of someone too embedded within debased national structures, Emerson chides Thomas Carlyle for being "practically in the English system" [*LL2* 323]). Those able to pursue intellectual activity that is freed from such restrictions, he writes, "exist in England, as in France, in Italy, in Germany, and in America. The inspirations of God, like birds, never stop at frontiers or languages, but come to every nation. This class, like Christians, or poets, or chemists exists for each other across all possible nationalities" (*LL2* 333). While it is true that the depiction, both here and in *English Traits*, of England's decline from a position of imperial dominance has a strong nationalist strain, the possibility of a cosmopolitan network of kindred thinkers evaluates national aesthetics by the degree to which they attain of communicability that transcends the conditions of their production.[81]

Emerson's "optative mood" (*CWE* 1: 342) has become a kind of critical millstone around his neck; that powerful phrase has underwritten a tradition of liberal individualism keen to assert and celebrate its national separateness. It would be foolish to deny that there is a strand of Emerson that is complicit in the high ideals of American self-definition. Yet his intellectual work manifests an unwillingness to settle into such a reading. Despite its utopian appeal, the absolute perspective of Edward Said's exile does not fit easily with an Emerson who is implicated in a series of cultural and institutional ties that he sometimes embraces and sometimes resists. "Emersonianism" itself represents one such ideological and rhetorical framework that Emerson works to confute. The poet Arthur Hugh Clough is credited with the first usage of that label. Writing in 1848, the same year he first met Emerson, he noted that "Emerson is much less Emersonian than his Essays" (*Oxford English Dictionary*), a statement that formulates a set of principles through which Emerson is read and one that acknowledges the inadequacy of the formulation.[82] Clough realizes that Emerson, the individual, does not conform to the textual image of him. I have tried to suggest that within Emerson's prose, the kind of consistency denoted by locating him within an ideological box is regularly confounded by his practice of resistance to that positioning. Emerson slips outside the categories that attempt to contain him. Nowhere is this more evident than in *English Traits*, where the reassuring prophet of an American future does not quite subscribe to his own message.

2

THOUGHT AND ACTION

My thoughts are murder to the State.
—HENRY DAVID THOREAU

Translating the Nation

On September 10, 1856, Ralph Waldo Emerson spoke in Cambridge, Massachusetts, at a meeting to raise funds to provide relief for antislavery settlers in "Bleeding Kansas," as it came to be known. With the passage of the Kansas–Nebraska Act in 1854, and its effective authorization of the expansion of slavery under the principle of popular sovereignty into territories north of the line 36°30′, Kansas had become an increasingly violent settlement, effectively governed by two opposing administrations, one antislavery and the other proslavery, with the federal government, led by President Franklin Pierce, firmly siding with the latter.[1] Emerson's speech, reprinted in the *Miscellanies* volume of the Centenary Edition of his works, is a powerful indictment of the political machine, at both national and state levels, and evinces a deep suspicion of language as the tool of public discourse. Lamenting a polity "so choked and stultified by forms" (*CWE* 11: 258) that it can no longer recognize "the known foundation of all law, that *every immoral statute is void*" (*CWE* 11: 261), Emerson asserts that "language has lost its meaning in the universal cant." The foundational vocabulary of American identity has become no more than a series of empty shibboleths that misrepresents the actual state of the nation's contested affairs:

> *Representative Government* is really misrepresentative; *Union* is a conspiracy against
> the Northern States which the Northern States are to have the privilege of paying for;
> the *adding of Cuba and Central America* to the slave marts is *enlarging the area of*
> *Freedom. Manifest Destiny, Democracy, Freedom,* fine names for an ugly thing. They
> call it otto of rose and lavender, — I call it bilge-water. (*CWE* 11: 259)

As Jenine Abboushi Dallal has noted, this passage identifies the "ugly thing"
not as the project of U.S. geographical expansion, but rather as the specific extension of slave territory. The contours of "*Manifest Destiny*," a term which for
Emerson, Dallal suggests, offers a "vision of the self expanding into free space
. . . as if it were acquired ahistorically and aphysically," are distorted by the all
too physically tangible and historically scarring structures of slavery.[2] Language
struggles to signify beyond or above the level of *Realpolitik*: "Our poor people,"
he declares, are "led by the nose by these fine words" (*CWE* 11: 260).

Emerson's response to this impasse is to revert, characteristically, to smaller
units of authenticity, where federal government is replaced by "the primary
assembly" and society is ignored in favor of "the private man." In a polemi-
cally antinomian vein, governments are only effective at the instant of their
formation, "in the moment when they are established," thereafter lapsing into
habits of accreted corruption; likewise only the "private man" "is qualified to
be a citizen" because he remains untarnished by forms of collective immorality
(*CWE* 11: 258). The history lesson that follows is fiction, to be sure, but it serves
to underscore Emerson's attachment to a politics of liberal individualism that
remains suspicious of — and at times explicitly hostile to — communal structures
of governance: "Massachusetts, in its heroic day, had no government — was an
anarchy. Every man stood on his own feet, was his own governor; and there
was no breach of peace from Cape Cod to Mount Hoosac" (*CWE* 11: 261–62).
Likewise California, another experiment in self-reliant pioneering "a few years
ago," possessed "the best government that ever existed. Pans of gold lay drying
outside of every man's tent, in perfect security. The land was measured into little
strips of a few feet wide, all side by side . . . Every man throughout the country
was armed with knife and revolver, and it was known that instant justice would
be administered to each offence, and perfect peace reigned" (*CWE* 11: 262). Exhibiting in this passage the kind of decontextualized affirmation of American
expansionism of which Dallal writes, Emerson's celebration of a purified self
signally fails to acknowledge either location as a geography already populated
by indigenous peoples and as contested, often dangerous environments. Instead
we read a vision of utopian anarchism, one that presents a scenario, as Dallal
notes, in which "U.S. expansion organizes the encounter of the United States

with itself—its own destiny; the ideology admits no dialectic and no Other."[3] It is "the Saxon man," significantly, who under such conditions "links himself *naturally* to his brothers" (my emphasis) in a way that does not detract from his inalienable autonomy and that also chooses to ignore the violence that may lie behind such a conjoining.

Emerson's inability to rest in this secure comfort of connection is signaled by the start of the speech's penultimate paragraph, where a telling "But" initiates a change of direction: "But the hour is coming when the strongest will not be strong enough," he intones (*CWE* 11: 262). Compared to the War of Independence, with its "simple" aim and "united" combatants, Emerson's present moment is one in which the linguistic opacity noted earlier matches a social and political complexity that seems to approach unreadability. The conjunction works to unsettle the mood once again: "But now, vast property, gigantic interests, family connections, webs of party, cover the land with a network that immensely multiplies the dangers of war." Immensity of size and the proliferation of attachments render the American scene vulnerable to the kind of corruption that Emerson sees being enacted in Kansas, where unnatural modes of association, characterized as partisan economic and political interests, conspire to produce a vision of imminent apocalypse:

> Send home every one who is abroad, lest they should find no country to return to. Come home and stay at home, while there is a country to save. When it is lost it will be time enough then for any who are luckless enough to remain alive to gather up their clothes and depart to some land where freedom exists. (*CWE* 11: 263)

The deflating certainty of the final sentence ("When it *is* lost") works to suggest the inevitable failure of voices such as Emerson's, overwhelmed by the weight and pervasiveness of a debased political culture. That the failure is also one of language is central to the preoccupations of this chapter, where the relationship between public utterance and political activism is brought into focus by the actions of John Brown, the radical abolitionist whose (sometimes violent) campaigns against slave-holding in Kansas, and whose execution in 1859 following a failed raid on the Harpers Ferry arsenal in Virginia, caught the attention of New England's intellectual elite. The apparent pessimism at the end of Emerson's Kansas address points to the inability of discourse—of intellectual work as the articulation of ideas—to have any tangible, material effect on the social or national body; the intellectual whose authority is invested in linguistic eloquence appears impotent amid such trauma. Speaking in 1857, Thomas Wentworth Higginson, one of New England's most ardent antislavery activists, lamented the ineffectiveness of political and legal structures in the face of the successful demands of Southern slaveholders. Instead, the time had come, he thought, for direct action: "All the intellect, all the genius, all the learning ever expended upon the point of Constitutional interpretation are not worth, in the practical solution of the slavery question, a millionth part so much as the poorest shot that ever a fugitive slave fired at his master."[4] As Ethan Kytle has recently noted, Higginson "insisted that the fight against slavery was *the* enlightened avenue out of the dusty library that constrained the American mind."[5] In the following year, 1858, as secessionist tensions heightened, he wrote in the pages of the *Atlantic Monthly* of the "intense egotism" that keeps men "from all demand for human sympathy." Detecting a preference in some "to belong to a party conveniently small" for fear of being compromised by "the slightest indications of popular approbation," Higginson criticizes those for whom intellectual detachment — what he calls "the abstract martyrdom of unpopularity" — is viewed as "clear gain." Yet in the face of "the rack and the thumbscrew, the revolver and the bowie-knife, the same habitual egotism makes them cowards."[6] In this chapter, I am concerned to explore what we might call an "anxiety of usefulness" in the context of Henry David Thoreau's response to Brown, where it is exactly Brown's refusal of rhetorical grandiloquence, along with his synthesis of words and actions, that provides Thoreau with a seductive model of antinomian effectiveness. In positing a transatlantic affinity between Brown and Oliver Cromwell, the leader of the victorious Republican forces in England's civil war (1642–46), Thoreau proposes the transmission of radical ideas across space and time, and, with Emerson's eulogy address after his death in 1862, the perceived protestant absoluteness of the Cromwellian stance is extended to Thoreau himself, although, as we will see, with certain reservations.

In the "Conclusion" to *Walden* (1854), Thoreau had noted with pleasure that "the volatile truth of our words should continually betray the inadequacy of the residual statement. Their truth is instantly *translated*; its literal monument alone remains" (*W* 580–81). Because of the evaporative nature of language, its inevitable translation into something else, the privileging of rhetorical eloquence as a marker of intellectual distinction comes under severe strain. In his lecture "Genius," delivered in 1838 as part of a series of ten on "Human Life," Emerson had imagined an ideal speech act in which orator and audience, words, and listeners, combined to construct a cultural space that was unified and coherent. The orator, Emerson's "chosen man," begins to speak:

> With his first words he strikes a note which all know; his word goes to the right place; as he catches the light spirit of the occasion his voice alters, vibrates, pierces the private ear of every one; the mob quiets itself somehow, every one being magnetized, — and

the house hangs suspended on the lips of one man. Each man whilst he hears thinks he too can speak; and in the pauses of the orator bursts forth the splendid voice of four or five thousand men in full cry, the grandest sound in nature. (*EL* 3: 83)

In contrast to Thoreau's exhilaration at language's volatility, and in contrast to his own subdued tone at the end of the Kansas address, Emerson's early lecture describes an unhindered communicative circuit, where the exceptional rhetorical qualities of the speaker are marked through their ability to provoke recognition in the minds of his listeners. Uttered thought of this kind—"A note which we all know"—is exceptional *and* representative, having the power to still the unruly crowd with its acute penetration and to initiate a response *from* that crowd which is equally impressive ("the grandest sound in nature"). The establishment of representative eloquence is crucial to Emerson's understanding of his intellectual role and of the kind of work that it enables. As James Perrin Warren notes in his account of oratory as an aesthetic and political mode, eloquence "becomes a figure for both the possibilities and the failures of the culture of antebellum America," where a measurement of the disparity between its ideal incarnation (as we find here in "Genius") and its concrete embodiment (in the political rhetoric of the day) is an indication for Emerson of the nation's health.[7]

Thoreau's reference to the "translated" truth of words reverberates on a number of levels. It suggests a quality that is mobile and dynamic, constantly in the process of assuming alternative possibilities of meaning that might not be expressed in linguistic terms; in one of his addresses on John Brown, as we will see, "translation" is also deployed to suggest removal to a higher, transcendent plane of being. Furthermore, the word marks a moment of relationship—or perhaps more accurately of tension—between the familiar and the foreign, where the normative force of an articulated word might be challenged and thus translated into a new form, an act which, following Stanley Cavell's reading of *Walden*, is intrinsic to the project of what he calls "*placing* ourselves in the world" in a manner that acknowledges the shifting terrain of any such placement. This model of translation involves establishing a sense of distance from the reassuring intimacies of a native language, creating what Cavell calls a "perpetual nextness" that prevents thoughts from settling into finished meaning.[8] Wai Chee Dimock's recent work proposes a recalibration of American writing along wider temporal and spatial axes than those that serve to re-enforce texts merely as instances of national exemplification. For Dimock, the significance of Thoreau's reading of the *Bhagavad Gita* (which causes him to declare that "the pure Walden water is mingled with the sacred waters of the Ganges" [*W* 559]) lies in the chain of transnational associations that constellate around it, a "threading [that] maps the deepest of time."[9] This ancient Sanskrit text, so concerned with debates about the nature and justification of war, is read by Thoreau, a nineteenth-century American proponent of aversive thought, who in turn influences both Mahatma Gandhi's acts of civil disobedience in South Africa and India, and the civil rights movement led by Martin Luther King in the United States in the 1960s. As Dimock notes, "Swept by that text [the *Bhagavad Gita*] and its torrents of time, *Walden* in turn flows outward, circumnavigating the globe, gliding past Europe and Africa on its way back to India" (9). Indeed her work has been instrumental in extending the possibilities of literary history beyond both the nation-state and standard temporal archives, to imagine a cosmopolitanism that sees the planet as "a plausible whole" (5) in which semantic networks can be discerned across time and space. Reading of this kind situates Thoreau not as a quintessentially New World figure in the mould of F. O. Matthiessen's *American Renaissance* but rather as someone positioned within a cross-cultural matrix that transgresses the boundary—and translates the idea—of America altogether.

In Thoreau's work, such acts of translation also occur at the point of confrontation with another culture *within one's own*, a process in other words that starts from within the native language. Cavell writes that "such visions [as Thoreau's] prepare for self-criticism of one's culture, preparing us for a change of our lives, to become deliberately not blindly strange to our conceptions of ourselves,"[10] This kind of internal estrangement, as Dimock shows, is enabled by the teachings of other cultures whose significance does not lie in the degree to which they can be incorporated into a native framework; neither is Thoreau interested in the mere juxtaposition of foreign and familiar elements as an act of disinterested comparison. Instead, the work of translation pushes against the linguistic norms of the native, introducing elements that interrupt the assumed transparencies of meaning upon which forms of governance and affiliation depend. Samuel Weber notes that translation

> unfolds *the ways* of meaning by moving words *away* from the meanings habitually attached to them, and which are generally construed as points of arrival rather than of departure. Meaning is generally conceived as a self-contained, self-standing universally valid entity, one that precedes the words that express it. Translation's way to go, by contrast, leads in the direction of other words and other meanings, exposing a complex and multidimensional network of signification in which word occurrences are inevitably inscribed.[11]

This movement away from interpretative closure toward a proliferating epistemology suggests that translation involves the creation of what Weber calls "instances" of meaning (66), instances that need not necessarily be expressed in a different language but which nevertheless embody transformed potentialities of understanding. The significance of this for Thoreau's project of cultural critique is recognized by Cavell, who argues that *Walden* "can be taken as a whole to be precisely about the problem of translation, call it the transfiguration from one form of life to another," by which Thoreau is able "to make human existence, or show it to be, strange to itself."[12] Cavell's word "transfiguration," with its connotations of death and rebirth, suggests how Thoreau's writing seeks to awaken us from the illusory stability of the immediate and familiar, inviting us to notice (and keep noticing) the strange within the same; words accrue a generative force, creating an afterlife of signification that loosens the hold that the guardians of meaning have over them.

Even when the text does not directly focus on cross-cultural dialogue, the reader is required to assume the role of a translator, experiencing the process of Thoreau's *own* translation of the native into the foreign through his internal criticism of the American social and political body. Offering "a continuous rebuke to the way we live" from within the contested space of where we live,[13] Thoreau's transformative aesthetic imagines thought not as an end in itself, or as the desire to create an enclosed system that can incorporate all particulars, but instead as an approximation of what we might become as we produce ourselves. In Stanley Cavell's terms, thought should be charged with the task of instilling moral perfectionism, which he defines as "becoming intelligible to oneself, as if the threat to one's moral coherence comes most insistently from that quarter, from one's sense of obscurity to oneself, as if we are subject to demands we cannot formulate, leaving us unjustified, as if our lives condemn themselves."[14] The capacity of the self to take responsibility *for* the self is dependent upon it being able to resist the pull of conformity—as Thoreau laments, "How worn and dusty, then, must be the highways of the world, how deep the ruts of tradition of conformity!" (*W* 579). Conformist thought is not one's own, and is therefore incapable of constituting an act of self-expression; the conformist is "subject to" others rather than responsible for his or her own self, a state of affairs which, following Cavell, leads to the obscurity and incoherence of failed self-intelligibility. For Thoreau, the political implications of this failure, in the context of antebellum debates over the Fugitive Slave Bill and the conflict in Kansas, were profound, and in the figure of John Brown he describes an example of radical nonconformity whose strangeness transforms the nation from a state of moral turpitude to one of perfectionist redemption through his uncompromising stance, which includes the right to use violence in the pursuit of abolitionist goals. If the persuasive powers of the intellect are exhausted at the end of Emerson's Kansas address, Brown represents the possibility of thought's translation into decisive action; he is both a model of effectiveness to be emulated and a rebuke to transcendentalism's nervous uncertainty regarding the value of practical power.[15] As Thoreau remarks in *A Week on the Concord and Merrimack Rivers* (1849), "The word which is best said came nearest to not being spoken at all, for it is cousin to a deed which the speaker could have better done" (*W* 85); language might be most effective at the point where it approaches silence, when it is most intimately related (i.e., no mere "cousin") to action. Imagining John Brown as a transcendent force, whose antinomian character displays the kind of self-intelligibility that marks the genuine nonconformist, Thoreau challenges the reader—and himself—to aspire to his subject's elevated plane of influence, where empty linguistic eloquence gives way to enacted thought.

Models of Transgression

Thoreau's public celebration of Brown at a meeting in the Concord Town Hall, at which he delivered his most extensive commentary on the Harpers Ferry episode, "A Plea for Captain John Brown," offers us the opportunity to explore his conception of action. As Jack Turner has noted, "it contains elaborate praise of Brown's actions . . . [and] the defense itself constitute[s] Thoreau's own purposeful political act."[16] The performance of the lecture is both a statement of self-validation *and* an invitation to Thoreau's listeners (and subsequent readers) to participate in a process of self-reform that will prepare them for responsible citizenship—and the creation of what he calls in "Resistance to Civil Government" (1848) "a corporation of conscientious men" (*PW* 2). John Brown's narrative provides a model of tangible intellectual engagement, and by locating Brown alongside himself and Emerson as "a transcendentalist above all, a man of ideas and principles" (*PW* 140), Thoreau can hope to lay claim to the mantle of purposive politics that he ascribes to his subject.

In "A Plea," we find a curious but, I want to suggest, telling temporal anomaly. Discussing Brown's "immortality," his transfiguration from "Old Brown" to "an Angel of Light," Thoreau declares: "I see now that it was necessary that the bravest and humanest man in all the country should be hung . . . I *almost fear* that I may yet hear of his deliverance, doubting if a prolonged life, if *any* life, can do as much good as his death" (*PW* 156). These lines, of course, announce Thoreau's sense of the inevitability of Brown's fate; yet they also offer Brown's execution as a *completed* deed, not as something still to be enacted. Thoreau's address was delivered in Concord on October 30; Brown was hung on December 2. The deployment of a past tense here ("was necessary") is indicative of the degree to which Brown's life takes on a trajectory for Thoreau that transcends the problematic particularities of it. To read Brown's narrative as a completed, teleological arc allows Thoreau to dispense with those elements of his radicalism that might challenge conventional notions of the relationship between acts of individual, often violent will and the need for social and legal structures to regulate and, at times, prevent such acts. In "A Plea," Thoreau's need to interpret John Brown as a figure who has managed to escape the oscillating dialectic of self and society leads to an explicit admission of temporal disregard: "I am aware that I anticipate a little, that he was still, at the last accounts, alive at the hands of his foes; but that being the case, I have all along found myself thinking and speaking of him as physically dead" (*PW* 148). The phrase "but that being the case" is an important hinge here, for what we might call Brown's textual death takes on greater importance than the biological fact of his actual living. Despite evidence to the contrary, Thoreau is keen to frame Brown in a past tense that initiates an afterlife. I want to suggest in this chapter that the form this afterlife takes for Thoreau is that of the idealized dissenting critic, the exemplary figure uncontaminated by material and local forces, whose actions offer a model for our better selves. Yet such a position is complicated by the recognition that the idea of a transcendent space is politically problematic, at the same time as it is epistemologically essential. Thoreau's fascination with John Brown derives, in part, from his belief that, in death, Brown had achieved the most effective form of cultural critique possible. If it is the role of the intellectual to diagnose and prescribe, Brown's deliberate act of martyrdom represents its most radical manifestation. There is no little element of self-promotion involved in all this as well: as Brown's steadfast interpreter, one of the very few who has managed to read him correctly, Thoreau takes up the mantle that a prematurely deceased Brown has lain down.

Theorists within the burgeoning academic study of terrorism have increasingly addressed the vexed relationship between instances of violence and their subsequent cultural mediation. Violence and discourse are viewed as conjoined components in the performance of terror, where the significance of the "event" is established in the subsequent "process" of narrating it. Joseba Zulaika and William A. Douglass make the claim that "whatever else it might be, 'terrorism' is printed text," whether a newspaper report, a celebration of its exponents, or a political bill condemning them. Terrorism "is a genre of 'emplotted' action in which narrative sequence is a moral and discursive construct" and where meaning is to be found in "the halls of the collective imagination."[17] Anthony Kubiak also highlights the role played by various forms of media in offering terrorists and their acts an afterlife. "Terrorism first appears *in culture* as a media event," he writes. "The terrorist, consequently, does not exist before the media image, and only exists subsequently *as* a media image in culture."[18] As Kubiak recognizes, however, the danger attendant in both this time-lag between act and interpretation, and the apparent prioritizing of the latter as that which makes sense of the former, is the occlusion of violence as an immediate experience. "For us, the *terror* of mediated terrorism does not exist, because it has been obliterated by the repetitions of its own abstracted image. This repetition deadens the initial impact" (2). The sharp moment of terrorism, as felt by its victims, runs the risk of being neutralized by the proliferation of narratives that transform it into theory, archetype, or telos; or, as in the case of Thoreau, that mediate the events at Harpers Ferry as interventions of untarnished nonconformity. Thoreau writes of Brown, "I shall not be forward to think him mistaken in his method who quickest succeeds to liberate the slave":

> I know that the mass of my countrymen think that the only righteous use that can be made of Sharp's rifles and revolvers is to fight duels with them, when we are insulted by nations, or to hunt Indians, or shoot fugitive slaves with them, or the like. I think that for once the Sharps' rifles and the revolvers were employed in a righteous cause. (*PW* 153)

Thoreau's critique of forms of internal and external colonialism is clear: America's relations with its neighbors (the war with Mexico would have been fresh in his memory), and her acts of persecution against African- and Native Americans, offer themselves as examples of collective conformity perpetuated by "the mass of my countrymen." Yet, as Lewis Hyde has recently noted, there is a "grim confusion" here between "eloquence and literal statement."[19] The effectiveness of Thoreau's disdain of certain forms of violence is matched by his apparently uncomplicated advocacy of it when performed under the rubric of a "righteous cause." The pressure he places on such a homiletic word as "righteous" is typical of Thoreau's wider insistence that we think more carefully about the kind of language we use.[20] Yet the unsettling of consensual definitions of words, however useful that may be as a rhetorical and ideological tactic, is not necessarily the same as being able to distinguish successfully between them so as to assert forms of moral superiority. The translation of "righteous use" into "righteous cause" in this passage, with the latter viewed as a just usage of the word and the former a corruption of it, runs the risk of glossing over the bloody effects of tangible violence common to both.

Thoreau's allegiance to Brown was not immediate. He met and heard him twice, in March 1857 and in May 1859, on the first occasion willing to contribute a small sum of money but irritated by Brown's unwillingness to specify what the money was to fund. Following Harpers Ferry, Thoreau made an entry in his journal: "I subscribed a trifle when he was there three years ago, I had so much confidence in the man, — that he would do right, — but it would seem that he had not confidence enough in me, or in anybody else that I know, to communicate his plans to us" (*Journal* 12: 437). This statement reveals the distance of Thoreau's self-proclaimed position of ignorance from what was happening around him in Concord and Boston. As David Reynolds has shown, Brown's insurrectionary intentions were circulating — if in an ill-defined form — among reformist circles, specifically the "Secret Six" of Franklin Sanborn (later to be Thoreau's biographer), Thomas Wentworth Higginson, Theodore Parker, Gerrit Smith, Samuel Gridley Howe, and George Luther Stearns.[21] Thoreau's eventual preoccupation with Brown has a belated element about it, which perhaps in part accounts for its unwavering zeal. What is beyond question is that by the time of Harpers Ferry in 1859, Thoreau's engagement with the political crisis of the moment had grown more focused and his textual response consequently more adamant.

"A Plea" is a powerful piece of rhetoric that occludes as much as it asserts. As we shall see, it assumes a position of righteous anger at the way in which Brown's acts are mediated and distorted within the culture, through the pulpit and in newspaper reports. However, Thoreau's clarity of perspective, his unwavering belief that Brown has undertaken "a brave and humane deed" (*PW* 146), detaches the story of Harpers Ferry from the problems of political philosophy and moral accountability that this episode explicitly raises. If we adhere to Thoreau's position — if we give our consent to his reading of Brown's narrative as a viable and just one — we are faced with the potentially troubling dilemma in which a principle (such as an ethics of antislavery) is upheld by (perhaps unprincipled?) acts of violence. Stanley Cavell proposes a model of consent that is more than simply a question of obedience but also of membership:

> What I consent to, in consenting to the contract, is not mere obedience, but membership in a polis, which implies two things: First, that I recognize the principle of consent itself; which means that I recognize others to have consented with me, and hence that I consent to political *equality*. Second, that I recognize the society and its government, so constituted as *mine*; which means that I am answerable not merely to it, but for it, my obedience to it is obedience to my own laws; citizenship in that case is the same as my autonomy; the polis is the field within which I work out my personal identity and it is the creation of (political) *freedom*.[22]

Consent involves the acknowledgment of community for it to have any political valency; it cannot be offered in isolation because it assumes the existence of at least one other with whom one is in relationship. The creation of "equality," of a consensual realm, also carries with it an ethical responsibility whereby one recognizes the congruence between individual beliefs and those articulated by larger structures of governance. Consent is the condition of having a political voice; and claiming a political voice is the expression of consent. Cavell is clear, however, that granting consent does not imply the attainment of a finished position or the completion of a political project. It is, instead, a tactic aware of its own contingency: "Consent is, on earth, always a risk, as democracy is, and hence is always accompanied by a knowledge of being compromised. So understood, consent is the show of a readiness for change, of allegiance to a state of society responsive to a call for change."[23]

To consent, then, is to propose an active participation in a particular politics. While acknowledging the attendant dangers in such an offer, its enactment supposes the possibility of transformation, of a perfectionism still to be achieved but nevertheless more nearly approached: "The idea is not to hedge consent, as if your commitment were incomplete, but to give it in the knowledge that its object is still in essential part idea, its existence incomplete" (108). As Stephen Mulhall has argued, the granting of consent brings with it the necessity for conversations about degree and amount. Consent — and its etymological relative "consensus" — is not an absolute position, but rather a contested one. In such situations we need, Mulhall writes, "to *discover* how far our consent reaches, for what it makes us responsible, and to what we are prepared to continue to consent."[24] "If one cannot possess a political voice without allowing that others may speak for you" (62), John Brown's nonconformism, the profound absoluteness of his position, sets in play the possibility that others might feel similarly mandated to act with extreme violence on the basis of a conviction not necessarily widely shared. At the heart of this chapter, then, are two related questions: Does Thoreau's admiring consent to Brown's actions distort them, to the extent that the principles upon which action can be based overrun and outweigh the extreme manner by which those principles are promulgated? And what are the implications for discursive intellectual work in the face of radical acts that seem to dispense with the need for rhetorical persuasion altogether?

In their book *Crimes of Art and Terror*, Frank Lentricchia and Jody McAuliffe explore the interconnectedness of political extremism and romantic artistic endeavor. Both, they argue, derive from a principled desire to overturn "the West's economic and cultural order," to induce a "terrifying awakening" by standing outside that order, "so much the better to violate and subvert the regime itself."[25] Both transgressive artistic desire and acts that we might call "terrorism" are generated, the authors suggest, at and beyond the margins of the mainstream, by individuals who refuse to conceive of themselves as "quintessential insiders, cultural enforcers, comfortably contracted" (19). Such a projection of the artist/

terrorist as a deracinated exile, freed from the constraints of social interaction and deformation in the interests of artistic/ideological purity, suggests an affinity with a version of the intellectual figure as self-fashioned and autonomous, one whose critique is all the more powerful because of its uncompromised status. Julien Benda's 1927 work *La Trahison des Clercs* (*The Betrayal of the Intellectuals*) asserted this position of detachment as axiomatic, and Benda's book has, in turn, become a critical touchstone for any discussion of intellectual self-definition.[26] The true intellectual, Benda thought, must be indifferent to the passions and associations of ordinary men and women, to the extent that "he *plays* human passions instead of living them." He (and with Benda the intellectual is always gendered as such) is "guided by the desire for truth alone, apart from any concern with the demands of society."[27] Intellectuals must resist the temptations of governing structures and institutional forces through a geographical or ontological position of distance, an embraced alienation from the centers of power. In this sense, then, Lentricchia and McAuliffe's thesis forces us to confront the possibility of viewing the writer/terrorist as a kind of intellectual figure, if by that we understand the term to mean one whose exile from the mainstream authorizes forms of critique and whose diagnoses enact patterns of textual/ actual resistance. *Crimes of Art and Terror* cites the transgressive acts of the Unabomber, Theodore Kaczynski, as indicative of the terrorist's impulse to oppose what is believed to be "a corpsed world": Kaczynski offers himself as "the one undegraded opponent" of a corrupt and corporatized culture (22).[28]

Such a transcendent position, disdainful of the dehumanizing impulses at work within the social and political body, recalls Thoreau's words in his 1849 essay "Resistance to Civil Government":

> The mass of men serve the State thus, not as men mainly, but as machines, with their bodies. They are the standing army, and the militia, jailers constables, *posse comitatus* &c. In most cases there is no free exercise whatever of the judgement or of the moral sense; but they put themselves on a level with wood and earth and stones, and wooden men can perhaps be manufactured that will serve the purpose as well. (*PW* 3)

Here, the political realm is equated with the marketplace, where our status as a commodity in the latter is mirrored by the instrumental nature of our participation in the former. As a result, Thoreau's skepticism of political representation of all kinds is explicit: "There are thousands who are *in opinion* opposed to slavery and to the war, who yet in effect do nothing to put an end to them . . . They hesitate, and they regret, and sometimes they petition; but they do nothing in earnest and with effect . . . At most, they give only a cheap vote, and a feeble countenance and God-speed, to the right, as it goes by them" (*PW* 5–6). Public culture conceived in this way is at some remove from the kind of consensual progression imagined by Stanley Cavell, for Thoreau judges that his contemporaries' acts of political representation have become timid and ineffective: "Even voting *for the right thing* is *doing* nothing for it. It is only expressing to men feebly your desire that it should prevail" (*PW* 6). As soon as action is located within the forms and institutions of representation, it is evacuated of moral power; the self-intelligibility so central to Cavell's perfectionism is, Thoreau argues, impossible when mediated through traditional patterns of linguistic or political visibility. Indeed, Thoreau's ideal government is one that is *invisible*: "The character inherent in the American people has done all that has been accomplished; and it would have done somewhat more, if the government had not sometimes got in its way" (*PW* 2).[29] At the root of Thoreau's political vision, then, is the belief that thought can be translated directly into action, without the interference of structures of representation that might exert a drag on the immediacy of the transition.

In contrast to the enervations of compromised expression, Thoreau proposes a countervailing model, precious in its rarity, that, in a journal entry of May 1851, he offers as a statement of self-definition:

> We are enabled to criticise others only when we are different from, and in a given particular superior to, them ourselves. By our aloofness from men and their affairs we are enabled to overlook and criticize them. There are but few men who stand on the hills by the roadside. I am sane only when I have risen above my common sense, when I do not take the foolish view of things which is commonly taken, when I do not live for the low ends for which men commonly live. Wisdom is not common. To what purpose have I senses, if I am thus absorbed in affairs? My pulse must beat with nature. (*Journal* 2: 267–68)

The position of social critic described here exerts legitimacy through distance; as we saw in chapter 1, Thoreau is advocating a model of intellectual prestige that is defined by its autonomy and imagined elevation over the "common," a word which (along with its adverbial relative) tolls like an insistent bell, warning against that sense of self-dissipation ("I am thus absorbed") that destroys integrity. The scarcity of those able to resist the deadening charms of the everyday is apparent if we return to "Resistance to Civil Government," where "A very few, as heroes, patriots, martyrs, reformers in the great sense, and *men*, serve the State with their consciences also, and so necessarily resist it for the most part; and they are commonly treated by it as enemies" (*PW* 3). Genuine, italicized manhood is to be found in those whose service to the state lies in their opposition to it;

Matthew Arnold would later describe it as the mind "refusing to lend itself to any idea of those ulterior, political, practical considerations" that impede the "current of true and fresh ideas."[30] Martyrdom, often seen by its advocates as the end-point of terrorist activity, signifies cultural critique of the profoundest kind. (On the day of Brown's execution, Thoreau gave an address called "The Martyrdom of John Brown.") Indeed, Julien Benda's formulation of the intellectual proposed dissociation from the contingencies of the everyday to such an extent that the intellectual's most potent occasion for influence is a posthumous one: "it seems to me that human affairs can only adopt the religion of the true 'clerk' under penalty of becoming divine, i.e., of perishing as a human."[31] Only in death might Benda's intellectual find a vantage point from which to exert influence. One of the reasons Thoreau gives for labeling Brown "the most American of us all" lies in the fact that "He did not value his bodily life in comparison with ideal things" (*PW* 147). A genuine American self is one for whom self-dissolution marks the profoundest statement of identity. As Jack Turner notes, one of the most controversial aspects of this paradoxical claim is its rejection of liberalism's standard focus on bodily integrity as a bulwark against monarchical power (Thomas Hobbes) or against religious persecution (John Locke). Instead "Thoreau suggests that there are times when it is appropriate to sacrifice bodily life for ideal things."[32]

Such an absolute disjunction between the life of the mind and that of corporeal existence has been a characteristic element of Western thought from its classical beginnings. Hannah Arendt records that both Plato and Aristotle establish "the enormous superiority of contemplation over activity of any kind," so that the "later Christian claim to be free from entanglement in worldly affairs, from all the business of this world, was preceded by and originated in the philosophic *apolita* of late antiquity." This type of activity (the *vita contemplativa*) inscribes an ideal mode of ontology that "can reveal itself only in complete human stillness," apart from and located above "external movement and activity of every kind."[33] Such a notion of transcendence, one in which the requirements of the corporeal and socialized self might be left behind, has become a foundational element in defining the terms by which an idea of the "intellectual" might be constituted. Arendt's categorization of the purely unfettered mind that owes no loyalty to forms of everyday life is a seductive self-image for Thoreau, as we have seen, yet the hard evidence of John Brown's "*vita activa*" (in Arendt's terms), a radicalism in which social detachment is exhibited by a violent flouting of conventional legal and moral frames of reference, creates an uncomfortable melding of models of social critique. Part romantic outcast, part Protestant prophet, part military insurgent, Brown is both an appealing instance of effectiveness and a rebuke to an intellectual culture such as Thoreau's that is unable, finally, to match his uncompromising stance.[34]

What I am suggesting, then, is the possibility of reading a confluence of perspective which traces connections between the romantic ideal of the writer as transgressive, the terrorist figure as fired by comparable (if more extreme) notions of disruptive critique, and the intellectual as the descendant of what Lewis Coser calls "those inspired madmen who preached in the wilderness far removed from the institutionalized pieties of court and synagogue," "biblical prophets . . . who never seem satisfied with things as they are."[35] Framing the function of the intellectual in the theocratic language of the jeremiad suits Thoreau's project of rehabilitating Brown. Thoreau's Brown creates and inscribes a holy narrative. His story functions as a scriptural text about an object of veneration whose example of absolute, unsurpassable influence is offered for earthly imitation: "Some eighteen hundred years ago Christ was crucified; this morning, perchance, Captain Brown was hung. These are two ends of a chain which is not without its links" (*PW* 156). Again we can note the equivocation over Brown's status — "perchance" he is already dead, in which case the line of succession that tethers him to his revolutionary antecedent can be completed.

But if we go back to Thoreau's words from "Resistance to Civil Government" and look at them a little more closely, there are flickers of qualification that serve to muddy the apparently pristine Manichean opposition between "men . . . as machines" and "*men* . . . in the great sense." Cultural critique that attains its authority from detachment might not be the sole position that Thoreau's heroes take: even his nonconformists can only uphold their "necessarily" purified position "for the most part," a phrase that highlights the major tension in Thoreau's work between the desire for self-reliant emancipation and the recognition that representational ties are inevitable. "Resistance to Civil Government" is itself an act of rhetorical representation that participates in a tradition of political discourse, and we should not forget that *Walden* is a text that faces the dissenter's social entanglement with a comic irony that allows the reader to value the motives behind the experiment of solitary utopian living, even as we recognize, along with Thoreau, the inevitably compromised nature of that utopia. Eric Sundquist has succinctly described how the urge for escape in Thoreau is continually thwarted by a material world that "trails naggingly behind as soon as he shoves off in search of that other . . . he can never have."[36] "Slavery in Massachusetts," a lecture delivered in the same year as *Walden*'s publication, shows Thoreau pushing against the confines of textual representation to propose violence as the only viable option left after the passing of the Fugitive Slave Bill and the failure of abolitionist Boston to protect the liberty of Anthony Burns and Thomas Sims. "The words of Massachusetts" are ineffective, Thoreau asserts, after he momentarily assumes the identity of a reformer whose timidity is satirized and roundly condemned: "It will indeed grieve me if you hurt them, if you deliver them to overseers to be hunted by hounds or to be whipped to death; but nevertheless, I will peaceably pursue my chosen calling on this fair earth, until perchance, one day, when I have put on mourning for them dead, I shall have persuaded you to relent." An awareness of the horrors of the slave system does nothing to jolt the speaker out of his delight in the "fair earth" or to shake his less than committed belief that the power of discourse will work to defeat the slaveholder. Against the prevarications of persuasion, Thoreau proposes an alternative route: "Rather than do thus, I need not say what match I would touch, what system endeavor to blow up, — but as I love my life, I would side with the light, and let the dark earth roll from under me, calling my mother and my brother to follow" (*PW* 131). The commitment to act remains undefined ("I need not say"), as if the gesture of consent resides in the performance rather than the articulation of intent: utterance negates the force of enacted thought. But even within this statement of discursive rejection, Thoreau resorts to the rhetorical artfulness of syllabic parallelism ("but as I love my life" / "I would side with the light"), and with the repeated stresses in "dark earth roll" he emphasizes a sense of heroic resistance to the forces of despair. The call for an unmediated act is itself bolstered by the arts of textual representation.

With his reading of John Brown, Thoreau's oscillation between untarnished disconnection from and renewed recognition by the center, raises anxious questions about how Brown's acts might be interpreted and built upon after his death. Thoreau cannot afford to pitch his model of ideal human behavior at too high a level without running the risk of isolating Brown in his own transcendence. Brown's greatest influence may be exerted after death (his "translation" [*PW* 168] is both from a mortal state and toward realms of influence that, following Dimock, stretch beyond his geographical and historical moment); but for those who continue to live with unpredictable contingency, the figure of transfigured power still requires rooting in a recognizable landscape. The emphatic denial of social connections—one that corresponds with Brown's radical antinomianism—is modified by a conceptual framework that, anticipating Gramsci's notion of the intellectual, relocates those assertions of independence and autonomy (an imagined "social utopia") into the flux of the everyday. Assumptions of transcendence, Gramsci noted, are "not without consequences in the ideological and political field," where the power that they generate is exerted in "the complex of superstructures, of which the intellectuals are, precisely, the 'functionaries.'"[37] He advocated "forms of new intellectualism" — "directive" in nature — that were explicitly located in the quotidian (10). While Thoreau would probably regard the idea of the functionary intellectual as an oxymoron, Gramsci's Marxist revision of Benda's theory nevertheless lays out the dilemma contained within Thoreau's response to John Brown. The extreme individualism of Brown's actions, his total rejection of any form of social or institutional framework by which those actions might be judged, dislodges him from shared cultural discourse. It creates an alienation that is difficult to answer or discuss. As Sam Worley has recently asked, in such a situation where the normative parameters of debate and conversation are explicitly rejected, "how is a society to affirm or extent a gesture that bespeaks complete alienation and opposition?"[38] How is Benda's intellectual to effect a Gramscian reconnection with the society he so disdains?

As noted in chapter 1, the lure of transcendence, and the position of authority it affords, is understandable. In an era in which subjects increasingly conceive of themselves as self-divided, when the national imaginary itself appears to lack coherence, the desire for integration drives intellectual work into a space withdrawn from the unsatisfying and fractured worlds of politics and material interaction. In such a realm the individual can cultivate and project such fantasies of integration and superiority that seem impossible within the contingencies of the everyday. Transcendence becomes, then, the possibility of retaining power in the face of that which would conspire to negate authority and autonomy. Critics who identify themselves on both the "right" and the "left" have argued for the centrality of transcendent values to combat the dangers of skepticism and relativism.[39] However conflicted the history of transcendence is, and however politically inflected the idea has become, the appeal to its values is still fundamental to the work that intellectuals do. This is an uncomfortable position, one in which an aspiration toward the transcendent is acknowledged as the foundation for critical work at the same time as the concept of transcendence becomes invested with politically and historically determined frames. George Konrad and Ivan Szelenyi's assertion that "we do not wish to deny the existence of transcendent elements in the activity of intellectuals, only to make them relative" encapsulates the paradox that marks what they call a certain "schizophrenia inherent in the intellectual's role."[40]

Adorno and Horkheimer's influential critique of the appeal to a transcendence that lies at the heart of the Enlightenment project theorizes the strategies of occlusion and disenfranchisement that underwrite the acquisition of power and its maintenance. Assertions of transparency and universality, they argue, inevitably mask strong blocs of self-interest that police the borders of social acceptability. For those who find themselves outside the coordinates of prescribed values that acquire the status of normative transcendence, what is generated is discord and resistance to the injustices that might accompany such policing.[41] Even so, despite our awareness of the dangers inherent in positing transcendence as the location of universal worth, it seems impossible to imagine an act of intellectual intervention that does not, at some level, appeal to it as an idea — something that is absent from a hypothetical present context but whose future possibility offers amelioration or, more radically, transformation. Without the ability to look beyond (and above) the immediate moment, intellectual work cannot take place.

Such ambivalent doubleness — an understanding of transcendence's unsavory history and yet the inevitable recourse to its framework — is at the heart of Thoreau's writing on Brown, and signifies the centrality of the intellectual type to both his own self-image and that which he projects onto his subject. Just as Matthew Arnold's assertion of intellectual detachment, mentioned earlier, proved to be a position that his later work, *Culture and Anarchy* (1869), inevitably revised, Thoreau is similarly alive to the dangers of constructing a critique that insists upon a perspective that might appear too aloof. In preserving an image of John Brown that conflates the roles of intellectual, artist, and activist he is keen to reattach him to recognizable coordinates — thus embracing the paradox of a historically grounded transcendence. One of the strategies undertaken to achieve this is an insistent focus on locality and region. In many of the tributes voiced to Brown by abolitionists there is a shared referencing of his New England — specifically Connecticut — heritage. Writing two days before Thoreau delivered "A Plea," William Lloyd Garrison, although no advocate of Brown's violent tactics, could nevertheless admire him as a devotee of "the logic of Concord, Lexington and Bunker Hill."[42] Ralph Waldo Emerson similarly asserted that Brown was "a fair specimen of the best stock of New England; having that force of thought and that sense of right which are the warp and woof of greatness" (*CWE* 11: 279). Not only placed at the heart of the dominant national imaginary, Brown's American credentials were also re-enforced by Emerson's (arguably specious) reconstruction of his impeccable ancestry: "He was happily a representative of the American Republic. Captain John Brown is a farmer, the fifth in descent from Peter Brown, who came to Plymouth in the Mayflower, in 1620" (*CWE* 11: 267). Echoing Garrison, Thoreau was similarly quick to locate Brown within recognizable co-ordinates, being "by descent and birth a New England farmer . . . He was like the best of those who stood at Concord Bridge once, on Lexington Common, and on Bunker Hill" (*PW* 138). In judgments such as these, as Joseph Conforti has observed, what is at stake is the consolidation of "the nationalist triumph of the Yankee" as "the ascendant signifier of the American character."[43] Reading Brown in such a context has the effect of sidelining anxiety over the moral legitimacy of his actions in favor of promoting his status as a New England saint *redivivus*, one whose regional identity becomes rapidly synecdochic of national self-fashioning.

Brown's ascension to a place of impregnable, posthumous authority is similarly modulated by Thoreau's initial, bald resolve in "A Plea" to situate his subject: "First, as to his history." The lines that follow ingeniously play with the conceit of shared knowledge: "I will endeavour to omit, as much as possible, what you have already read. I need not describe his person to you, for probably most of you have seen and will not soon forget him." Thoreau establishes a community of the like-minded, taking for granted degrees of interest and sympathy that, although surely present among his listening audience, nevertheless has the effect of pushing rhetorically all the members of that audience (and his subsequent readers) into intellectual and ideological alignment. Moreover, Thoreau's own credentials as documenter of Brown's history are immediately underscored by framing phrases that suggest or assert personal contact: "I am told that"; "I heard him say"; "He said that." Thoreau's design in these paragraphs is simultaneously to assume shared knowledge and to reveal his own privileged position—evidence of that certain "schizophrenia" of perspective mentioned earlier. That he is acutely conscious of his constituency is apparent in the address's opening lines, where he subscribes to the well-worn convention of authorial self-effacement in introducing his topic. "A Plea" begins on an apologetic note—"I trust that you will pardon me for being here"—and continues with Thoreau seemingly reassuring his audience that what they are about to hear will be in the New England tradition of genteel temperance. He has no desire to "force" his opinions, although with characteristic linguistic playfulness, he admits to feeling "forced" himself to express them. Acting out of some kind of moral compulsion, Thoreau wants to insist at the outset (at least) that his role will be to act as a moderator of the interpretative community that has built itself around Brown. Revisionist rather than revolutionary, he would "fain" (i.e., willingly, with pleasure [*Oxford English Dictionary*]) correct the widely disseminated image of Brown ("the tone and the statements of the newspapers") in a modest attempt "to be just," to "*at least* express our sympathy, and admiration of, him" (my emphasis). There is little suggestion at the start of the speech of the more radical—and more problematically transcendent—position that Thoreau will eventually come to articulate. His concern here instead is to appeal to common values: those held by him and his audience; and those of geography and history that they all share with Brown. Thoreau's narrative intent, it seems, is not to do anything to disrupt this sense of community; rather, his more reassuring ambition is to adjust its focus in ways that will seem entirely reasonable.

This unwillingness to alarm is continued in the way in which Thoreau chooses to represent Brown's pre-Harpers Ferry activities. It becomes important, for instance, that Brown's knowledge of army planning is made explicit. "He learned by experience how armies are supplied and maintained in the field," Thoreau states (*PW* 137). Instead of leading a group of disorganized, ill-disciplined men (as many of the anti-Brown newspaper reports had suggested), Thoreau wants to insist upon his skill and knowledge, a professional authority based upon recognizable rules and procedures. But more than this, such tactical experience, he asserts, convinced Brown of the righteousness of pacifism: "He saw enough, at any rate, to disgust him with a military life, indeed to excite in him a great abhorrence of it . . . He then resolved that he would never have anything to do with any war, unless it were a war for liberty" (*PW* 137–38). The combination here of an avowedly nonviolent Brown who nevertheless possessed all the requisite skills to be a successful army leader in the right circumstances is effective or disingenuous—depending upon the degree of intellectual license we are prepared to allow. On the one hand, by asserting professionalism and pacifism Thoreau seeks to neutralize powerful prejudices operating against Brown; on the other, the easy transition from peace to war generated by the word "unless" in the above quote might cause Brown's trenchant pacifist assertions to be viewed with more skepticism. With Brown's actions in Kansas, culminating in the "Pottawatomie Massacre" of five slave-state settlers in May 1856, Thoreau finds it rhetorically and ideologically necessary to slide over what has come to be seen as one of the most controversial aspects of his subject's career. Michael Meyer has shown that reports of the events at Pottawatomie Creek appeared in many of the Democratic newspapers that Thoreau is known to have read, but that such accounts failed to temper the degree of his support for Brown.[44] In "A Plea," this often-violent conflict over questions of settlement and slavery is translated into the less emotive and insistently nonjudgmental phrase, "the troubles in Kansas." What is elided is the specific event that has come to mark Brown's intervention in the sectional politics of the state. My interest here is not so much in judging Brown's actions (others have offered their sentences on him),[45] but rather in noticing the textual reconstruction that Thoreau undertakes to position his subject in the role of principled actor. Thoreau is required to clear a space in the historical record to allow for Brown's reincarnation as a transcendent force, one whose action might serve as a model for our own, inevitably more compromised, acts. To this end, Brown's intervention is reduced to a more benign one of assistance "with his hand and counsel," through whose "agency" (a delightfully vague choice of word) "Kansas was set free" (*PW* 138).

In narrating a Brown who oscillates between forms of resemblance and of exceptionalism, Thoreau ascribes to him multiple identities that serve successively to include and exclude his audience. We have seen already how he adopts a familiar strategy of asserting Brown's shared New England ancestry as a means of establishing a sympathetic willingness in his listeners to consent to what becomes a more disquieting, accusatory speech. One aspect of this ancestry was the connection that Thoreau (and others) drew between Brown and Oliver Cromwell, a transatlantic and transhistorical sympathy that was given greater intellectual purchase by the gradual rehabilitation of Cromwell within the United States during the nineteenth century. Post-revolutionary Enlightenment America was intent on ensuring the stability of its social and political forms. Cromwell's reputation as the perceived exponent of a civic rupture that failed led Thomas Jefferson, as early as 1776, to worry about the permanence of his own nation's brand of Republicanism. Writing to his fellow Virginia politician Edmund Pendleton in August of that year, Jefferson considered the possibility of "a reacknowledgment of the British tyrant as our king": "Remember how universally the people run into the idea of recalling Charles the 2d after living many years under a republican government."[46] Such anxieties about revolutionary excess had given way, by the mid-nineteenth century, and with the help of Thomas Carlyle's *On Heroes, Hero-Worship, and the Heroic in History* (1840) and *Oliver Cromwell's Letters and Speeches with Elucidations* (1845), to a reinterpretation of Cromwell as a figure of righteous heroism and religious purity. The admiring reviewer in the *New Englander and Yale Review* of Carlyle's edition of the *Letters* is typical of this revisionary historiography. Carlyle's Cromwell was "not that quintessence of cant, falsity and the devil; that red-nosed Noll, who was a mere savage fighter, snorting death-fire upon St. Charles I." Instead he is presented as "A real hero; a deep, earnest, sincere, godly man; a reality and not a sham; veracious, not lying, — truly religious, and as far from cant and hypocrisy as any other."[47]

Among New England Transcendentalists, perhaps the earliest extended engagement with Cromwell was Charles Lane's piece in the Emerson-edited *Dial* of October 1842. Lane, English-born but recently relocated to Concord, constructs a more absolutist figure whose role in the scourge of a corrupt English polity earns his admiration. A "sharp, gray-eyed fanatic," Cromwell's "real, soul-inspired manhood" is "an instrument" for the working out of a providential cleansing.[48] Central to Lane's reading of his subject is the supplanting of ineffective political discourse by action. "Reverie is, for the moment, past for him," he writes. "He has the revelation, and now he comes forth to action. To frail argument and long-drawn speech he never descends. His tactics are not talkative, but active. To place his cause on the rotten stage of logical precision were to forecast defeat." The suspicion, shared by both Emerson and Thoreau, that eloquence might be insufficient as a tool of transformation is made explicit in this account of Cromwell's politics of enactment. To resort to speech is to lapse from the purity of action; the significance of Cromwell lies in the fact that his inspiration to act ("the revelation") was immediately channeled into a purposive response that evades the weakness and inertia of discourse. For the practically minded Lane (he was later to be the cofounder, with Bronson Alcott, of the short-lived experiment in utopian living Fruitlands), the appeal of such a translation is clear (and one might almost be tempted to suggest that his indictment of reformist intellectuals who refrain from tangible engagement was aimed at his editor): "Here lies the point. We all see, we all feel eternal rectitude, but we do not all act it. We do not even verbally affirm it . . . [M]ultitudes . . . can talk of heroism, and applaud the actor, but can no more" (260). Cromwell's eventual failure, for Lane, is marked by his fall into language-use, for revolutionary zeal gives way to the corruptions of political rhetoric. "Courting his opponents with the words of peace on his lips," Cromwell performs the art of "conscious diplomacy, which must fail . . . Oscillating between the substance and the shadow, true to neither, he is no longer heart-whole" (263, 264). Cromwell's failure leads to Lane's perorating call that "We need a new Cromwell," and to his belief that the presence of such a figure — or more precisely of the attributes that Cromwell displayed — might be located in New England: "The wrongs he temporarily addressed have not yet passed away; the rights he claimed are not yet conceded. Old England is still corrupt; New England is still the land of hope" (264).[49]

That John Brown represented a possible Cromwell *redivivus* was not lost on a number of New England abolitionists. Wendell Phillips regarded him as "a regular Cromwellian, dug up from two centuries." For George Stearns he was "a Cromwellian Ironside introduced in the nineteenth century for a special purpose," and his fellow "Secret Six" member Franklin Sanborn, in his 1909 autobiography, judged that "Like Cromwell, whom in certain rare qualities he much resembled, [Brown] had 'cleared his mind of cant'; the hollow formulas of scholars, priests and politicians had little force with Brown."[50] Reynolds notes that Brown had read with enthusiasm the first biography of Cromwell by an American writer, Joel Tyler Headley's 1848 *Life*, in the preface to which Headley is explicit about the role his own national identity has played in writing the book: "That as an American, I should wish to defend the founder of the first true commonwealth, and expose the slanders that have been heaped upon him, is most natural."[51] Aligning English Republican and U.S. identities in this way created a usable Old World past from which American intellectuals might draw inspiration and analogy.

Thoreau's contribution to this act of transhistorical translation is to focus on speech as a political mode. Brown, he asserts, "was not in the least a rhetorician

... had no need to invent any thing; but to tell the simple truth, and communicate his own resolution; therefore, he appeared incomparably strong, and eloquence in Congress and elsewhere seemed to me at a discount. It was like the speeches of Cromwell compared with those of an ordinary king." The deliberate inversion of rank in that last sentence is typical of Thoreau's disruptive tactics. Similarly, Brown's eloquence resides precisely in its lack of rhetorical visibility, for by speaking "within bounds" so that he "did not overstate any thing," Brown becomes "a volcano with an ordinary chimney-flue." Such restraint is analogous to that demonstrated by "an experienced soldier," and compares favorably to the inflated language of the professional politician: Brown "was not talking to Buncombe or his constituents any where" (PW 140).[52] The reference to Cromwell provides a transatlantic historical referent that had increasing currency in New England intellectual circles, for whom a divinely inspired revolutionary soldier could reappear as an incarnation of American transgression.

As with his highlighting of Brown's eloquent lack of eloquence, Thoreau's account of his subject's education similarly reverses conventional expectations of intellectual authority:

> He did not go to the college called Harvard, good old Alma Mater as she is. He was not fed on the pap that is there furnished. As he phrased it, "I know no more of grammar than one of your claves." But he went to the great university of the West, where he sedulously pursued the study of Liberty, for which he had early betrayed a fondness, and having taken many degrees, he finally commenced the public practice of Humanity in Kansas, as you all know. (PW 139)

Thoreau's comic resituating of education away from the institutional structures of legitimacy has a double effectiveness. Clearly positioning Brown outside of the formal learning to be found at "the college called Harvard" (what other could there be of significance to a Concord crowd?), Thoreau removes the possibility that the traditional privileged centers of intellectual life might alienate Brown's potential supporters. For Thoreau, genuine intellectual activity happens away from such environments, and the only actions that have the potential to be transformative are those unencumbered by conventional disciplinary parameters. The ineffective "pap" served up at a cloistered Harvard, then, is set against a model of education received on the frontier of the United States where the founding principles of the nation still have a moral currency. The "study of Liberty" prepares Brown for the direct and active "public practice of Humanity." As Worley has remarked, Brown thus becomes a recognizable type, in the mould of such American incarnations of natural nobleness as Daniel Boone and Andrew Jackson.[53] But in addition to this, Thoreau begins to construct a powerful taxonomy of intellectual legitimacy, one that insists upon unfettered detachment and a sense of estrangement from the normative practices of society. Harvard, instead of signifying metonymically an ideal of American intellectual life, becomes in the eyes of Thoreau a place of conformity and mediocrity, an unwelcome site against which he exerts a willed alienation. Such a felt sense of exile at the heart of the national imaginary is more explicitly stated later on in the address. "Foreign countries" that are imagined as spaces of difference, provoking feelings of isolated dislocation, are in fact, Thoreau says, to be seen on every street corner. "This strangeness between us and our nearest neighbors" replicates the anxiety we project onto unknown lands. Our fellow citizens, he asserts "are our Austrias, and Chinas, and South Sea Islands," to the extent that "the thoughtful man" finds himself "a hermit in the thorough-fares of the market-place." Where the beginning of "A Plea" had sought to reassure with its advance-ment of a communal identity, now "impassable seas"; "impassable boundaries"; and "difference" are what is most registered. Thoreau's deployment of "we"; "us"; and "our" at this point still gestures at a notion of group solidarity, but it is one now irrevocably distanced from all the forms of organization—religious, legal, educational, governmental—by which life is regulated. In positing such an op-position, it becomes inevitable that Thoreau's collective "we" is translated into modes of singularity—the distinction to be drawn is one "between individuals and between states" (*PW* 145). There can be little security invested, it seems, in a pronoun that grammatically embodies the risk of reduced selfhood.

Indeed, one of the fascinating problems that Thoreau's "A Plea" presents to its readers is exactly this sense of a shifting subject position: what is the relationship between the speaker and his audience, and how is that relationship mediated by the presence of Brown as both representative and ideal figure? One paragraph, in particular, illustrates the nature of Thoreau's pronounal flexibility:

> Our foes are in our midst and all about us. There is hardly a house but is divided against itself, for our foe is the all but universal woodenness of both head and heart, the want of vitality in man, which is the effect of our vice; and hence are begotten fear, superstition, bigotry, persecution, and slavery of all kinds. We are mere figure-heads upon a hulk, with livers in the place of hearts. The curse is the worship of idols, which at length changes the worshipper into a stone image himself; and the New Englander is just as much an idolater as the Hindoo. This man was an exception, for he did not set up even a political graven image between him and his God. (*PW* 144)

This passage begins with a clear confrontation between an "our" / "us," constitut-ing Thoreau and his like-minded friends, and a ubiquitous enemy that is ev-erywhere "about." However, the plotting of such close yet separately identifiable positions immediately begins to unravel in the next sentence: whereas before the "foes" were "in our midst," now they are internal to the body (politic) itself. Referencing Lincoln's "House Divided" speech of June 1858, the possibility of distinguishing between "we" and "they" has disappeared. In its place, a non-discriminating "universal" malaise affecting both mental and emotional faculties has blurred the strict demarcation of adversarial positions. "Our foes" are ourselves, caused by "our vice." The dubious status for Thoreau of the pronoun "we" as a marker of nonconformist resistance is apparent here: instead of heroic solidarity, "we are mere figure-heads upon a hulk," toothless cheerleaders for a monstrous and degraded society. At the start of "A Plea," as we saw, a New England identity was promoted as representative of certain core national ideals, as something definitively American. Now this is startlingly no longer the case: what was recognizable and cherished has become foreign and idolatrous. If all forms of collective identity have failed in this way, Thoreau's celebration of Brown depends upon his singular status: "This man was an exception" (again we have the premature past tense), to the extent that Brown was able to transcend the man-made structures that interpose themselves between us and God. The nobleness of an Andrew Jackson or a Daniel Boone is distilled into a pure antinomianism in which Brown is figured as uniquely different from a collective identity that, here at least, includes Thoreau himself: "He [Brown] could not have been tried by a jury of his peers, because his peers did not exist." Brown is identifiable in absolutist national terms ("he was the most American of us all" [*PW* 147]) and yet remote from that nation's citizenry ("he was not our representative in any sense" [*PW* 149]). This unresolved dialectic calls into question those accounts of "A Plea," such as Worley's, that seek to smooth out Thoreau's less reconcilable tensions. While acknowledging that Thoreau might wish the address to be read as a celebration of a form of sociability in which Brown's identity is "merged" with that of a community that recognizes his value (Worley writes that Brown "represents values that penetrate the entire culture,")[54] it is important to place alongside such "authorised" interpretations those moments of rhetorical or ideological resistance that pull the argument of the text in other, potentially distorting, directions. "A Plea" reveals a movement across and between assertions of uniqueness on the one hand and those that stress Brown's representative status on the other, an opposition, I have been arguing, that is characteristic of Pierre Bourdieu's "bidimensional" intellectual.

By incorporating into his account of Brown his own acute reading of the culture that he and Brown share, Thoreau manages to effect a relationship with his subject that not only authorizes a version of Brown's life, but also validates his right to draw on the moral capital that Brown has established. A form of intellectual succession, Thoreau hopes, is performed by the address. Yet, it is in perhaps the epistemologically most opaque section of "A Plea" that Thoreau's ability to wear Brown's mantle finds itself compromised. Before discussing this passage at some length, I want to preface it by returning to the issue of consent as a philosophical and moral problem in the text. What is the value of that which we agree to countenance? Does consenting to acts undertaken with the aim of ushering in a more just society absolve us of responsibility for the form those acts might take? On several occasions in "A Plea" Thoreau raises the issue of consent as a kind of moral weathervane: the health of the individual body and the body politic might be measured by looking at the kind of things to which we, individually and collectively, agree. Thoreau's examples are usually negative: "The modern Christian is a man who has consented to say all the prayers in the liturgy, provided you will let him go straight to bed and sleep quietly afterward"; "He has consented to perform certain old established charities, too, after a fashion, but he does not wish to hear of any new-fangled ones" (*PW* 144); "when a government takes the life of a man without the consent of his conscience, it is an audacious government, and is taking a step toward its own dissolution" (*PW* 156). These models are indicative of a narrow, morally bankrupt culture of which Thoreau despairs. Yet at the start of what I think is the most resistant passage of "A Plea," he assigns to himself a more radical, less compromising form of consent:

> It was his [Brown's] peculiar doctrine that a man has a perfect right to interfere by force with the slaveholder, in order to rescue the slave. I agree with him. They who are continually shocked by slavery have some right to be shocked by the violent death of the slaveholder, but no others. Such will be more shocked by his life than by his death. I shall not be forward to think him mistaken in his method who quickest succeeds to liberate the slave. I speak for the slave when I say, that I prefer the philanthropy which neither shoots me nor liberates me. At any rate, I do not think it quite sane for one to spend his whole life in talking or writing about this matter, unless he is continuously inspired, and I have not done so. A man may have other affairs to attend to. I do not wish to kill nor to be killed, but I can foresee circumstances in which both these things would be by me unavoidable. (*PW* 153)

Brown's moral position is regarded here as unusual ("peculiar"), in a way that re-enforces his transcendent status. Immediately Thoreau gives his consent to it—"I agree with him." The relationship between the two men is orchestrated around sympathetic recognition: Thoreau is exceptional enough to see beyond the apparent peculiarities of Brown's stance and is prepared to affirm it in a way that gives it a wider legitimacy.

In comparison with the other versions of consent described in the address, Thoreau's simple four-word sentence asserts itself with bald, bold force. But as we have seen in other passages, clarity begins to waver as the lines proceed, almost as if the troubling personal and moral implications of such a statement begin to obscure the uncompromising view. Those who continue to find slavery shocking, Thoreau continues, have a "right" to be troubled by the killing of a slaveholder, "but no others." In other words, only those who are unaware of slavery's brutality are entitled to feel shock at the death of a white slaveholder. The use of the word "right," of course, is troublingly ambivalent, for a noun ordinarily invested with legal and moral force here resonates with a deflating irony: what kind of "right" is appropriate to confer to the profoundly ignorant? The grammatically imprecise "Such" that begins the next sentence refers, I take it, to those "others" for whom slavery's horrors elicit no surprise. Thoreau suggests that these "others" are more alarmed by the actions of the slaveholder in life than in the brutal manner of his death. Yet such a distinction sits uneasily alongside the parallel claim that these same people are no longer shocked by slavery's degradations. In working with the structuring opposition of life/death here, Thoreau teeters on the brink of sacrificing transparency of exposition for rhetorical effect: behind the linguistic playfulness, his argument begins to loosen into contradiction and ambivalence.

Perhaps sensing that his prose has lost its way, Thoreau is keen to focus it on that which he might be able to control more effectively—himself. As with the earlier "I agree with him," a second statement of consent is now offered: Thoreau will not criticize any form of action that "quickest succeeds to liberate the slave." Once again, this is directed explicitly at Brown and establishes an alliance between the two men. However, it is immediately followed by what may well be the strangest sentence in the address: "I speak for the slave when I say, that I prefer the philanthropy which neither shoots me nor liberates me." The ambiguity lies in the words "I speak for." Cavell, as we have noted, believes that the act of consent brings with it the responsibility of acknowledging forms of collectivity, a sense of shared intent that works to elicit moral perfectionism that, if not attained, is nevertheless targeted as an ambition. To "speak for" someone else, as Thoreau claims to be doing here, might indeed be intended by him as just this kind of act, yet what is actually spoken in this moment of ventriloquism remains problematic. Should we perceive "speaking for" as a Whitmanian gesture of democratic voicing or an act of race- and class-bound appropriation? Indeed, as we consider in chapter 5, does a rhetoric of inclusivity (like Whitman's) inevitably result in a politics of homogenized incorporation? Given the consent that Thoreau has just offered to Brown's tactics, why would he and/or the slave feel more comfortable with an action that does not result in freedom? This line refuses to come into focus, resisting interpretation in a way that is fascinating for literary criticism but damaging for the ideological and moral impetus behind Thoreau's speech. The apologetic "At any rate" that follows suggests the inadequacy of his position, and a second attempt is made at articulation, this time more securely focused on the "I" pronoun. But instead of returning to the claims of moral equivalency between himself and Brown, Thoreau now chooses to draw attention to what appear to be incompatible interests and lifestyles. Brown's Ahab-like fixity of purpose that had commended itself to Thoreau earlier in the address becomes something alien to his (Thoreau's) experience. This is disarmingly honest on Thoreau's part, yet it works against one of the central trajectories of "A Plea," which is to say Thoreau's acquisition, as Brown's interpreter and kindred spirit, of his intellectual and moral authority. The wish not to kill or be killed is understandable enough, but in the face of Brown's intensity of purpose and clarity of vision, the statement "I can foresee circumstances in which both these things would be by me unavoidable" is more tentative than we might expect.

I have focused on this passage not with the desire to catch Thoreau out, but to show how "A Plea" as a whole resonates with the kinds of irreducible tension that can be found in concentrated form here. Thoreau's admiration for Brown is not in question; what is less clear, for Thoreau and for us, is how he could use Brown's narrative most effectively as a form of cultural critique. Thoreau's most individualist self was able to see in Brown's most antinomian incarnation the possibility of an effective intellectual life, transcendentally unimpaired by material existence. The "sublime spectacle" of Brown's narrative suggested an image of the dissenter as prophet and hero. Yet the Thoreau who in *Walden* found himself unable to describe nature except through metaphors and analogies from the man-made world is also aware of the inevitably compromised status of transcendence; he strives to connect Brown to a series of recognizable coordinates and types. Lentricchia and McAuliffe's notion of the terrorist as transformative artist describes a romanticized, utopian paradigm that Thoreau wants to believe in. Yet the text finds itself torn between such a radical model of externally located influence and a need to locate that influence among others. This oscillation between exceptionalism and representativeness never gets to grips, as we have seen, with the key moral problem posed by Brown's actions. By consenting to violence, Thoreau seems to share his subject's values; yet the paradox of acting immorally in the service of a moral *telos* is never entirely resolved, however much Thoreau chooses to elide the violent specifics of Brown's campaign. What resonates is the suggestion that Brown's purified intellectual, despite its appeal, is finally unsustainable: "A man may have other affairs to attend to" (*PW* 153).

Thoreau's admiration for John Brown, and the affinity with Cromwell that he imagines for him, is directed by a belief that thought can be translated into action without the interference of representational structures, either linguistic or institutional. Enacted thought is purified of the inertia induced by corrupt discourse and represents the possibility of genuine political transformation. Thoreau judged that Brown, "this comparatively unread and unlettered man," was superior to "our professor of belles-lettres, or of logic and rhetoric" because he knew that "the *art* of composition is as simple as the discharge of a bullet from a rifle" (*PW* 167). This equivalence of text and action gave him an eloquence that was at once exemplary and exceptional.[55] Brown's presence as both a familiar avatar of nonconformity and a figure of foreignness within the American body politic results in the kind of instability we have noted in Thoreau's text. Translating Brown into terms that are recognizable *and* retain the force of productive estrangement pushes Thoreau's account in unstable, if hermeneutically interesting, directions.

In Emerson's eulogy address to Thoreau, later printed in the August 1862 edition of the *Atlantic Monthly*, the oscillation between representativeness and exceptionality is once more apparent. Like Brown, Thoreau is the embodiment of national identity ("No truer American existed" [*CWE* 10: 459]) and yet at the same time he is most comfortable in his absolute resistance to the edifices of that nationality ("he did not feel himself except in opposition" [*CWE* 10: 455–46]). For the most part, Emerson enjoys the tension that inheres in such a combination, and elements of Thoreau's nonconformity remind us of the Brown-Cromwell alliance already mentioned. Thoreau "was a born protestant" (*CWE* 10: 452), Emerson declares, "a protestant *a outrance*" (*CWE* 10: 454) who was "somewhat military in his nature" (*CWE* 10: 455). As with the accounts of Cromwell and Brown, Thoreau is remembered as "a speaker and actor of the truth" (*CWE* 10: 457) whose impulse was always to run counter to prevailing opinion: "his first instinct on hearing a proposition was to controvert it, so impatient was he of the limitations of our daily thought" (*CWE* 10: 456). The iconoclastic nature of Thoreau's stance Emerson finds attractive, recognizing in him aspects of his own carefully cultivated self-image of guide and interpreter, "the man of men, who could tell them all they should do" (*CWE* 10: 465). The disdain that Thoreau had for his audience also chimes with Emerson at his most unapologetically individualist; what he says of Thoreau's alienation from ordinary structures of polity ("it is needless to say that he found himself not only unrepresented in actual politics, but almost equally opposed to every class of reformers" [*CWE* 10:

460]) could apply equally as well to the Emerson of "The American Scholar" and "The Divinity School Address."

Those early blasts of nonconformity (1837 and 1838, respectively) had, however, been followed by an increasingly professionalized literary career that saw Emerson enter the public sphere as a widely traveled lecturer and, belatedly, convert to the antislavery cause. While I do not wish to endorse Stephen Whicher's influential narrative of Emerson's decline from early radicalism to middle-aged conservatism — indeed, later texts such as *The Conduct of Life* (1860) demonstrate a continuation of Emerson's nimble elusiveness, as Stanley Cavell and Pamela Schirmeister have shown[56] — it is nevertheless important to recognize the location of Emerson's intellectual career within structures of knowledge that, while offering him a potentially wider audience, might also have the effect of corralling his ideas into predetermined shapes. Thoreau certainly worried about the damage popularity might do to the effectiveness of thought, noting in *Walden* that "the orator yields to the inspiration of a transient occasion, and speaks to the mob before him, to those who can *hear* him" (*W* 404); and Emerson incorporated a journal entry into his eulogy that displays Thoreau's suspicion of successful (and, for Emerson, increasingly remunerative) acts of oratory: "Talking, one day, of a public discourse, Henry remarked that whatever succeeded with the audience was bad. I said, 'Who would not like to write something which all can read, like Robinson Crusoe? and who does not see with regret that his page is not solid with a right materialistic treatment, which delights everybody?' Henry objected, of course, and vaunted the better lectures which reached only a few persons" (*CWE* 10: 456–57).[57] What looks like Emerson's goading here of Thoreau's purist position (surely he must have realized that, to a transcendentalist, a "materialistic treatment" of anything was never going to be acceptable?) marks the first point in the address where the celebration of Thoreau's Brown-like antinomian qualities modulates into more skeptical treatment.

This reported exchange between the two friends, one that hinges on a disagreement over the appropriate audience for intellectual claims, encapsulates Emerson's reluctance to endorse completely the radically unconnected force he has spent many pages remembering. Thoreau's independence of thought ran the risk, he feels, of becoming unnecessarily obstructive, a stance held for its own sake rather than directed at tangible, transformative ends. Thoreau's inclination "to put every statement in a paradox," rather than a strategy of radical defamiliarization, becomes for Emerson a rhetorical tic, "a habit of antagonism" that "defaced his earlier writings" and was "not quite outgrown in his later" (*CWE* 10: 479). Thoreau may have "scoffed at conventional elegance" (*CWE* 10: 481), in much the same way that he admires Brown's insistence on "no idle eloquence, no made, nor maiden speech, no compliments to the oppressor" (*PW* 149), yet Emerson finds his position unacceptable because, *unlike* Brown's, it did not result in action, at least in the kind of action that Emerson considers to be valuable here. In a damning paragraph he makes his judgment of Thoreau's disengagement explicit:

> Had his genius been only contemplative, he had been fitted to his life, but with his energy and practical ability he seemed born for great enterprise and command; and I so much regret the loss of his rare powers of action, that I cannot help counting it a fault in him that he had no ambition. Wanting this, instead of engineering for all America, he was the captain of a huckleberry-party. Pounding beans is good to the end of pounding empires one of these days; but if, at the end of years, it is still only beans! (*CWE* 10: 480)

What Maurice Lee has called Emerson's "mean-spirited edge"[58] here is provoked by a sense of Thoreau's failure to enact thought. Despite the impetus of the preceding pages, which have worked to admire Thoreau's refusal to submit to regimes of meaning and which seek to translate him into someone whose significance might continue after his death, Emerson nevertheless wishes Thoreau had managed to locate himself within the parameters of "great enterprise and command." Lack of ambition consigns him to the status of an unheroic John Brown or Oliver Cromwell, one who is unable to make the transition from revolutionary impulse to its tangible manifestation. The reference to "captain," of course, reminds us of these earlier military models; but it also brings us right up to the present of the Civil War, for by the time of Thoreau's death in May 1862 the conflict had reached new levels of slaughter with the defeat by Stonewall Jackson of the union forces in the Shenandoah Valley. (The bloodiest day of the war, the Battle of Antietam, was only four months away.) In this context, choosing to captain a huckleberry-party signals a retreat from the duty of serving a nation in crisis. Such a critique might strike us as hypocritical, given Emerson's self-confessed contortions over the competing realms of thought and action. These moments of disapproval in the text are difficult to read in the knowledge of their author's own very belated embrace of conventional political action. Yet as a textual whole, Emerson's eulogy is a succinct reminder of the challenges posed to solitary intellectual activity by events that seem to demand organized and collective forms of response. John Brown had provided Thoreau with an ideal example of purposive living; the martyred abolitionist, in his reading, was able to unite the life of the purified mind and its performance in righteous violence. But even here, as we saw, Thoreau cannot quite escape the worry that antinomian action might be unsustainable, and that more representative forms of enactment might have to suffice. Emerson's account of Thoreau similarly oscillates between admiration of his subject's uncompromising alienation and scorn that such alienation cannot, paradoxically, be put to better use. The eulogy closes with Emerson softening his tone, likening Thoreau to a botanist in search of a "summer plant called 'Life-Everlasting,'" a man whose untimely death means that he leaves incomplete "his broken task which none else can finish" (*CWE* 10: 484). The move from huckleberries to *Edelweisse* embodies the return of the romantic naturalist in Emerson's figuration, and the final sentence of the address maintains this transcendental register: "His soul was made for the noblest society; he had in his short life exhausted the capabilities of the world; wherever there is knowledge, wherever there is virtue, wherever there is beauty, he will find a home" (*CWE* 10: 485). In the shadow of Emerson's reservations, and in the shadow of Shenandoah, these words register both the precious value of such a location and America's distance from it.

3

CONVERSATION AND COSMOPOLITANISM

We would live with them, rather than be taught by them how to live.
—MARGARET FULLER

If Ralph Waldo Emerson and Henry David Thoreau were ambivalent as to how best to intervene in the intellectual life of the nation—at times emboldened by their sense of moral independence, and at other moments doubtful of their ability to furnish an effective language of change—Margaret Fuller more convincingly embraced the possibilities for intervention offered by the emergence of a literary marketplace served by advances in publishing technology. The localized intimacy of the pulpit congregation or the Lyceum audience was, if not surpassed, then in increasing competition with an anonymous public granted easy access to affordable newspapers and journals. As Adam-Max Tuchinsky has recently noted, Fuller was located in a culture "where ideas were exchanged as a commercial transaction, and where the intellectual's relationship to the public was detached and anonymous," a facet of America's burgeoning modernity that offered a challenge to the willed autonomy of New England's literary avant-garde.[1]

Fuller's intellectual maturity had been reached at a point subsequent to the intense theological debates between American Unitarianism and an emerging American Romanticism, debates that had been focused around very powerful personalities and intellectual enmities and that were situated within the worlds of Boston and Harvard. Her move to New York in 1844 to begin work as literary editor on Horace Greeley's New York *Tribune*, one of the most widely read American newspapers of the mid-nineteenth century, symbolizes Fuller's dissatisfaction with the amateur intellectual tradition of the Concord circle; a culture of literary professionalism within the republic of letters made possible a larger audience and a greater influence. It also had the effect of challenging those elements of Romantic culture that stressed the solitary, deracinated figure as the model for the American intellectual. Advances in commercial printing inaugurated anxieties over intellectual authority, such that Ralph Waldo Emerson could frame his suspicion of the popular press in terms of its corrupting transience: "The newspaper of course will defame what is noble and what are you for but to withstand the newspapers & all the other tongues of today; you do not hold of today but of an age, as the rapt & truly great man holds of all ages or of Eternity. If you defer to the newspaper, where is the scholar?" (*JMN* 7: 76). The "of course" here has the effect of inscribing as obvious and inevitable Emerson's position, as he establishes a familiar hierarchy between eternal virtues and temporal vicissitudes, between succumbing to contingencies and upholding one's true intellectual nature.[2]

In an 1844 letter to his friend, Samuel Ward, written shortly after Fuller's arrival at the newspaper, Emerson repeated his skepticism:

> The Tribune office may be good treatment for some of his [Emerson is referring to William Ellery Channing, then employed by Greeley] local distempers, but it seems a very poor use to put a wise man & a genius, to. Is it any better with Margaret? The Muses have feet, to be sure, but it is an odd arrangement that selects them for the treadmill. Our grand machine of Society must be sadly disjointed & ricketty, if this is its best result. (*Letters* 7: 618)

Emerson locates Fuller in the secondary role of female muse who finds her influence blunted by participating in the debased mechanics of knowledge distribution that, for him, characterize newspaper publishing. As Gustavus Stadler has observed, in his analysis of the taxonomy of the idea of "genius" in American nineteenth-century letters, "in a cultural sphere of a mass scale," the worry for intellectuals like Emerson was that they might come to be seen as "undifferentiated from their readers, with whom they participated in the cultural marketplace, as laborers in a literary *profession* subsuming an older, vocational model of authorship."[3] In contrast to Russell Jacoby's influential definition of public intellectuals as having "a commitment" to "a public world — and a public language, the vernacular,"[4] Emerson's skepticism about the appropriateness of popular impact for the conveyance of ideas leads him to value the comforts of an imagined intellectual peer group. In "The Progress of Culture," an address read in 1867 to the academic elite of the Phi Beta Kappa Society at Harvard, he laments the fact that "a certain enormity of culture makes a man invisible to his contemporaries"; genuine intellect risks being lost in a society that values majority opinion and the power of popularity, such that, Emerson suggests, "it is always hard to go beyond your public" (*CWE* 8: 215). Faced with this kind of inattention he seeks refuge in the company of the like-minded:

> Every book is written with a constant secret reference to the few intelligent persons whom the writer believes to exist in the million. The artist has always the masters in his eye, though he affect to flout them. Michel Angelo is thinking of Da Vinci, and Raffaelle is thinking of Michel Angelo. Tennyson would give his fame for a verdict in his favor from Wordsworth. Agassiz and Owen and Huxley affect to address the American and English people, but are really writing to each other . . . The importance of the one person who has the truth over nations who have it not, is because power obeys reality, and not appearance; according to quality, and not quantity. (*CWE* 8: 219, 220)

The production of culture here is brought about by a relationship of intellectual titans who provoke it, as well as aimed at such men who are its consumers. This model, while evincing healthy suspicion of the collective articulation of national affect, nevertheless operates according to an airless law of circularity.

As early as 1836, Fuller had considered the potential benefits and drawbacks of commercial publishing for the transmission of ideas. In a journal record from December of that year, she notes a conversation with Richard Henry Dana in which he

> railed against newspapers and periodicals, professing his willingness to give them up entirely. I plead in favor of reading them moderately, and asked whether it was not better to use the time in its own way than to lose all benefit from it and waste strength in useless opposition to its course. Would not he allow such reading to stand in the same relation to real reading that street compliments do to real conversation. No! nothing of the sort would he tolerate; total abstinence was the only way to keep the mind healthful and thoughtful. Go into society without caring or thinking any thing about common ground; speak out directly from your own interests and you will be likely to drop some good seed (Here I thought of Mr Emerson)[.][5]

Dana, then completing his education at Harvard before entering into a highly successful legal career, reacts against the burgeoning development of the popular press with an absoluteness that chimes, as we have seen, with Emerson's response (Fuller's parenthetical reference is appropriate); it signifies the anxiety over loss of influence felt by elements of Brahmin Boston, the traditional arbiters of public opinion, in the face of a transformed cultural authority brought about by expanded newspaper publication.[6] Fuller's attempts at countering Dana's onslaught configure around the necessity of engagement with a discourse that cannot be avoided; while acknowledging the secondary, inferior nature of journalism (it is figured as "street compliments" rather than "real conversation"), she nevertheless argues in favor of its inclusion within the realm of intellectual discussion. "Street compliments" may be no more than empty social niceties, yet they might also encode possibilities of dialogue and exchange with portions of society ordinarily beyond the reach of the republic of letters. For Fuller, the "common ground" dismissed by Dana becomes an increasingly politicized and transnational space as her writing career progresses. This chapter plots aspects of Fuller's relationship to the possibilities of newspaper publication; as a space within which intellectual work might be possible, Fuller conceives of her journalism within explicitly comparativist and cosmopolitan terms. The first section examines the question of intellectual authority within the new print culture by considering the contrasting responses Fuller and Emerson articulate to the question of criticism's form and function within the literary marketplace. That this marketplace had a reach beyond the parameters of the national is the focus of the second part of the chapter, where I offer some ways of thinking about the relationship that Fuller's critical project has to notions of the cosmopolitan that she inherits from Goethe. The final section looks specifically at instances of her textual engagement with the Italian Revolutionary uprising of 1848–49, in which the possibilities for a transformed European polity enabled Fuller to orchestrate a critique of American national ideologies. Throughout, I want to argue for Fuller's role as a mediator of foreign cultures for the United States, a role that is made textually visible by the discursive and structural diversity in her writing, yet one which, when faced with political failure, runs the risk of translating cultural mediation into redemptive orchestration.

The Literary Marketplace and Intersubjective Criticism

The problem of reconciling the competing demands of the marketplace with those qualities of purified self-assertion cherished by the romantic intellect is evident in two texts—one by Emerson, the other by Fuller—that served to introduce readers to the *Dial*, the house journal of American Transcendentalism whose first issue appeared in July 1840. The *Dial*, although not widely read during its four-year lifetime (its subscription list never rose above three hundred), nevertheless marked a key moment in the development of New England intellectual history as debates over U.S. culture moved from the institutional authority of the pulpit and theological discourse to the more secular (if still, at times, idealized) space occupied by the cultural critic. The journal represented Transcendentalism's first foray into a potentially more diverse democratic culture, and as such it exhibited from the start an uncertainty as to how it wished to be perceived within that culture.[7] The kinds of resistance to Jacksonian America advocated by Emerson and Thoreau had suggested a model of unaffiliated intellectual work in the face of capitalist conformity; yet in the pages of the *Dial*, the avant-garde nature of Transcendentalism was venturing, however tentatively, into the more market-driven parameters of modern journal publishing. The three figures most involved in its establishment — Fuller, Emerson, and George Ripley — had great difficulty in agreeing the purpose and general tone of the publication. As editor, Fuller drafted an introductory essay that she hoped would set out the *Dial*'s aims and objectives, but after reading it Emerson's response was not encouraging: "This paper [Fuller's essay] addresses the public; and explains; it refers to contemporary criticism; it forestalls objection; it bows, though a little haughtily, to all the company; it is not quite confirmed in its own purpose" (*Letters* 2: 285). He is instinctively reluctant to have the journal speak to a populist constituency; its cognizance of modernity detracts from what should be its more legitimate focus on "Universal aims" (*Letters* 2: 286). Rather than expressing concern about the relative position of the *Dial* within an ever-expanding marketplace of cultural critique, Emerson asserts a characteristically combative position of intellectual autonomy:

> With the old drowsy Public which the magazines address, I think we have nothing to do; — as little with the journals & critics of the day. If we know any other Journal, certainly we should not write this. This Journal has a public of its own; its own *Thou* as well as *I*; a new-born class long already standing waiting for this voice & wondering at its delay. They stand before their doors in the highway on tiptoe looking down the road for your coming. (*Letters* 2: 285–86)

The established public sphere of intellectual exchange is regarded here as an economy with which, and in which, the *Dial* need have no purchase; the uniqueness of *this* publishing endeavor, Emerson maintains, lies in its relationship to an expectant constituency that is itself already alienated from the mechanics of the marketplace. Emerson imagines a separate space in which "I" and "Thou" can communicate, one which need pay no attention to the enervated forms in which a culture of letters is conventionally articulated. Fuller accepted Emerson's offer of an alternative introductory essay, yet it is clear from a letter he sent her in May

1840 that there remained a lack of consensus as to its value or purpose: "I hope ere this you have digested your chagrin concerning the Introduction I sent you Nay have fairly got Mr Ripley at work to try his hand in drafting a Declaration of Independence. When he has tried, suppose we apply to Dr [William Ellery] Channing — indeed I would send the requisition all round the Table to every member" (*Letters* 2: 294).

When the first number of the *Dial* appeared in July, Emerson's "The Editors to the Reader" was indeed the opening piece, followed by Fuller's "A Short Essay on Critics." While both texts confront the problem of the literary marketplace for the Transcendentalist intellectual, their responses to this dilemma are subtly different, with Fuller's suggestive of a more dialogical sense of cultural critique than Emerson's insistence on transcendent values and the expression of private emotion. Emerson chooses to focus on those who have "paid their vows to truth and freedom," a constituency of readers who are united in their rejection of forms of association and collective performance. They "have no external organization, no badge, no creed, no name. They do not vote, or print, or even meet together. They do not know each other's faces and names." As we saw was the case with Thoreau, Emerson's revolutionaries are also skeptical of modes of representation, both political and textual, preferring instead to inhabit private spaces of resistance that, Emerson hopes, might be conjoined through the pages of the *Dial* into effective voices of American futurity. These potential readers, he suggests, are located across the nation's economic and social structures, and are not confined to the educated or reading classes that constitute the conventional demographic for literary journals. The cross-section Emerson imagines is worth quoting at length:

> They are of all conditions and constitutions. Of these acolytes, if some are happily born and well bred, many are no doubt ill dressed, ill placed, ill made — with as many scars of hereditary vice as other men. Without pomp, without trumpet, in lonely and obscure places, in solitude, in servitude, in compunctions and privations, trudging beside the team in the dusty road, or drudging a hireling in other men's cornfields, schoolmasters, who teach a few children rudiments for a pittance, ministers of small parishes of the obscurer sects, lone women in dependent condition, matrons and young maidens, rich and poor, beautiful and hard-favored, without concert or proclamation of any kind, they have silently given in their several adherence to a new hope, and in all companies do signify a greater trust in the nature and resources of man, than the laws or the popular opinion will well allow.

Emerson's choice of vocabulary consistently enforces a sense of shared conditions that pertain within the apparent diversity of his sociological sweep. "Lonely and obscure"; "solitude"; "obscurer sects"; "lone women"; "matrons and young maidens"; "silently"—these all work to solidify an accumulated sense of the unaffiliated nature of his ideal readers, all of whom voice "without concert" an eagerness for transformation, such that the "spirit of the time is felt by every individual with some difference."[8] Within the common cause of personal and social revolution, then, exists a variety of response that, for Emerson, guards against the myopic ineffectiveness of a collective identity. As I discuss in the context of William James in chapter 4, negotiating a position that acknowledges diversity and yet aims for authoritative coherence provides a challenge to the antifoundationalist impulse of pragmatism; for Emerson, the centrality of individualism to his concept of American ontology works to imagine a readership of solitary souls. Yet he fears that even this constituency of the disassociated elect might not be best served by the material products of intellectual work, for in comparison with the natural world, "we wonder how any book has been thought worthy to be preserved. There is somewhat in all life, untranslatable into language. He who keeps his eye on that will write better than others, and think less of writing, and of all writing" (3). While not going so far as to doubt the durability of the new journal at its birth, Emerson's skepticism about writing as the means by which to convey profound ideas (which, after all, were the only ones that mattered to him) strikes an uneasy note. Instead of exhibiting "the pens of practiced writers," the *Dial* will focus on "the discourse of the living," those, as it becomes apparent, alienated from and by the mechanics of conventional publishing. Drawing from the "recesses of private thought," the "secret confession of genius," and the "tear-stained diaries of sorrow and passion" (4), the journal's putative writers appear as similarly isolated in their romantic purity as do its imagined readers.

Emerson's positioning of the *Dial* as essentially a transcript of private experience reflects his distaste for the vulgarities of commercial publishing. While Margaret Fuller, as we will see, concurs with much of her friend's analysis, her opening intervention in the journal, "A Short Essay on Critics," represents a more savvy reading of the form and function of criticism within the literary marketplace. As such, it is also one of Fuller's earliest meditations on the responsibilities of the intellect in American life. From the opening paragraph it is apparent that taxonomical structures will regulate her essay:

> [T]hough this age be emphatically critical, the writer would still find it necessary to investigate the laws of criticism as a science, to settle its conditions as an art. Essays, entitled critical, are epistles addressed to the public, through which the mind of the recluse relieves itself of its impressions. Of these the only law is, "Speak the best word that is in thee." Or they are regular articles got up to order by the literary hack

writer, for the literary mart, and the only law is to make them plausible. There is not yet deliberate recognition of a standard of criticism, though we hope the always strengthening league of the republic of letters must ere long settle laws on which its Amphictyonic council may act.[9]

As Julie Ellison has remarked, amid the categorizing certainties of this passage lie inconclusive judgments and definitional shifts.[10] An age that is "emphatically critical" is nevertheless devoid of a "standard of criticism," such that the paragraph's insistence on standards of "law" is ironically undermined by the admission that these are anything but "settled." In classic Enlightenment terms, Fuller hopes that the "republic of letters," independent of sectarian or national affiliation, will be able to resolve the matter once and for all. Meanwhile she locates the *Dial* somewhere between the private "epistles" of the intellectual recluse and the "regular articles" of the professional scribe, between the romantic alienation of Emerson and the knowing, "plausible" commercialism exhibited in newspapers such as the Boston *Courier* and *Daily Times*. Her taxonomical focus on types of critic, rather than on types of criticism, allows Fuller to deploy a characteristically romantic trope of personification to explore aspects of national, spiritual or (as here) aesthetic importance. She outlines three categories of critic, "subjective," "apprehensive," and "comprehensive," the transition from one to the next characterized by increased degrees of intellectual range and sympathy.

"Subjective" critics, as Fuller denotes them, believe in the absolute authority of their own judgments, displaying a solipsistic confidence that brooks no need of dialogue or conversation; under these conditions, thought is not required to exert any influence beyond its moment of expression. The "subjective" critics discount the possibility that "it [thought] may live to others when dead to them." Lacking the intersubjective sympathy Fuller regarded as essential for the role of the critic, "They state their impressions as they rise, of other men's spoken, written, or acted thoughts. They never draw of going out of themselves to seek the motive, to trace the law of another nature. They never dream that there are statures which cannot be measured from their point of view" (5). The "subjective" critic is tied to the circumstances and conditions of his existence, "his nation, his church, his family even," and, in a damning sentence, Fuller charges that "He is content to be the creature of his place" (6). Intellectual provincialism that passes as solipsistic assertion will also characterize Fuller's critique of nationality in her letters to the *Tribune* sent from Europe at the end of the decade. "A Short Essay on Critics," then, marks an early call for the kind of critical cosmopolitanism so evident in those dispatches, and is a quality present in the second category of intelligence Fuller describes. "Apprehensive" critics, she asserts, "can go out of themselves and enter fully into a foreign existence": "They reproduce the work of which they speak, and make it better known to us in so far as two statements are better than one." In an act of intellectual translation that adds to the sum of human knowledge, the "apprehensive" critic exhibits the kind of receptiveness to a work that matches "the dignity of disinterested friendship," to the extent that her reading might surpass the original in beauty—"melodies will sometimes ring sweetlier in the echo," Fuller asserts (6). Finally, within this increasing scale of value, the "comprehensive" critic augments the qualities of her "apprehensive" colleague by being able to locate her judgments of a work not only according "its own law," but also within what Fuller calls the "analogies of the universe," that "absolute, invariable principle" that acts as a standard against which ideas can be evaluated: "Sustained by a principle, such as can be girt within no rule, no formula, he can walk around the work, he can stand above it, he can uplift it, and try its weight. Finally he is worthy to judge it." Here, the cosmopolitan specificities of a "foreign existence" are rendered interpretable in a move reminiscent of the transcendentalizing potential of Emerson's "transparent eyeball." The "comprehensive" critic assumes different vantage points offering multiple perspectives on a work, but instead of inducing hermeneutic confusion, she is able carefully to weigh the evidence in front of her before offering a classification in the light of universal values.

Yet what follows in "A Short Essay on Critics" illustrates an oscillation that is characteristic of Fuller's intellectual life as a whole, for the Emersonian hue that is evident in her denotation of the "comprehensive" critic is soon modified by a series of statements that seek to reassert a dynamic relationship between artist, critic, and the reading public. If Fuller's third critical category appears overly distant from the experience of the ordinary reader, she is quick to reassure the *Dial*'s subscribers that the role of her ideal critic is to establish a new partnership with the reader, to expand the circulation of ideas by "making others appreciate" them. The critic "sees" the divinity of the creator, "but brings it down to humanity": "Next to invention is the power of interpreting invention . . . [E]very step is explanation down to the lowest" (7). Explanation, as she envisages it, should not be didactic, for "dictatorship in the reviewers" and the consequent "indolent acquiescence of their readers" has been largely responsible for the poor reputation of journal culture (8). However, in a more positive vein than we found in the Emerson piece, Fuller is prepared to maintain a belief in the usefulness of such publications—"They afford too convenient a vehicle for the transmission of knowledge;—they are too natural a feature of our time to have done all their work yet" (9)—such that her final paragraph outlines a striking manifesto of collaboration and intersubjectivity:

Able and experienced men write for us, and we would know what they think, as they think it not for us but for themselves. We would live with them, rather than be taught by them how to live; we would catch the contagion of their mental activity, rather than have them direct us how to regulate our own. In books, in reviews, in the senate, in the pulpit, we wish to meet thinking men, not schoolmasters or pleaders. We wish that they should do full justice to their own view, but also that they should be frank with us, and, if now our superiors, treat us as if we might some time rise to be their equals. It is this true manliness, this firmness in his own position, and this power of appreciating the position of others, that alone can make the critic our companion and friend. We would converse with him, secure that he will tell us all his thought, and speak as man to man. But if he adapts his work to us, if he stifles what is distinctively his, if he shows himself either arrogant or mean, or, above all, if he wants faith in the healthy action of free thought, and the safety of pure motive, we will not talk with him, for we cannot confide in him. (10)

Fuller's desire to encounter "thinking men" in an environment of intellectual reciprocity and exchange, freed from the impositions of authority and instruction, establishes a model of solidarity with her readers. The insistent "we" pronoun introduced at this point underscores what Capper describes as Fuller's "community of self-reflective readers,"[11] and imagines conversation as the form around which ideas are circulated. She is open to the possibility of encountering such ideas in the conventional locations of public discourse—the government, the church, the printed text—but it is clear that the excessively circumscribed voice of class, party, or nation must be rejected in favor of interactions that acknowledge the permeability of such borders. Thought, after all, is transmitted here by "contagion," a word which, as James Snead has noted in another context, etymologically joins con and tangere ("touching together") to render obsolete the barriers to thought's transmission.[12] Communicability is delicately balanced with an uncompromising genuineness, where ideas are only exchanged (and exchangeable) so long as they do not pander to the expectations or limitations of those who receive them. Within the networks of intellectual encounter that Fuller envisages, authenticity remains central. Julie Ellison regards the hierarchy of critics in "A Short Essay" as "facile, if feisty,"[13] yet, while the schematized structure of the piece does indeed determine the framework for its ideas, Fuller, as Ellison herself has shown, is unable or unwilling to contain them completely within its contours. The doctrinaire rigidity of Fuller's taxonomy is finally inconducive to an intellectual *habitus* that thrives on encounters with alterity—indeed often with subaltern alterity—for its motivation. Her pieces in the *Tribune* were frequently concerned to highlight the plight of disenfranchised groups—women, the urban poor, Native Americans, African-Americans, and Irish-Americans were all discussed in the pages of the newspaper, such that, as Christina Zwarg has pointed out, "Fuller makes a direct correlation between the activity of reading and the process of social change, for reading can offer a way to disrupt certain ideological assumptions."[14] Among her papers at the Houghton Library are four sheets in Fuller's hand dated "Boston 20 September 1840," placing them at the start of her tenure as editor of the *Dial*. While it is unclear if what follows is her own composition or instead one of the many transcriptions from other works that fill her notebooks, its focus on intellectual activity as ongoing and dynamic nevertheless supports Zwarg's characterization of Fuller as a writer always keen to dislodge—and to be dislodged from—the securities of the status quo. The text begins: "How vast is the sea of Knowledge that spreads before us—How far we look out over its horizon—How little progress do our frail Barks make—The letter that concludes the alphabet of knowledge is that sublime saying of the great man, that all he had done was but the picking up of a few pebbles on the shore of this mighty water." Our disappointing incompleteness, in which "the progress we make seems little," is enforced, Fuller's text suggests, by the jolting encounter with a perspective that undermines any notion of intellectual mastery: "suddenly a little word, a young untaught person, a child in his playful style, touches a sounding note on the chord we have stretched with so much pains, that is more musical than all we can play—Then our knowledge seems to us nought."[15] The example here of the untutored child reminds us of Fuller's experience as a teacher in 1836–37 at Bronson Alcott's Temple School in Boston, where Alcott sought to demonstrate the innate superiority of children through their possession of universal truths and which resulted in the publication of the scandalous *Conversations with Children on the Gospels* (1836–37).[16] Fuller's focus on the unlettered mind as the repository of eternal values is more than a conventional (if, in the case of Alcott, at times controversial) Romantic trope. It also signals her belief in the generation of thought through unexpected moments of encounter, where knowledge might be furthered by interaction with subaltern groups hitherto deemed inconsequential to the republic of letters. Her "Boston 20 September 1840" text closes with a commitment to intellectual work that, in a daring reversal of the standard opposition between nature's permanence and the transience of those edifices of human creation, warns against complacency and stasis, advocating instead the exemplary role of the striving mind:

> And knowledge too, pursuing from year to year its steady course, shall be our earthly occupation, our daily bread. Generations may lie beneath the forest shade, and say it

is beautiful enough, it shelters us, and we are happy — By and by comes one that is not happy enough — He is not warm enough in the shade of the trees — he must cover his head with the rude work of his own hands — so rises his low roof — He gazes sadly as he contrasts it with the majestic groves where lie his brethren — He says "It is not beautiful, but it is my own" — The groves pass away with the innocent and beautiful that were sheltered by them; they leave no trace behind — But he that for & by himself has laid one stone upon another, his work shall endure, & all that come after shall be sheltered. He is a tutelary god to all who follow in his road after.[17]

Literature's "Great Mutual System of Interpretation"

For many women, the emergence of literary modernity, coinciding as it did with the wider leveling effects of Jacksonian democracy, facilitated easier entry into intellectual culture and the kind of "tutelary" role that Fuller envisaged. Surrendering her marginality through employment at the *Tribune*, Fuller relinquished her romantic singularity and obscurity, as well as the collegiality of a small, sympathetic readership. As a participant in, rather than a mere observer of, this new mass culture, she was faced with a wider constituency of unknown readers than anything with which Emerson had to contend. She was also writing in a form — the newspaper article — that was gaining increased importance as the purveyor of opinion and shaper of national identity, offering Fuller the opportunity to belong to what she called "the advanced guard in all liberal opinions."[18] In Benedict Anderson's influential theory of the building of modern nationalism outlined in *Imagined Communities*, the newspaper is significant because it reflects and enables modern conceptions of time and also because its consumption is communal. What Anderson (following Walter Benjamin) calls "homogenous empty time"[19] — the impression that readers shared an identical moment with the columnist and with each other whilst reading the article — created an epistemological framework within which Fuller's audience might identify a textual and ideological connection to themselves. The act of reading is thus centrally connected with the creation of an imagined community; printed and consumed on a national scale, the newspaper becomes the common link for a republican nation confronting any given issue as a shared whole. "The printed word became the primary avenue of national enculturation" in this era, according to Ronald Zboray. "Type was well suited to the work of constructing a national identity," because texts were portable and unchanging, and thus they facilitated "a common reading experience."[20] The mass circulation of newspapers and the immediacy of the telegraph allowed for wide-ranging forms of national deliberation, as James Russell Lowell noted in a eulogistic flourish in 1865:

In one respect, and no unimportant one, the instantaneous dispersion of news and the universal interest in it have affected the national thought and character. The whole people have acquired a certain metropolitan temper; they feel everything at once and in common; a single pulse sends anger, grief, or triumph through the whole country; one man sitting at the keyboard of the telegraph in Washington sets the chords vibrating to the same tune from sea to sea; and this simultaneousness, this unanimity, deepens national consciousness and intensifies popular emotion. Every man feels himself a part, sensitive and sympathetic, of this vast organism, a partner in its life or death. . . . It is no trifling matter that thirty millions of men should be thinking the same thought and feeling the same pang at a single moment of time, and that these vast parallels of latitude should become a neighborhood more intimate than many a country village. The dream of Human Brotherhood seems to be coming true at last.[21]

Lowell's belief that the "newspaper and telegraph gather the whole nation into a vast town meeting" (193) had important implications for those men and women who would present themselves as cultural leaders. As a tool of considerable force, the modern newspaper, as Lowell and before him Fuller recognized, maps the co-ordinates of national identity in a way that rescues it from provinciality (cultivating instead "a certain metropolitan temper") and provides group cohesion, despite the absence perhaps of any other kind of direct connection between the members of that group. What both Lowell and Anderson overlook in this alliance of communication technology and national imagining is the extent to which, even in the nineteenth century, the newspaper was thought capable of articulating a constituency that expanded beyond the contours of the nation-state. In 1887, the German sociologist Ferdinand Tönnies published his influential work *Gemeinschaft und Gesellschaft* (*Community and Society*), in which he described the press as possessing a "universal power" that "is not confined within natural borders, but, in its tendencies and potentialities, . . . is definitely international."[22] Tönnies serves to remind us that the power of the newspaper to permeate across and between nations was recognized well before the emergence, in our own time, of multinational media corporations.

While Fuller's readership in the *Tribune* remained distinctly American, she nevertheless imagined her writing in its pages as a space to broaden the "imagined community" of those readers and to articulate the possibility of a transnational politics of republican democracy that was no longer the preserve of any particular nation. Liberated from the claustrophobic coterie world of New England intellectuals, Fuller's Romantic sensibility was exposed, through her position as first literary editor and then foreign correspondent on the *Tribune*, to a cosmopolitan and eventually transatlantic set of influences. If the newspaper could re-enforce cultural and national positions, Fuller's work in this form often sets out to disrupt them—or at least to demonstrate their constructed nature—through its often fragmentary structure, its regular incorporation of translated texts, and its attention to unconventional subject matter. Her 1845 review in the *Tribune* of the vernacular Scottish poet William Thom's *Rhymes and Recollections of a Hand-Loom Weaver* is a striking example of Fuller's advancement of a democratic intellectual purview that incorporates writing beyond the contours of the respectable or expected. Thom's life—as the title of his volume indicates, he combined literary ambition with work as a weaver in Inverurie, Aberdeenshire—provided Fuller with the basis for an intervention on the topic of literary legitimacy that matches anything similar we may find, for example, in Walt Whitman. Thom "has a poetical mind, rather than is a poet," but the deficiencies in his technical skill are more than compensated for by what Fuller judges to be his "delicate perception of *relations*" (my emphasis). Confronted by literature of this type, criticism has two choices. It can hold on to standards of aesthetic excellence and moral universality, of literature as the manifestation of "kernels of permanent value" whereby the reader is satisfied only with the "Iliads and Odysseys of the mind's endeavor." Alternatively Fuller posits the view that "literature may be regarded as the great mutual system of interpretation between all kinds and classes of men. It is an epistolary correspondence between brethren of one family, subject to many and wide separations, and anxious to remain in spiritual presence one of another." The dialogic and reciprocal aspects of this model are immediately apparent, and its emphasis on diversity contained within forms of resemblance (the "brethren of one family") both echoes the design of America's *e pluribus unum* motto and anticipates questions of philosophical and political pluralism that would preoccupy William James at the turn of the century. The inevitabilities of distance—whether structured through gendered, racial, economic, or national parameters—become more easily managed once contained within Fuller's notion of familial affinity. Then, shifting the terms of the discussion to an extended horticultural riff to enforce her distinction, she imagines the critic who polices the literary space as one who "weeds well the garden, and cannot believe that the weed in its native soil may be a pretty graceful plant." Such selective cultivation is set against a more holistic understanding:

> There is another way which enters into the natural history of everything that breathes and lives, which believes no impulse to be entirely in vain, which scrutinizes motive and object before it condemns, and believes there is a beauty in its natural form, if its law and purpose be understood. It does not consider literature merely as the

garden of the nation, but as the growth of the entire region, with all its variety of mountain, forest, pasture and, tillage lands. Those who observe in the spirit will often experience from some humble offering to the Muses, the delight felt by the naturalist in the grasses and lichens of some otherwise barren spot. These are the earliest and humblest efforts of nature, but to a discerning eye they indicate the entire range of her energies.

By locating William Thom within such a widened artistic tradition in which, importantly, he has a stake, Fuller envisages a literature that does more than merely display its aesthetic qualities for complacent consumption. The ordered "garden" of America becomes a diverse "region," and, in the context of her Scottish subject matter and New York readers, this geography in turn widens to become a genuinely extranational space of critical inquiry in which the "naturalist" is poised to encounter the unexpected and conventionally overlooked. Although Fuller's next move is to reconcile the opposition she has spent time establishing — she imagines a moment when "[t]he highest sense of fulfilled excellence will be found to consist with the largest appreciation of every sign of life" — it is clear that the impetus of her discussion is as much ethical as literary, for in her analysis of Thom's poetry lies the desire to construct a theory of cultural interaction that allows for expanded and plural significances.[23]

In a review of Thomas Arnold's *Introductory Lectures on Modern History*, published only five days after the Thom piece, she reiterates this position by quoting with approval her subject's insistence that "a mixed knowledge is not a superficial one. . . . [H]e who reads deeply in one class of writers only, gets views which are almost sure to be perverted, and which are not only narrow but false."[24] As Amanda Anderson points out, in her discussion of what she calls "communicative ethics," such an holistic approach enables one to hold "self-reflexive questioning of norms, or postconventionality, as the moral ideal that undergirds the subject's acts of affiliation and disaffiliation." Political stances, in other words, remain porous and receptive to a range of possibilities that allow for multiple forms of belonging. "The subject's relation to a specific cultural identity," Anderson writes, "may extend from strongly expressed attachment, to radical redefinition, to outright rejection and negation. Communicative ethics should promote practices that can remain flexible and open-ended in the face of multiple and shifting attachments and detachments."[25] Fuller's concern to promote such a diversity of political and aesthetic positions ensures that her relationship to notions of U.S. national identity remains anything but stable, inflected as it is with a cosmopolitan and self-critical impulse which, both ideologically and structurally, unravels the comforts of a narrowly exceptionalist reading of the nation's health.

In this, Fuller's key intellectual debt lay with Goethe, whose impact upon American letters she was largely responsible for initiating. The first historian of transcendentalism, Octavius Brooks Frothingham, noted that "No author occupied the cultivated New England mind as much as [Goethe] did," although the occupation itself was not always a comfortable one.[26] Most transatlantic intellectuals recognized Goethe's pre-eminence, but many were disturbed by his work: he was condemned by both religious conservatives because of his supposed Pantheism, and condemned by political liberals because of his supposed political conservatism. Elizabeth Peabody regarded him as an "Epicurean"—he "had no ideal—no moral standard of perfection."[27] Francis Jeffrey, the influential editor of *The Edinburgh Review*, did not hold back in attacking *Wilhelm Meister's Lehrjahre* for being "eminently absurd, puerile, incongruous, vulgar, and affected . . . almost from beginning to end, one flagrant offence against every principle of taste, and every just rule of composition . . . throughout altogether unnatural."[28] The German-educated American historian George Bancroft was just as damning when he concluded that "in everything that relates to firmness of principle, to love for truth itself, to humanity, to holiness, to love of freedom, [Goethe] holds perhaps the lowest place."[29] Emerson's response to Goethe is most comprehensively detailed in his chapter on him in *Representative Men*,[30] but an earlier journal passage from 1844–45 indicates the co-ordinates around which he was able to articulate his appreciation:

> [George] Putnam pleased the Boston people by railing at Goethe in his ΦBK oration because Goethe was not a New England Calvinist. If our lovers of greatness & goodness after a local type & standard could expand their scope a little they would see that a worshipper of truth and a most subtle perceiver of truth like Goethe with his impatience of all falsehood & scorn of hypocrisy was a far more useful man & incomparably more helpful ally to religion than ten thousand lukewarm church-members who keep all the traditions and leave a tithe of their estates to establish them. But this clergyman should have known that the movement which in America created these Unitarian dissenters of which he is one, begun in the mind of this great man he traduces; that he is precisely the individual in whom the new ideas appeared & opened to their greatest extent & with universal application, which more recently the active scholars in the different departments of Science, of State, & of Church have carried in parcels & thimblefuls to their petty occasions. (*JMN* 9: 145–46)

Putnam's rigidly New England hermeneutics diminishes his ability, Emerson contends, to read Goethe with the kind of liberated perspective his subject deserves. The narrowness of the Calvinist "local type" is set against the benefits to be derived from even only a moderately expanded intellectual curiosity, the effect of which would be to recognize the essential kinship between American nonconformity and its European equivalents (or, as Emerson suggests here, antecedents). The exceptionalism that lies behind Putnam's claim of intellectual and moral superiority is revealed to be a sham, Emerson insists, once we realize that not only did Goethe initiate those impulses of dissent that America claims for itself, he was also the most uncorrupted and complete representative of them. Compared with Goethe's total embodiment, the United States presents itself as divided, its separate parts working to little effect.

Goethe represented for Margaret Fuller both an intellectual ideal and a challenge, and her response to him was a fluctuating one. In an undated journal fragment on Goethe and Herder, her assessment of the former's skills as a poet is far from effusive:

> In poetry altho he has bequeathed so much to posterity, he seems, like Pope!, to display rather a systematic versification of prose than a spontaneous effusion of verse! He had neither the poet[']s timidity nor the poet's flights. Mankind he took as he found them, neither seeking nor causing to make them better.[31]

Yet in an 1832 letter to James Freeman Clarke, she confesses her disquiet when faced with the perfection of Goethe's mind:

> It seems to me as if the mind of Goethe had embraced the universe . . . I am enchanted while I read; he comprehends every feeling I ever had so perfectly, expresses it so beautifully, but when I shut the book, it seems as if I had lost my personal identity — All my feelings linked with such an immense variety that belong to beings I had thought so different. What can I bring? There is no answer in my mind except "It is so" or "It will be so" or "No doubt such and such feel so."[32]

For Fuller, contemplating writing a biography of the German writer that she would never complete, Goethe's overpowering mind worked to reduce difference and to suppress individuality, including her own. The "immense variety" of "beings I had thought so different" is rendered homogenous under Goethe's comprehending gaze, such that the possibilities of intellectual exchange are reduced to a finite number of inadequate affirmations. As Colleen Boggs has explained, in an astute reading of the politics of Fuller's practice of translation, the danger of Goethe's "universal genius" lay in the threat it posed to Fuller's ontological status.[33] Yet in a later, more considered essay on Goethe, published in the *Dial* in 1841, offered ostensibly as a rebuke to a harsh assessment of the German writer by the conservative critic Wolfgang Menzel, Fuller's stance has changed. While acknowledging his importance as a spur to intellectual development ("he obliges us to live and grow, that we may walk by his side"), Goethe is now also seen as fallible: "Had he but seen a little farther, he would have given this covenant a higher expression, and been more deeply true to a diviner nature." As it is, "a too determined action of the intellect limited and blinded him for the rest of his life."[34] Moreover, Fuller feels that her subject was unable to locate himself in any particular circumstance: "Nature having given him power of poetical sympathy to know every situation, would not permit him to make himself at home in any" (342), a homelessness that has the effect of diminishing national affiliation in favor of cosmopolitan curiosity. The appeal of this kind of worldliness to a writer like Fuller cannot be underestimated, for her conception of cultural identity was not determined by the securities of bounded space but by the relational possibilities of transnational encounter, of conversation within and between different contexts that pose, in Boggs's words, "challenging questions about the nation's relation to a collective world culture and the individual's relation to national and international collectives."[35] As Wai Chee Dimock remarks, failure of the kind Fuller attributes to Goethe paradoxically initiates the possibility of continuing influence and inspiration, an afterlife that will always signal Goethe's "incompleteness" (Fuller's word).[36] Dimock understands this kind of incompleteness as translating "into a collective injunction for the entire species,"[37] one that aims for the kind of Cavellian perfectionism that, as we noted in chapter 2, is an inevitably elusive but nevertheless noble aspiration. Fuller writes that Goethe "has failed of the highest fulfilment of his high vocation," yet in this failure resides his "claim to all our study."[38] The nature of the response to Goethe that she envisages here is central to her conception of intellectual activity. Instead of passively echoing the thoughts of others, Fuller advocates encounters that, as studies like Christina Zwarg's have demonstrated, are structured around a polyvocal engagement with conflicting identities and subjectivities.[39] Fuller's first substantial intervention in the intellectual life of mid nineteenth-century Boston was the publication in 1839 of her four-hundred page translation of Johann Peter Eckerman's *Gespräche mit Goethe*, a record of Goethe's conversations as recorded by his reverential young secretary, which appeared in George Ripley's "Specimens of Foreign Literature" series, an early venture in introducing a more cosmopolitan perspective to American letters whose motto (taken from Milton) expressed the desire that "ripe understanding, and many civil virtues, be imported into our minds from foreign writings; — we shall else miscarry still, and come short in the attempts of any great enterprise."[40] Rather than supporting the image of the Weimar poet as a morally suspect writer who had created the tempestuous, tortured *Werther* or the profound, but in America little-read, *Faust*, Fuller's translation introduced Americans to a keen and accessible critic overflowing with wise reflections on social ethics, art, and the literary vocation. In the preface to the translation,

Fuller's resistance to an obedient submission to intellectual mastery is clear. Eckermann, she judges, is too happy to voice his subject's ideas:

> The simple reverence, and thorough subordination to the mind of Goethe, which make Eckermann so transparent a medium, prevent his being of any value as an interpreter. Never was satellite more completely in harmony with his ruling orb. He is merely the sounding-board to the various notes played by the master's hand; and what we find here is, to all intents and purposes, not conversation, but monologue. . . . Perhaps there is no instance in which one mind has been able to give out what it received from another, so little colored by its own substance.[41]

In noting Eckermann's accuracy, Fuller was unaware that he had scrupulously edited Goethe's speeches and had reconstituted the conversations of 1823 from correspondence. Indeed, Eckermann's preface (which Fuller translated) would seem to dispute her estimation of his "simple reverence," for he notes that "this is *my* Goethe. And this applies not merely to his manner of presenting himself to me, but to my incapacity for fully receiving and reproducing him" (5).[42] Despite this confession of subjective fallibilism, Fuller is insistent that Eckermann's "translation" of Goethe's spoken words manifests itself as an exact transcription that undermines their usefulness. In her reading journal from March 1835, she noted the collaborative manner of Goethe's intellectual life: his "manner of learning was to investigate as far as he could from his then state of knowledge or being and *after* to ascertain what others had thought[,] done[,] or written on the subject."[43] She thus encapsulated a praxis that emphasized intersubjectivity as its central mode, one that organized intellectual exchange through structures of difference in a manner that also came to animate Fuller's own work. By contrast, Eckermann's form of literary devotion, she judged, closes down the opportunities for mutual sympathy which, in turn, diminishes the possibility of transforming private discourse into public communication. The formal heterogeneity of texts such as the Eckermann–Goethe conversations (as well as the correspondence of two aristocratic German women, Karoline Günderode and Bettine von Arnim, which Fuller translated, but did not finish, between 1840–42) appealed to Fuller's desire to expose noncanonical literary genres to a reading public, as well as to explore models of ideal intellectual affiliation. In "Bettine Brentano and her Friend Günderode," an essay published in the *Dial* in 1842, Fuller claims that the two women's letters represent "the soul made manifest in the flesh, and publication or correspondence only furnishes them with the occasions for bringing their thoughts to a focus."[44] Her work translating these texts focused her attention on the benefits of productive, reciprocal exchange, as well as highlighting the dangers of relationships structured around mastery and dominance. Moreover, as

Karen English has observed, Fuller's theory of translation as dialogic and intuitive also informed the hybridity of her own major works, *Summer on the Lakes, in 1843* and *Woman in the Nineteenth Century*, whose formal and generic variety militate against neat hermeneutic closure.[45] As she noted in the latter text, in the context of gender categorizations, "History jeers at the attempts of physiologists to bind great original laws by the forms which flow from them. They make a rule; they say from observation what can and cannot be. In vain! Nature provides exceptions to every rule. She sends women to battle, and sets Hercules spinning . . . Presently, she will make a female Newton, and a male Syren."[46] This model of ceaseless flux and transition, in which attempts at organized taxonomy are immediately undermined by nature's willed perversity, establishes a dialectic of pattern and dispersal that can offer only momentary respite from a terrain of heterogeneity.

In Fuller's autobiographical sketch, composed in 1840 but published posthumously in 1852, she had drawn a distinction between the kind of neoclassical education "of considerable severity" advocated by her father, Timothy Fuller, and the release from this offered by her reading of Ovid's *Metamorphoses*.[47] Of her father's regime, she recalls that "he demanded accuracy and clearness in everything: you must not speak, unless you can make your meaning perfectly intelligible to the person addressed . . . 'But,' 'if,' 'unless,' 'I am mistaken,' and 'it may be so,' were words and phrases excluded from the province where he held sway" (I, 17). Timothy Fuller's firmness of will found an analogue in Roman culture, knowledge of which his daughter was encouraged to acquire. There she noted that "Everything turns your attention to what a man can become, not by yielding himself freely to impressions, not by letting nature play freely through him, but by a single thought, an earnest purpose, an indomitable will, by hardihood, self-command, and force of expression" (I, 18). Acting as a counterpoint to this expression of masculine strength, Ovid enabled Fuller "to get away from the hum of the forum, and the mailed clang of Roman speech, to these shifting shoes of nature, these Gods and Nymphs born of the sunbeam, the wave, the shadows on the hill" (I, 21). Thus is established in her early intellectual life an oscillation between systematic thought, with its impulse to classify and monumentalize, and the kind of flexible, contingent mode of discourse that transforms thought into a form of conversation. The contrast between the stressed hardness of "mailed clang" and the softer assonances of "shifting shoes," "sunbeam," and "shadows" helps Fuller to make her point. Pattern and diversity as polarities in constant negotiation is a central component of Goethe's natural history, as Eric Wilson has pointed out.[48] In Goethe's journal *On Morphology* (1817–24), he notes (in terms that seem to anticipate the antifoundationalism of pragmatism) that

"Natural system: a contradictory expression. / Nature has no system: she has—she is—life and development from an unknown center toward an unknowable periphery. Thus observation of nature is limitless, whether we make distinctions among the least particles or pursue the whole by following the trail far and wide." The endless horizon of Goethe's nature, like the "shifting shoes" of Fuller's nature, render provisional any attempt at codification, although Goethe allows for the possibility of a coalescing structure to come into view. (Again, the affinity here with William James's desire for order amid pragmatist flux, as chapter 4 explores, is worth remarking.) For Goethe, a world of transition is, with relief, momentarily stilled by the appearance of those aspects of the natural world that have achieved final coherence: "The idea of metamorphosis deserves great reverence, but it is also a most dangerous gift from above. It leads to formlessness; it destroys knowledge, dissolves it. It is like the *vis centrifuga*, and would be lost in the infinite if it had no counterweight; here I mean the drive for specific character, the stubborn persistence of things that have finally attained reality. This is the *vis centripeta* that remains basically untouched by any external factor."[49] Goethe's ambivalence about the value of "metamorphosis"—it is deserving of reverence as a divinely transformative gift and yet has the power to inaugurate an intellectual apocalypse—appears to be weighted in the direction of anxiety, if the rhetorical force of the warning of formlessness, destruction, and dissolution is allowed to register fully. Yet "it" (i.e., metamorphosis) can be rescued as a productive dynamism if viewed in relation to those instances of stability and focus that offer co-ordinates around and through which we can plot our otherwise unpredictable course. The centripetal and centrifugal forces that he identifies are in perpetually creative strife, with impulses of transition checked from becoming random incoherence by moments of resistance.

The quality of Fuller's translation of Goethe's *Gespräche* has been addressed by several commentators, most notably Christina Zwarg. Instead of revisiting these issues, I want to draw attention to Goethe's confident belief, as translated by Fuller, in the imminent benefits of *Weltliteratur*. "I therefore gladly make excursions to other countries," Goethe asserted, "and advise everyone to do the same. National literature is now rather an unmeaning term; the epoch of World literature is at hand, and each one must strive to hasten its approach."[50] For Fuller, keen to promote an American literary culture that was confidently multilingual and global in its significance and circulation, difficult questions were raised about the nation's relationship to a world culture and the individual's relationship to national and communal groupings. Goethe's ability to explore these relations drew Fuller to his writing. In her translator's preface she expressed admiration for his possession of a mind "which has known how to reconcile individuality of character with universality of thought" (xx). Most recently David Damrosch has explored the parameters of Goethe's notion of "world literature," the extent to which its cosmopolitanism exists in a state of tension with Goethe's sense of his own provinciality, and the degree to which *Weltliteratur* was an inevitably circumscribed, Eurocentric concept.[51] It has remained a problematic, nebulous idea to those working within the field of comparative literature. Its coinage, however, suggested the possibility of enhanced intellectual co-ordinates, of different cultures struggling to interpret, appropriate, and judge each other's forms. "World literature" helps observe a rapidly diversifying field and, at its most ambitious, envisions transnational circuits of intellectual advance, what Goethe described in an 1830 introduction to Carlyle's *Life of Schiller* as "relatively free intellectual trade relations."[52] Wherever familiar practices cross into other cultures, the term predicts the potential for new learning, seeking to conceptualize an international and more widely mediated flow of transnational scholarly interest, unconfined by the parameters of the nation-state.

One of the potential pitfalls in constructing narratives of national history lies in the powerful impulse to reproduce certain essentialized values from within; such epistemological and discursive modalities—in the context of the United States, phrases such as "Virgin Land," "American Adam," and "melting pot" come to mind—work to imagine the coherence of the nation and so inscribe a narrative that becomes naturalized and inevitable. In her book *Writing Outside the Nation* Azade Seyhan details an alternative model through which the "dialogic and self-reflexive tone of exilic writing . . . registers its distance from social and cultural norms by questioning the logic of the traditions it has inherited." Writing produced under these circumstances, she suggests, produces an "exteriority" in relation to "a dominant or national culture" through which textual forms of "self-alienation" can effectively question the "representational certainty" of such symbolic shapes as the nation.[53] The possibility of a narrative "free of official doctrine and rhetoric" (20) is the reward, Seyhan proposes, for a stance that refuses the comforts of those authorized and teleological national imaginaries that work to efface difference. While such emancipation from ideology may seem to approach a dangerously utopian condition of posthistorical transcendence—as we saw in chapter 1, far more telling are those moments of textual interference where sanctioned epistemologies rub up against dissident ones—Seyhan's critique of the protocols that determine national narratives, nevertheless, points to the prismatic networks of comparative exchange within which more complex understandings of connection might be achieved. Membership of groupings of any kind—intellectual, political, national—is accompanied by a responsibility, as J. Hillis Miller points out, "to be as self-conscious about this as possible."[54] The difficulty with the idea of American uniqueness, for Miller, lies in its ascription of "a unity and a reified existence to an entity (American romanticism) which is a fictitious creation of the critic, made by ignoring all sorts of differences from one text to another" (223). It is both too narrow and not general enough: rather than seeking out qualities that mark a text for its national coherence, he suggests instead a supranational perspective that extends across borders and chronologies. The texts of transatlantic romanticism are "permutations of linguistic materials at least two and a half millenia old": every work, regardless of its national provenance, is implicated in "an overdetermined network of associations, influences, constraints, and connections, often connections leaping far over chronological or geographical contiguity." The result of such entanglement is the inevitably compromised nature of classification itself, cautioning the critic to resist what Miller calls "the almost irresistible lure of premature generalization" (225).

As a methodology for the practice of literary criticism, Miller's strictures are daunting, to say the least. One of the anxieties pertaining to the concept of world literature, a concept with which Miller's argument has affinities, is the spectre of amateurism. Perhaps lacking the kind of deep knowledge of textual interaction and development that Miller advocates, is the critic fated to remain tied to a limited range of material or else to succumb to what David Damrosch has called "scholarly tourism"?[55] How to mediate between these two stances by acknowledging the particularity of a text and the relevance of its position within certain groupings necessitates a practice of reading that is alive to transitional moments between singularity and representativeness, the kind of textual encounter that Edward Said characterizes as "contrapuntal." What is at issue is not the idea of cultural difference itself, but the means and efficacy of identifying it and the purposes to which such identification is put. Rather than seeking simply to transcend national boundaries in the name of a universal humanism or in accordance with Miller's potentially labyrinthine nodes of intersection, my concern through reading Margaret Fuller is to explore what happens when different national formations collide or interact with each other. The contrapuntal path between the familiar and the hitherto unexplored hollows out the symbolic power of national identities, even as those identities are granted a contingent, strategic value. From this angle it might be possible to explore another kind of literary history, one more sensitive to a dialectic of familiarity and alterity, domesticity and estrangement, that works to questions assumptions about national identity without abandoning the concept of the national altogether.[56] By plotting the sometimes awkward and interrupted processes of transition between the local and the global, one is able more clearly to recognize those external points of reference that pull the circumference of national identity into strange shapes.

Certainly, Goethe was not in a position in the early nineteenth century to foresee the potential effects of the vigorous commingling taking place in the current age of multicultural exchange on a global scale. However, his emphasis on "fremde Teilnahme" ("foreign participation")[57] within and among discrete national traditions expands the geographical and historical reach of the hybrid cultural space Homi Bhabha, for one, sees inscribed in postcolonial literature. Such national reshaping, Bhabha writes, manifests itself "in the narrative temporalities of splitting, ambivalence and vacillation."[58]

At first glance, the writings of American Romanticism might seem precisely the wrong place to look for signs of an emerging transnationalism. The decades before and after the Civil War have been read as the era in which the nation's identity seemed to assert itself as never before, thanks in part to conscious efforts by intellectuals to articulate a national profile that circumvented lingering anxieties about the cultural cringe of postcolonial inferiority. The "Young America" grouping in mid-century, for example, was explicit in its advocacy of exceptionalism, a position regularly trumpeted in the pages of its journal, the *Democratic Review*. One article therein, a review of a collection of poems by William Cullen Bryant, hymned that Americans "are fresh, like a young people unwarped by the superstitions and prejudices of age, free, like a nation scorning the thought of bondage, generous, like a society whose only protection is mutual sympathy, and bold and vigorous like a land pressing onward to a future state of glorious enlargement."[59] What is striking here is the simultaneous disavowal of Old World tethering and the imperial ambition of New World expansion, a powerful and characteristic duality in much of the writing of the period. Yet such self-confident diagnoses raise the question as to how the idea of the transnational can be of such importance when the work of nation-building is still underway? The force of such a question might lead us to expect that if the global and the national were proceeding side by side, then they would have been the occasion of noisy conflict; those desiring to "condense . . . nationality," in Walt Whitman's phrase,[60] would have found themselves at odds with those pointing to wider filiations and vaster sympathies. Incipient nationalism would want to protect itself against the force of a global perspective; conversely, forms of transnationalism would seek to undermine the entrenched myopia of national models.

This relationship of seeming incompatibility, however, is complicated when we understand how imbricated and mutually constitutive the discourses of nationalism and globalism are. To be sure, the globalizing imperatives of capitalism, communication and travel undermined the development of rigidly distinct national forms. As Karl Marx and Friedrich Engels famously observed in 1848, "In place of the old local and national seclusion and self-sufficiency, we have intercourse in every direction, universal inter-dependence of nations . . . National one-sidedness and narrow-mindedness become more and more impossible, and from the numerous national and local literatures, there arises a world literature."[61] Such universalizing forces however might trigger a reactionary assertion of national specificity—sometimes reductive, and sometimes more nuanced (as I argue is the case with Margaret Fuller). The ways in which globalization might simultaneously undermine and provoke national allegiances was something that Friedrich Nietzsche fully understood. In *Human, All Too Human* (1878) he predicted "a weakening and finally an abolition of nations, at least the European: so that as a consequence of continual crossing a mixed race, that of European man, must come into being out of them," while at the same time realizing that forces of national identity would emerge as a counter-reaction to this, working "consciously or unconsciously" to produce an "artificial nationalism."[62] Margaret Fuller's conception of American identity, and her role as diagnostician of it, sits exactly at this hinge-point between the economic and cultural impulses of transnational exchange and the very tangible political drives of national expression. While noting a degree of admiration for English literature in an essay of 1846, for example, she finally felt compelled to distance herself from it: "what suits Great Britain, with her insular position," she wrote, "does not suit a mixed race, continually enriched with new blood from other stocks the most unlike that of our first descent."[63] Rather than identifying cultural identity as an organic, original given—in the way that exceptionalist readings of the United States have done—Fuller imagines a model of cultural transplantation that disrupts the shape of a powerful national imaginary based on, as she says, "our first descent." National units—whether celebrated in the rhetoric of the *Democratic Review* or fought for in mid-century European revolutions—become understood as a reaction to transnational realities, rather than as the expression of some solely domestic national process operating in proud isolation. As Pascale Casanova has recently argued, this imbrication of national and international perspectives is fundamental to the operation of a globalized literary space. "Literatures are . . . not a pure emanation of national identity," she contends. Instead "they are constructed through literary rivalries, which are always denied, and struggles which are always international . . . In a sense, there is nothing more international than a national state: it is constructed solely in relation to other states, and often in opposition to them."[64] As we will see, Margaret Fuller's keen sense of a U.S. national imaginary—and of her intellectual role in its articulation—is bound up with the impact of events and contexts beyond the nation's borders.

In a different national context, Declan Kiberd, writing of the myths of Irish national character, points out that "if huge numbers of people believed in them, then they also must be accorded their place as decisive agents of history."[65] Instead of looking beyond such agency, as Hillis Miller's textual capaciousness proposed, a properly self-conscious reading might be said to situate itself at that awkward, liminal place where the national meets the global.[66] Within contemporary discourses of cosmopolitanism, the relationship between national and global forms of affiliation exerts, as one might expect, particular attention. In a review triggered by Martha Nussbaum's 1994 essay "Patriotism and Cosmopolitanism," Bruce Robbins suggests one model of cosmopolitan thinking as the choice to regard "distant strangers neither as objects of loving concern nor as objects of policy, but as interlocutors with whom one must enter into a dialogue, common participants in a transnational public sphere whose goal would be co-ordinated action."[67] Inspired by the Stoics and Kant, Nussbaum presents cosmopolitanism as an ethos, a structure of loyalties to a vision of humanity as a whole: "We should recognize humanity whenever it occurs, and give its fundamental ingredients, reason and moral capacity, our first allegiance and respect."[68] Nussbaum's Kantian "high minded universalism," with its appeal to a transcendent, elevated notion of the cosmopolitan self, while utopian in its purity, tends to overlook the contested and porous nature of actual transnational encounters, those instances of interaction that exhibit what Robbins calls "the messy, soiling compromises between a normative and a descriptive cosmopolitanism." The desire to imagine a cosmopolitan perspective that overrides such tangled political and cultural realities runs the risk, as Timothy Brennan has argued, of substituting imperial values of national aggrandizement for imagined universal ones of benign worldliness: as the masthead of the American journal *The Cosmopolitan* tellingly proclaimed in 1886: "The world is my country and all mankind are my countrymen."[69]

In *The Ethics of Identity* Kwame Anthony Appiah, while acknowledging suspicions that cosmopolitanism enacts a hidden form of imperial ambition ("liberalism on safari," as he phrases it),[70] proposes an alternative, perhaps less ambitious but nevertheless more nuanced model that speaks to the competing and irreconcilable impulses operating in Margaret Fuller's work. He is resistant to the distinction drawn between cosmopolitanism defined as "principles of moral universalism and impartialism" on the one hand, and as "the values of the world traveler, who takes pleasure in conversation with exotic strangers" on the other (222). To regard the cosmopolitan as either an Olympian universalist or a thrilled tourist, Appiah argues, results in an unhelpful simplification of the possibilities of cultural exchange, in which one is caught between a sterile abstraction and the danger of reductive stereotyping. Instead, an engaged cosmopolitanism needs to marry its transcendent ideals with an awareness of the cultural particularities in which those ideals might strive to gain a purchase. "A tenable cosmopolitanism," Appiah writes, "must take seriously the value of human life, and the value of particular human lives, the lives people have made for themselves, within the communities that help lend significance to those lives" (222–23). What he labels "a cosmopolitanism with prospects" needs to balance both the vantage point of universal worldliness with the various loyalties of specific location; it "must reconcile a kind of universalism with the legitimacy of at least some forms of partiality" (223). That this notion of "partiality" might take shape in national form is something that Appiah is willing to acknowledge: the "ethical salience" of national groupings remains a powerful force in constructions of identity, with cosmopolitanism constituted as "debate and conversation across nations" (246).

As I have been suggesting in this chapter, Margaret Fuller advances a form of cultural exchange where traditional identities find themselves traversed by the forces of difference. That point of intersection results in a dialogue with others, in a nation whose culture emerges in global contexts. Such a vision is explicitly relational ("I need to be called out," she wrote, "and never think alone, without imagining some companion")[71] and opposes the solipsistic boundaries that Emerson erects, for example, to establish the difference between himself and what he called in *Nature* (1836) the "NOT ME." Indeed, at one point the tensions in Fuller and Emerson's friendship were expressed by the latter in terms of failed national exchange. In a letter of October 1840 he writes: "We use a different rhetoric. It seems as if we had been born and bred in different nations. You say you understand me wholly. You cannot communicate yourself to me. I hear the words sometimes but remain a stranger to your state of mind" (*Letters* 2: 353). Fuller's foreignness to Emerson, his estrangement from her discourse, is explicitly staged as a failure of language. The phrase "You cannot communicate yourself to me" suggests both Fuller's inability to convey her thoughts and Emerson's refusal to translate them into a language he might understand. For Emerson the famously reluctant traveler, "being born and bred in different nations" becomes an impediment to cultural and intellectual exchange. His impulse here is to collapse difference into a metaphysical model in which variety reassuringly gestures at the same foundational essence; only then could Emerson construct a fantasy of unity that negated the randomness and potentially inchoate nature of American pluralism.

Fuller's major statement on national literary traditions is her 1846 essay already referred to, "American Literature, Its Position in the Present Time, and Prospects for the Future," published in the *Democratic Review*. I have been arguing that Fuller's position as an intellectual within the American Romantic tradition complicates the powerful taxonomies that have been constructed to explain this literary-historical period. The beginning of her essay, however, appears to run counter to my contention: "Books which imitate or represent the thoughts and life of Europe do not constitute an American literature," she writes. "Before such can exist, an original idea must animate this nation and fresh currents of life must call into life fresh thoughts along its shores."[72] This is the very familiar "Young America" rhetoric of the mid-century, with unmistakable echoes of Herman Melville's review of Nathaniel Hawthorne's "Mosses from an Old Manse." Melville asserts that "No American writer should write like an Englishman or a Frenchman."[73] It is clear from the outset then that Fuller does not set out to negate the status or organizing power of the national within intellectual life; even at her most cosmopolitan, she incorporates the nation-state as a component of cultural classification. Lawrence Buell has nicely captured this sense of nationality's persistent presence by suggesting that "nations are utopian fictions . . . at once epistemologically suspect, economically obsolete, politically potent[,] . . . territorially determinate (except in warfare), and culturally porous."[74] A quality of porousness might be a useful way of thinking about Fuller's prose style because her writing resists the imperatives of organicism so as to retain its receptivity to difference, an intellectual nimbleness that is suited to, and encouraged by, the context of regular newspaper and periodical publication. In her essay, it becomes apparent that its opening salvos of literary exceptionalism are a form of impersonation, the voicing of a position in order to establish a relationship with it, so that Fuller's third paragraph begins very differently: "We have no sympathy with national vanity. We are not anxious to prove that there is as yet much American literature." "We are not impatient," she writes (contra Melville), "[o]f those who think and write among us in the methods and of the thoughts of Europe." America is in what she calls "a transition state,"[75] a resonant phrase for this discussion in terms of its connotations of mobility and permeability, "a transition state" in which it would be unwise to create intellectual and literary barriers to transatlantic interaction. The best in European literature offered, she thought, "an ideal manifestation in forms of national and individual greatness" (381–82), in other words, an achieved reciprocity between larger and smaller units similar to that which, as I mentioned earlier, she felt Goethe had attained. The practice of reading, then, might reveal how the individual's position within the nation-state might be transformed; likewise the imagined community of nationality itself, again through an ethics of relational reading, might be emptied of its more inflexible, isolationist incarnations.

Margaret Fuller's transnational, cosmopolitan Romanticism climaxes around the events of the Italian Revolution of 1848–49. Her complex engagement with an eruption of nationalist feeling in opposition to wider, pan-European political maneuverings is revealed in the thirty-seven dispatches she wrote for the *Tribune* between 1846 and 1850. When she arrived in Italy in 1847, the various Italian city-states were struggling to remove foreign monarchies, limit the pope's temporal power, and establish a centralized republican government. Fuller negotiates an encounter with European nationalism and translates it for her American readers as a manifestation of democracy. Such an act embodies a strategy of dialogic encounter that opens up the borders of the United States for a conversation that is at the same time global (Fuller's perspective encourages her readers to look outward) and national (she challenges them to face the complacencies of their own exceptionalism). For Fuller, the histories of other countries illuminate and magnify aspects of American culture, often ones that mark deep fissures in the unity of national identity. Her experience of, and response to, Italy illustrates the peculiarly itinerant nature of core U.S. values, for in the nineteenth-century American idea of Italy, American principles could travel, detached from the geopolitical entity of the United States. This dislocation from the anchor of the state made such principles available for reapplication in foreign situations, such that the Risorgimento and the Italian fight for national independence expressed the spirit of the American Revolutionary War, even as Fuller struggled to locate that same liberating spirit in the United States of 1848. The migration of home-grown principles allowed U.S. nationalists to take credit for elements of Italian history, so that, as Paolo Gemme has noted, the Italian dedication to democratic revolution was relayed across the Atlantic in terms of "representing Italians as confirming the American vision of the Risorgimento as derivative from the U.S. republican experience."[76] Closely wedded to this articulation of Italian derivativeness was an American sense of Italy's failure to match the purity of the original New World model. In 1852 the *North American Review* published an account of Italy's history since 1815, in which the journal's readers could feel doubly superior, both because Italy had sought to imitate their nation's principles and because Italy had signally failed to live up to the demands of them: "the Italians . . . are willing to be free, they can protest loudly against the tyranny of the rulers, and can form endless conspiracies against them. But they have not energy and patriotism enough to combine and make a manly fight for freedom."[77] For this writer, at least, it was clear that the United States remained the only extant incarnation of the republican principle.

Fuller's confrontation with conventional assumptions underlying the proprieties of statehood is profound and wide-ranging, involving not simply a matter of playing national stereotypes off against each other but, more significantly, of considering ways in which global horizons dislocate the grounds on which indigenous manners and styles of representation are predicated. Writing for the New York *Tribune* in May 1847, Fuller considered the difficulty of being able to truly "know" Italy, suggesting to her either affronted or self-satisfied readers that "an intimacy of feeling, an abandonment to the spirit of the place, [is] impossible to most Americans."[78] It is tempting to place this as a delayed riposte to Emerson's complacent refusal/inability to cross those borders of friendship that I mentioned earlier. It certainly names the problem that an intellectual strategy of relational thinking needs to overcome, if Americans are to become receptive to modes of sympathetic attachment. Writing in a later dispatch in the *Tribune*, Fuller describes the qualities she felt should characterize any potential candidate for the newly vacant U.S. Ambassadorship to Rome, following the election of Zachary Taylor to the U.S. Presidency in 1848. He should be "one that has experience of foreign life," having "knowledge and views which extend beyond the cause of party politics in the United States." Moreover, she felt that the possession of ethical and moral coherence should not detract from a sympathetic awareness of diversity, to the extent that, in a reversal of the trajectory of the *e pluribus unum* national motto, Fuller judged her ideal American representative abroad to be "a man of unity in principles, but capable of understanding variety in forms" (245).

The perceived myopia of Emerson's position—his failure to exhibit exactly this kind of sympathetic range—is given political edge in a December 1847 letter to Fuller from the Italian patriot Giuseppe Mazzini, with whom she established an enduring friendship. Failed "intimacy of feeling"—to quote again Fuller's phrase critiquing the inflexibility of American tourists—translates here into something more damning. "I ... feel fearful that he [Emerson] leads, or will lead man too much to contemplation," Mazzini writes. "His work, I think very greatly needed in America, but in our old world we stand in need of the one who will like Peter the Hermit, inflame us to the Holy Crusade and appeal to the collective influences and inspiring sources, more than to individual self-improvement."[79] Transcendentalism may have been instructive as a counterforce against American materialism, but the implication of Mazzini's letter was that it had no purchase in Europe, especially a Europe whose political climate was so radically volatile. For Fuller, the corollary to Emerson's self-culture was cultural pluralism; her theory of culture and of reading necessitated multiple viewpoints of sympathetic attachment. As Bell Gale Chevigny has remarked, her knowledge of a variety of languages produced what Chevigny calls "comparativist tendencies," an epistemological framework that made "her adept at discerning the edges or limits of certain . . . value system[s] or ideolog[ies]."[80] Such a self-consciously transnational perspective enabled Fuller to interrogate the shibboleths of American identity, to inhabit a position on the borders of conventional modes of belonging so as to excavate the language of presence and self-evidence that dominates the rhetoric of American exceptionalism. Moreover the formal qualities of the newspaper front page—its bricolage of discourses and textual registers—was perfectly suited to Fuller's vision of a pluralized intellectual space of competing and circulating ideas.

Fuller's participation within a wider discourse of European travel writing required her to position her own account of Italy in relation to such strong antecedents as Goethe, Byron, Dickens, and Fanny Trollope, as well as more imitative, generic examples. Her letters are highly conscious of the literary tradition to which she is contributing, and Fuller's mounting anger directed at those who produce what she calls the tourist "scorch and dust of foreign invasion"[81]—a pejorative allusion not just to the debris on the streets but also to the waste to be found in books and minds—evinces her desire to transcend touristic attitudes and what Brigitte Bailey describes as "American habits of visualizing."[82] In so doing, she fashions herself as a figure of cultural authority and distinctiveness, narrating a history of Italian transformation which both reflects and refreshes American cultural and political idioms. Writing in her journal in 1844, Fuller imagines herself as possessing "no real hold on life—no real permanent connection with any soul." Instead, she is keen to construct a persona of alienated homelessness that legitimates her emergent identity as a questing intellectual: "I seem a wandering Intelligence driven from spot to spot that I may learn all secrets and fulfil a circle of knowledge."[83] In the explicitly comparativist framework of her Italian letters, this declaration of a mobile, inquisitive mind is given a transatlantic focus in Fuller's description of the responsibilities of her ideal tourist, a figure she calls "the thinking American." He is

> a man who, recognizing the immense advantage of being born to a new world and on a virgin soil, yet does not wish one seed from the Past to be lost. He is anxious to gather and carry back with him all that will bear a new climate and new culture. Some will dwindle; others will attain a bloom and stature unknown before. He wishes to gather them clean, free from noxious insects. He wishes to give them a fair trial in his new world. And that he may know the conditions under which he may best place them in that new world, he does not neglect to study their history in this.[84]

This figure combines the twin impulses of American exceptionalism and cosmopolitan receptivity in a curious relationship of interdependency where New

World superiority is evidenced by a proper appreciation of the European scene. Opposed to the radical rejection of European models and influences advocated by the Young America movement, Fuller deploys the familiar Americanist trope of a "virgin soil" only to populate that landscape with cultural and political imports. It would be foolish to ignore, of course, the appropriative impulse that lies behind Fuller's denomination of the "thinking American"—she is, after all, describing a process of transatlantic transplantation in which some of the European arrivals attain a "bloom and stature unknown before" in their new environment; yet this needs to be seen alongside an awareness that, for Fuller, the most complete expression of American identity is brought about by its encounter with the unfamiliar and the foreign, such that what constitutes the idea of national character comes under a degree of pressure in the context of European political revolution.

In a dispatch from December 1847, the persona of self-fashioned connoisseurship is readily apparent in Fuller's sense of living in what she calls "the real Rome": "She [the city] reveals herself now; she tells me some of her life. Now I never go out to see a sight, but I walk every day, and here I cannot miss of some object of consummate interest to end a walk. In the evenings, which are long now, I am at leisure to follow up the inquiries suggested by the day" (168). The construction here of an identity opposed to the instrumental acquisitiveness of the regular tourist locates Fuller within the rhythms and patterns of Roman life, where the ordinary or the everyday has the potential to become invested with interpretative significance. The "leisure" she enjoys is contrasted implicitly with the administered regime of conventional sight-seeing. For this "child of Protestant, Republican America," as she calls herself, Rome nevertheless is "full of instruction for those who learn to understand" it (169). With the establishment of a French Republic in February 1848, following the removal of Louis-Philippe from the throne, Fuller regards the political upheavals occurring in France—and more widely across Europe—both as significant moments of resistance to Old World structures of authority and as triggers for American self-analysis. Her exclamation that "Those tremendous problems [of European governance] MUST be solved, whatever be the cost!" is swiftly extended to include a reassessment of those shibboleths of political republicanism that France shares with the United States. "To you, people of America," she writes, "it may perhaps be given to look on and learn in time for a preventive wisdom. You may learn the real meaning of the words FRATERNITY, EQUALITY: you may, despite the apes of the Past, who strive to tutor you, learn the needs of a true Democracy. You may in time learn to reverence, learn to guard, the true aristocracy of a nation, the only really noble—the LABORING CLASSES" (211). This insistently direct address to the *Tribune*'s readers demands that they reconsider their understanding of the vocabulary of democracy. Displacements in Europe, Fuller argues, have implications for other geopolitical spaces, to the extent that the comforts of a self-satisfied American exceptionalism are challenged by the embodiments of a transforming Old World polity. Significant here too is the precise nature of this embodiment. Fuller's celebration of the working class *as a social group* places her at some distance from the individualistic impulses of her mentor Ralph Waldo Emerson, indicative of her desire to think through the problems of social relations in terms that are more structural than Emerson could ever envisage. The transatlantic impetus behind this passage from Fuller's letter imagines a political economy in which national authority—the question of who or what can lay claim to the possession of founding principles—gives way to a transnational vision of politicized interconnection.

That the realization of this vision is located in some future moment is everywhere apparent in Fuller's reports. She returns insistently to the comparative framework that the combination of her Italian location and her American readership fosters, and the force of this comparison usually works to deny the hierarchy of New World privilege. In a letter published in the *Tribune* in June 1848 Fuller expresses her desire to attain what she calls a "higher knowledge" that would be unavailable to her back home. It is a passage worth quoting at length:

> My friends write to urge my return; they talk of our country as the land of the Future. It is so, but that spirit which made it all it is of value in my eyes, which gave all of hope with which I can sympathize for that Future, is more alive here at present than in America. My country is at present spoiled by prosperity, stupid with the lust of gain, soiled by crime in its willing perpetuation of Slavery, shamed by an unjust war, noble sentiment much forgotten even by individuals, the aims of politicians selfish or petty, the literature frivolous and venal. In Europe, amid the teachings of adversity a nobler spirit is struggling—a spirit which cheers and animates mine. I hear earnest words of pure faith and love. I see deeds of brotherhood. This is what makes *my* America. I do not deeply distrust my country. She is not dead, but in my time she sleepeth, and the spirit of our fathers flames no more, but lies hid beneath the ashes. (230)

Fuller's refusal to listen to the entreaties of her American friends to return home signals her ambivalence toward the rhetoric of U.S. exceptionalism, in which America both originates the principles that enshrine good governance and at the same time represents the best hope for a future manifestation of those principles. For Fuller, the migration of "words of pure faith and love" transforms Italy into a version of the United States that is untarnished by the geopolitical conflicts of her nation. Instead of the inevitable westward movement of civilization advocated in the *translatio studii* model of intellectual mobility—Bishop Berkeley's prediction in "Verses on the Prospect of Planting Arts and Learning in America" that "Westward the Course of Empire Takes its Way"[85] being the key instance of this—she reverses the direction. Italy demonstrates, albeit tentatively, the stirrings of a democratic nobility that an exhausted America has squandered through the prosecution of its sectional and imperial ambitions.

The dialogic structure that organizes much of Fuller's Italian correspondence—the sustained reflection on spatial and political differences, and the manner in which those differences might be traversed and challenged—is readily apparent in this example. Elsewhere, the number of perspectives incorporated into her reports proliferates, such that the reader is faced with a diversity of modes and voices that enacts the cosmopolitanism of Fuller's text. A letter published in April 1849 describing the establishment of the new Constitutional Assembly illustrates this strategy most explicitly in its multiple transitions between at least four different modes of discourse: a detached journalistic account of events as they unfold; a narrative describing Fuller's embedded participation in those events; a recounted dialogue between Fuller and an obtuse American tourist about those events; and the translated text of the constitutional declaration that gives the scene its political purpose. The rhetorical shifts involved in the construction of this sequence all work to underscore Fuller's intellectual authority over the scene being played out. Detachment affords her the gravitas of observational mastery, while participation ensures that the *Tribune*'s readers are aware of her claim to interpretative familiarity within the space she inhabits. One aspect of Fuller's strategy of policing the disruptive diversity of political upheaval is to orchestrate events as aesthetic spectacle, where what is emphasized is the impact of performance over the potential incoherence of violence. Between each declaration of the four articles of the fledgling Roman republic, Fuller describes how "the speaker paused; the great bell of the Capitol gave forth its solemn melodies; the cannon answered; while the crowd shouted, *viva la Republica! viva Italia!*" Politics is here represented as theatricality, and it is of a kind that serves to give refreshed impetus to political action, or more precisely to the emotional responses that might in turn generate such action. The "imposing grandeur of the spectacle," Fuller writes, "gave new force to the thought that already swelled in my heart; my nerves thrilled, and I longed to see in some answering glance a spark of Rienzi [Cola di Rienzo, a fourteenth-century politician who tried to restore the Roman Republic in 1347]."[86] Spectacle evokes sentiment in a way that can recalibrate a slumbering political consciousness. But it becomes immediately clear that the therapeutic effect of the scene is not felt by all. "The American at my side remained impassive," Fuller reports. "Receiving all his birthright from a triumph of Democracy, he was quite indifferent to this manifestation on this consecrated spot. Passing the Winter in Rome to study Art, he was insensible to the artistic beauty of the scene—insensible to this new life of that spirit from which all the forms he gazes at in galleries emanated" (257–58). An appreciation of the performance of politics, its presentation as spectacle, becomes the means by which Fuller is able to evaluate the political credentials of those around her. Necessary are "modest scrutiny, patient study and observation" in order to avoid exhibiting "a mind befooled rather than instructed" (258). Under a regime of appropriate tutelage then, Fuller suggests treating the Italian revolutionary moment as a matter of aesthetic taste, allowing her to negotiate a position that refashions political upheaval as art. In Julie Ellison's helpful formulation, "Spectacle, speaking to the informed eye, mediates between subjectivity and public life for Fuller."[87]

The willed embrace of violence that was evident in John Brown's highly masculinist political persona—and which, as I explored in the chapter 2, Henry David Thoreau went some way to endorsing—was not a position that Margaret Fuller could easily inhabit. Her desire for political change brought with it, as Ellison notes, "the problem of aggression, exacerbated by the question of gender" (261). To counter the dangers of an improper female violence, Fuller advocates a sensibility of restraint that would work to neutralize the risks of excessive action. In *Woman in the Nineteenth Century*, she assures her reader that "[i]ndividuals might commit excesses, but there is not only in the sex a reverence for decorums and limits inherited and enhanced from generation to generation, which many years of other life could not efface, but a native love, in woman as woman, of proportion . . . a Greek moderation, which would create immediately a restraining party, the natural legislators and instructors of the rest."[88] While the tension between a culturally developed sense of moderation ("enhanced from generation to generation") and one that is inherent ("native") presents perhaps the most immediately noticeable oscillation in this passage, significant too is Fuller's reliance on the restraining authority of "those natural legislators" to posit a bulwark of stability in the face of radical personal upheaval: "one who speaks with authority, not in anger or haste" (49). Whereas Thoreau could adopt—at least for a while—an antinomian position of unequivocal directness, in which thought and action were simultaneous processes, Fuller is careful to moderate between the righteousness of a rebellious impulse and society's need for an interpreter able to negate the excesses of that impulse. If the "thinking American" moderates between nativist and cosmopolitan perspectives, Fuller's "natural legislators" work to deflect the dangers of inflexible thought's enactment into unthinking violence. The harsh reality of war's destructive force shocks Fuller, even as she realizes the righteousness of the political case it is deployed to serve. Writing from Rome in May 1849, she attempts to romanticize its effects — "it has produced much fruit of noble sentiment, noble act" — but is rapidly forced to list instead its calamities: "but it still breeds vice, too, drunkenness, mental dissipation, tears asunder the tenderest ties, lavishes the productions of earth for which her starving poor stretch out their hands in vain, in the most unprofitable manner."[89] Yet, by translating the ravages of revolution into instances of sentimental mediation, controlled by the legitimizing figure of Fuller as interpreter, she is able to imagine the troops of the Republic, preparing to make a last stand against the invading French army, as "light, athletic, resolute figures" possessing the "finest manly beauty" and "sparkling" with "genius." Fuller's model for this incarnation of noble masculinity is, as she acknowledges, Walter Scott, who she "longed . . . to be on earth again" to witness the scene. In the face of imminent military catastrophe, Fuller turns to an aesthetics of the picturesque (observing Rome's "glittering mosaics of the early ages," the city "so richly strewn with ruins") through which to master the unfolding events.[90]

Fuller's final dispatch from Italy, dated January 6, 1850, and published in the *Tribune* on February 13, is typical of the rhetorical and generic diversity of her political journalism; the polyvocality that William Stowe and others have detected in her writing is present here at a pitch of intensity that manifests itself in astonishing shifts between registers of language and models of discourse. The letter begins with a conventional description of landscape invested with meaning, the device of the pathetic fallacy working to establish a contrast between an earlier moment of revolutionary optimism and Italy's current political malaise. "Last winter began with meteors and the rose-colored Aurora Borealis," she writes. "All the winter was steady sunshine, and the Spring that followed no less glorious." The political analogy is then made (perhaps unnecessarily) explicit: "as if Nature rejoiced in and daily smiled upon the noble efforts and tender, generous impulses of the Italian people."[91] The shift from such portentous and exciting intensity to a now blocked state of inertia is quickly established:

This winter, Italy is shrouded with snow. Here in Florence the oil congeals in the closet beside the fire — the water in the chamber — just as in our country-houses of New-England, as yet uncomforted by furnaces. I was supposing this to be confined to colder Florence, but a letter, this day received, from Rome says the snow lies there two feet deep, and water freezes instantly if thrown upon the pavement. I hardly know how to believe it — I who never saw but one slight powdering of snow all my two Roman winters, scarce enough to cover a Canary bird's wing. (320–21)

That New England and Italy share a meteorological condition points to other forms of stasis—of impeded conversation—that concern Fuller here, in the aftermath of the failure of the Republic. The unexpected covering of snow in Rome mirrors the smothering of that city's political hopes, where action "freezes instantly" into inertia in the face of what she goes on to describe as "[t]he seeds for a vast harvest of hatreds and contempts." However the failure of Italy's revolutionary moment—a combination of papal deception and the "foolish national vanity" of other European powers—generates the potential for a more comprehensive, transnational redemption. Fuller pushes her political reading into the rhetoric of religious apocalypse, determined to assert a teleology in which "the wishes of Heaven shall waft a fire that will burn down all, root and branch, and prepare the earth for an entirely new culture." Instead of the abortive experience of Rome, Fuller assures her readers that the future upheaval will be "uncompromising" in its ushering in of what she confidently calls the "New Era." The tonal shifts of this letter—its movement from pointed local color description, to political analysis, to utopian projection—suggest a mind flexible enough to marshal and juxtapose such contrasting modes of representation, yet the strong eschatological emphasis of its final paragraphs reveals Fuller's determination to salvage both the significance of what she has witnessed and the worth of her intellectual project of cosmopolitan conversation.

The teleological lure of this final dispatch is apparent in its author's abandonment of the idea of the "transition state"—recall her earlier use of this phrase in the context of America's cultural identity—for something more definite: "Men have long been talking of a transition state—it is over—the power of positive, determinate effort is begun" (321). Echoing both Milton and Emerson, she claims that "the film is hourly falling from [men's] eyes and they see" (321–22),[92] the results of such refreshed vision being that corporeality is overcome in favor of a consort of transcendent intellects. "Men shall now be represented as souls, not hands and feet, and governed accordingly. A congress of great, pure, loving minds, and not a congress of selfish ambitions, shall preside." The fading of political materiality from Fuller's Rome suggests itself further by her admission that "I take little interest now in what is going on here in Italy" (322), as if the concerns of that country's revolution have been superseded by a more globalized prospect of democracy. While Leslie Eckel is right to point to Fuller's desire to encourage "the productive juxtaposition of ostensibly diverging viewpoints" in order "to seek common ground, whether linguistic or political,"[93] there is nevertheless something a little forced about this shift of perspective, with her strategy of conversation as the structural basis for intellectual exchange at risk of giving way to the presumptions of proclamation. Indeed the final paragraph of the letter leaves the reader in no doubt that, with its geographical sweep and repeated rhetorical invocation, Fuller has determined to translate the failures of 1848–49 into the certainty of transnational redemption. "Joy to those born in this day," she intones. "In America is open to them the easy chance of a noble, peaceful growth, in Europe of a combat grand in its motives, and in its extent beyond what the world ever before so much dreamed. Joy to them" (322–23). Fuller, of course, did not live long enough to see her vision of New World democratic possibility severely tested by the sectional ruptures of Civil War, and her paean to the work of constructing universal harmony may sound naïve with the luxury of hindsight. Yet in a journal entry of 1851, one year after her death, Emerson acknowledges her importance in terms that resonate with those qualities of intersubjectivity, conversation and relation that characterize her mode of engagement. He writes: "A personal influence towers up in memory the only worthy force when we would gladly forget numbers or money or climate, gravitation & the rest of Fate. Margaret, wherever she came, fused people into society, & a glowing company was the result. When I think how few persons can do that feat for the intellectual class, I feel our squalid poverty" (*JMN* 11: 449).

4

VARIETY AND LIMITS

In his important book on the development of a black intellectual tradition at the end of the nineteenth century, Shamoon Zamir argues that William James, along with his intellectual precursor Ralph Waldo Emerson, "conceive of consciousness as passive perception and of action as unreflective activity," an epistemological perspective that belongs to a faculty of mind which "can only submit unquestioningly to the given social and political order."[1] Seeking to establish an intellectual antecedent for the subject of his book, W. E. B. Du Bois, Zamir correctly notices James's preference for the habitual, the requirement to choose between the manifold options of pluralist flux and thereby acquire a "groove of habit." Yet, his account fails to acknowledge the degree to which, even once the regularity of habit has been achieved, James does not settle into complacent comfort: the habitual is always at the mercy of the contingent, prone to adjustment and the kind of revisionary tensions we have already seen enacted within Emerson's supple prose in earlier chapters. *Dark Voices* proposes two contrasting models of intellectual perspective. If James is defined as Emersonian in his "willed transcendence" as a "wholly unconditioned agent" (12), Du Bois evidences the ontological contestations of a self "mediated by power and terror, but also by positive social location among others" (13). Although Zamir moves away from the apparently sharp contours of this distinction in later parts of his book, *Dark Voices* is nevertheless underpinned by a narrative of Jamesian exceptionalism that, it is argued, fits uncomfortably onto a racial politics at the start of the new century grappling with the effects of discrimination and prejudice.

While acknowledging the problems that forms of racial oppression posed to transcendentalist thought (especially in its Emersonian variation), my account of William James here proposes a very different intellectual engagement with those tangible and urgent issues of cultural plurality and diversity that Zamir suggests are missing from his philosophical horizon. This chapter argues that William James is located transitionally, between a Victorian culture of (often imagined) stability and a modernist one of flux, and that the friction generated between stasis and movement, retreat and intervention, produces a more complex figure than Zamir's avatar of a kind of belated romanticism would suggest. James is also located transnationally, in terms of his acute commentaries on the forms of American imperial expansion as they become manifest at the turn of the century. In the face of extra-territorial expansion, identifying nationality becomes an increasingly problematic undertaking, as earlier incarnations of bounded Americanness threaten to unravel. The influx of immigrants from eastern and southern Europe at the end of the nineteenth century undermined the Anglo-Saxon foundation of American citizenship; moreover, transformations in the U.S. economy placed individuals within forms of exchange that were far removed from traditional local or voluntary affiliations. The campaign for women's suffrage and the rise of a vocal African-American middle-class added to general anxiety about the dissolution of any normative sense of where American identity might be located.[2] William James's account of pluralism, then, is more than just a philosophical problem of epistemology. Rather it represents a timely intervention in some prevalent cultural anxieties surrounding the tense interaction of national collectivity and forms of difference, at the same time as it suggests a mode of intellectual work that, for James, is central to the health of the body politic.

In 1894, one of James's former students, Theodore Roosevelt, published an article entitled "True Americanism." In a particularly extreme variation on the idea of the melting pot, part of the political currency of the United States since at least de Crèvecoeur's articulation of the trope in 1782,[3] Roosevelt insisted upon the total erasure of cultural difference:

> Where immigrants, or the sons of immigrants, do not heartily and in good faith throw in their lot with us, but cling to the speech, the customs, the ways of life, and the habits of thought of the Old World which they have left, they thereby harm both themselves and us . . . It is an immense benefit to the European immigrant to change him into an American citizen. To bear the name of an American is to bear the most honorable of titles . . . We welcome the German or the Irishman who becomes an American. We have no such use for the German or Irishman who remains such.[4]

Roosevelt's later imperialist ambitions for the United States would earn James's scorn; in a 1900 letter to a friend, he called the expansionist ideas of the-then governor of New York "a combination of slime and grit, sand and soap" which would "scour anything away, even the moral sense of the country."[5] In "True Americanism," the ambitious politician was concerned to enforce an internal colonization of adopted Anglo-Saxon identity, one that, in its proud demonstration of nativist American virtues, dismissed those forms of European culture and education that had defined the formation of the entire James family: "Thus it is with that most foolish of parents who sends his children to be educated abroad, not knowing—what every clear-sighted man from Washington and Jay down has known—that the American who is to make his way in America should be brought up among his fellow Americans."[6] With its reference to George Washington and John Jay, two of the nation's founding figures, cosmopolitanism here is associated with a dangerous lack of patriotism, a derogation of filial duty to the home-grown ideals that Roosevelt saw embodied in the two men. "True Americanism" caught the eye of William's brother, Henry James, when he came to review the book in which the article was subsequently collected. Henry ridiculed Roosevelt's contention that the term "American" could be so easily inhabited and reductively defined. In an age that had seen, he wrote, "an inter-penetration that would have been the wonder of our fathers," Roosevelt's belief in a superior and singular American type displayed the kind of perception akin, for James, to wearing "a pair of smart, patent blinders."[7]

The melting pot had particular force as a metaphor in the early 1900s—Israel Zangwill's play, *The Melting Pot*, appeared in 1908 for example, with Roosevelt the dedicatee of its first printed edition.[8] Its hymn to the assimilative trajectory of American identity matches Roosevelt's in its stridency: "Ah, what a stirring and a seething! Celt and Latin, Slav and Teuton, Greek and Syrian—black and yellow. . . . Yes, East and West, and North and South, . . . —how the great Alchemist melts and fuses them with his purging flame!"[9] At the beginning of the twentieth century, the second great wave of immigration to the United States had been underway for some fifty years, consisting principally of Irish Catholics and German Protestants. These newcomers had threatened to disunite America—insofar as its self-definition rested on Anglo-Saxon foundations. By the time of Zangwill's play, as Marcus Klein has stated, the disruptions caused by a diversifying society had fractured the national narrative. "The traditional past," Klein writes, "could no longer authorize the non-traditional present because there could no longer be general agreement as to what the traditional past was."[10] The result was the instantiation of an alternative story, one in which American ideals would become the targets of identification, at the expense of lingering attachment to aspects of an indigenous culture. For Jack Pole, among the "undisclosed assumptions" about American democracy held by political leaders, the "most basic" was that "of a pervasive homogeneity of national character."[11] It is important to realize, however, as Pole's reference to these "undisclosed assumptions" attests, that the essentialized American identity that served to underwrite narratives of assimilation had always been viewed, even by its proponents, as a fiction, a strategic device to "forge" a national character to be imprinted on immigrants. Nina Baym has noted that, in the context of New England's geographical and cultural dominance, "Conservative New England leaders knew all too well that the nation was an artifice and that no single character undergirded it. And they insisted passionately that peace and progress called for a commonality that, if it did not exist, had at once to be invented."[12] In this sense, well before Benedict Anderson articulated his now canonical theory of nationhood as an imaginary construct, an organizing trope around which a diverse and distanced people are able to unite, teleologies of Americanization similarly recognized the importance of an invented coherence.

The melting pot, as a narrative framework and as a metaphor for the national imaginary, has retained its potency. Arthur Schlesinger, in a blistering jeremiad called *The Disuniting of America* (1991), sought to protect the metaphor's foundational force against the threat from what he perceived to be a disciplinary and intellectual rebellion by those charged with the teaching of American history. Educational programs dedicated to the study of race and ethnicity earned his suspicion, as did those for which concepts of the post- or transnational had more pedagogical relevance than the cherished shibboleths of an Americanized unity. What Schlesinger labels "the new ethnic gospel" undermines a precious "unifying vision of individuals from all nations melted into a new race."[13] Such a narrative of declension contrasts the promise of Enlightenment universalism with the particulars of romantic nationalism that had spawned a fragmentary politics of identity. Echoing the urgent nativism of Roosevelt, *The Disuniting of America* worries that "If the republic now turns away from Washington's old goal of 'one people,' what is its future?" offering some alarming potential scenarios: "Disintegration of the national community, apartheid, Balkanization, tribalization" (118). Schlesinger's assertion of the need for the United States to maintain "common ideals and a single society" (131) has, as we will see, affinities with a call at the end of the nineteenth century for a literary style through which social difference might be erased in the service of shared sympathy. The contextual specifics of his text are, of course, significant in accounting for the impulses that produce it: writing in the aftermath of the Cold War, his account of a splintering and factionalized American culture is a response to the removed ideological balance of east-west relations. The book appeared just two years after Francis Fukuyama first aired a version of his highly contested "end of history" thesis, in which the triumph of capitalist liberalism had evacuated the need for large-scale ideological confrontation. Fukuyama was clear, however, that more localized forms of ethnic and nationalist conflict could not be eradicated, even in a posthistorical era.[14] Schlesinger similarly writes in the wake of a perceived ideological vacuum, in which the end of the global stand-off results in a proliferation of internal claims for difference that risk undermining the project of American exceptionalism altogether.[15]

A political system that celebrates individualism and plurality of group identity has, then, historically—and paradoxically—subscribed to this stabilizing conception of Americanization. The national motto of the United States, *e pluribus unum* (adopted in 1782 but originating perhaps with Virgil's *Moretum*),[16] ratifies and institutionalizes a narrative of accomplishment. "Out of many, one" encodes as essential and self-evident a national definition that, from the moment of America's Constitutional creation to the present day, has nevertheless remained contested and fragile. As Jay Grossman points out in his account of the languages of American political representation, *e pluribus unum* insists on "the one true outcome toward which all events necessarily point."[17] In Emerson's famous 1845 journal passage on the "smelting pot," the relationship between diversity and unity is described in exactly these terms of teleological unfolding, but here with historical antecedents:

> It is the result of science that the highest simplicity of structure is produced, not by few elements, but by the highest complexity. Man is the most composite of all creatures, the wheel-insect, *volvox globator*, is at the beginning. Well, as in the old burning of the Temple at Corinth, by the melting & intermixture of silver & gold & other metals, a new compound more precious than any, called the Corinthian Brass, was formed so in this Continent, — asylum of all nations, the energy of Irish, Germans, Swedes, Poles, & Cossacks & all the European tribes, — of the Africans, & of the Polynesians, will construct a new race, a new religion, a new State, a new literature, which will be as vigorous as the New Europe which came out of the smelting pot of the Dark Ages, or that which earlier emerged from the Pelasgic & Etruscan barbarism.

Following this passage, and serving as a gloss on it, Emerson wrote in pencil: "La Nature aime les croisements" (*JMN* 9: 299–300).[18] His analysis of mixture and commingling as a means of instilling national vitality is linked here to the industrial process of refining raw ore to make a "more precious" metal; it is also described as an evolutionary process in which the minute or microscopic organism (the "wheel-insect," the "*volvox globator*") might develop into something more complexly unified. Multiplicity provides nutrients to the American soil, but rather than regarding this as an exceptional phenomenon in the New World, Emerson links it to processes already completed successfully in the remote past. The United States is in the middle of the same narrative, but Emerson's use of the future tense in the passage indicates his sense of its unfinished status.

This notion of variety's therapeutic value chimed with already-developed theories of diversity that regarded evolutionary progress as increasing hetero-geneity. (Karl Ernst von Baer's *Über Entwickelungsgeschichte der Thiere* [*On the Development of Animals*, 1828–37] had been the first to demonstrate that the early embryos of very distinct types of organism are quite similar, and that the various traits characteristic of specific organisms appear only later in the course of development.) For mid-century American romantics, Arnold Henry Guyot's Lowell Institute lectures, *Earth and Man* (1849), represented biological forma-tion as one of progressive complexity, in which the homogeneity of "primitive" species is supplanted by the "multiplicity and the variety of the special organs" that produce "a richer life." Social structures, Guyot judges, demonstrate a similar pattern: "Here again, homogeneousness, uniformity, is the elementary state, the savage state. Diversity, variety of elements, which call for and multiply exchanges; the almost infinite *specialisation* of the functions . . . [has] been the sign of a social state arrived at a high degree of improvement."[19] Moreover, as Günter Leypoldt has pointed out, Guyot applied this mechanism of advancing complexity to imagine a vision of transatlantic relations that perpetuates the *translatio imperii* topos.[20] If Europe is the location of fulfilled civilization, the relative homogeneity of the New World provides the stimulus for westward movement to the continent. Couched in explicitly gendered terms, America awaits its completion by a European colonization that will take advantage of her abundant natural riches, riches that have been neglected by an "incapable or careless" indigenous population:

> The two worlds are looking face to face, and are, as it were, inclining toward each other. The Old World bends toward the New, and is ready to pour out its tribes, whom a resistless descent of the reliefs seems to sweep toward the Atlantic. America looks toward the Old World; all its slopes and its long plains slant to the Atlantic, toward Europe. It seems to wait with open and eager arms the beneficent influence of the man of the Old World. No barrier opposes their progress; the Andes and the Rocky Mountains, banished to the other shore of the continent, will place no obstacle in their path. Soon the moment will come.[21]

This image of transcontinental cleaving in anticipation of consummation works to legitimize an idea of American exceptionalism that is determined by its diversity. America is a landscape able to contain within its geographical expanses the sophisticated varieties of European civilization, and, as a writer in the *Continental Monthly* put it in an essay of 1863, "American Destiny," "the leading races of mankind are becoming constantly more composite. The contact and intermixture of races have had a moral result, which, in its turn, acts upon the physical."[22] The essay asserts that democratic political systems, such as America's, are founded on racial and ethnic diversity, rather than the reverse. Complexity produces political unity.

E pluribus unum performs both the desire for and the assertion of a collective identity, one which, as Grossman notes, grammatically speaking is achieved only after the Civil War, when the "United States" becomes a unified nation consistently attached to a singular verb. In the tenth number of *The Federalist Papers* (1788), a text responding to an earlier moment of national crisis and potential fracture, James Madison famously argued that a strong federal government would have the effect of converting unruly factions into a form of benign difference essential to the security of the Union. His immediate purpose was to persuade reluctant New Yorkers into adopting the proposed new Constitution, which would sacrifice a degree of local and state power in order to strengthen the national government. *Federalist* number 10 is a consummate piece of political rhetoric that manages to appear entirely reasonable at the same time as it asserts a curtailment of direct democratic representation. Grossman reminds us that, in its defence of the Constitution, the text addresses, with some degree of anxiety, the status of that political entity denominated as "the people." For Walt Whitman, writing within the literary and political Romanticism of the mid-nineteenth century, it is precisely this constituency of "the people" that designates America's political project as exceptional. In his preface to the 1876 edition of *Leaves of Grass* Whitman's location of national identity is unequivocal:

> In my opinion, it is by a fervent, accepted development of comradeship, the beautiful and sane affection of man for man, latent in all young fellows, north and south, east and west — it is by this, I say, and by what goes directly and indirectly along with it, that the United States of the future, (I cannot too often repeat,) are to be most effectually welded together, intercalated, anneal'd into a living union.[23]

The recourse to an idea(l) of commonality, one that we have seen deployed elsewhere already, is Whitman's ideological (and, indeed, poetic) strategy for incorporating difference into an harmonious and democratic body politic. His representation of the United States as a teeming plurality relies on a strategic amnesia that flattens productive tensions and diminishes political conflicts. As Judith Butler has observed, such a desire runs the risk of effacing instances of particularity altogether. Echoing an earlier complaint by D. H. Lawrence, Butler writes in *Bodies that Matter* that "The ideal of transforming all excluded identifications into inclusive features . . . in appropriating all difference as exemplary features of itself, becomes a figure for imperialism, a figure that installs itself by way of a romantic, insidious, and all-consuming humanism."[24] For George Santayana, as we will see more fully in chapter 5, Whitman's embrace of the demos represented a false revolutionary dawn and a failure of aesthetic control, where "this abundance of detail without organization, this wealth of perception without intelligence and of imagination without taste, makes the singularity of Whitman's genius."[25] The poet's democratizing impulses teeter on the brink of bland inclusiveness, where the idea of "the people" is endorsed as a de-corporealized organizing principle rather than acknowledged as a highly differentiated and complex entity.

Grossman notes that, for James Madison, in his more cautious model of the relationship between populace and polity, it is the unpredictable, potential unruliness of "the people" that is the reason why government is required in the first place. As Madison asks in *The Federalist Papers*, "But what is government itself but the greatest of all reflections on human nature? If men were angels, no government would be necessary."[26] His Union exists in the face of a gothic world of competing voices and unstable meaning, of the type familiar to readers of Charles Brockden Brown's anti-Enlightenment novels. The new nation is faced with "mortal diseases," he writes, "under which popular governments have everywhere perished":

> The latent causes of faction are thus sown in the nature of man. A zeal for different opinions regarding religion, concerning government, and many other points, as well of speculation as of practice; an attachment to different leaders ambitiously contending for pre-eminence and power; or to persons of other descriptions whose fortunes have been interesting to the human passions, have, in turn, divided mankind into parties, inflamed them with mutual animosity.

Faction is defined as a "destructive agency" proposing "sinister views"; for Madison, it opens up the likelihood of perilous partisanship and the difficulty of establishing secure grounds for judgment. The implications of this bring the text to a crisis of meaning that seems to undermine the very possibility of representative government itself:

> No man is allowed to be a judge in his own cause, because his interest would certainly bias his judgment, and, not improbably, corrupt his integrity. With equal, nay with greater reason, a body of men are unfit to be both judges and parties at the same

time; yet what . . . are the different classes of legislators but advocates and parties to the causes which they determine? (124)

The effect of that rhetorical question is devastating to the structure of distinct spheres of claim and adjudication that Madison has set out to build. By acknowledging that faction can extend even to those charged with eradicating its dangers, his argument broaches the impossibility of arriving at an assessment—of naming and representation—that is not also already impartial and contingent. A text that sets out to establish the categories by which a central and centralizing body can justify political authority teeters on the brink of an antifoundationalism that will come to characterize a version of William James's pragmatist philosophy.

As if recognizing the epistemological and political implications of this move, *Federalist* 10 restores its equilibrium at the point at which Madison transforms the dissident and potentially ubiquitous concept of "faction" into a healthy and controlled plurality that is contained within a strong federal structure. Carrie Bramen has astutely pointed out that factionalism is reinterpreted as "variousness," through which the United States is able to reconcile harmoniously the many with the one, the each with the all. The "clashing interests" of unruly faction are reimagined as "a variety of parties" and "a variety of sects" that, as she notes, suggest an "abundance and plenitude . . . [that] provide a way of rhetorically diffusing strife within a strong federal government."[27] In October 1865, six months after the surrender of the Confederacy at Appomattox, the editor of the *North American Review*, Charles Eliot Norton, penned a lengthy encomium to the "moral community" of the United States as it had emerged from the fracture of the Civil War.[28] Norton's argument rested on a belief in America's fundamental political differences from European nations. The Old World offered a political system buttressed by the "supports of tradition, succession, and force," whereas the United States, "severed from the past," embodied the "product of the fresh efforts of men striving to do the best for themselves, unimpeded by traditionary forms and authority" (560). While America's unchanging "moral ideas" had first been articulated at the nation's founding, Norton argued that their "application" was prone to revision and adaptation, "according to the advance of mankind in moral culture and intelligence" (563). Of course, such a conception of a pragmatically evolving polity allowed Norton to view the brutal divisions of the previous decades as "excrescences" (551) that could be surpassed within a "political system constantly ductile and pliable" (562). It also presented him with the same kind of structural dilemma that, as we will see, William James would encounter as he tried to align an intellectual disposition for openness and provisionality with an instinct for stability and order. Alongside the standard exceptionalist stance (e.g., "From the height of our Pisgah we have beheld the promised land, not as in dream, but in actual vision" [551]), Norton, too, regarded the federal structure as key to the resolution of division and to the maintenance of order amid "the principle of the unlimited freedom of the individual":

> However self-governed the individuals of a community may be, yet, owing to the diverse wills and the variety of interests of individuals, the community requires, and must always require, an external government to control those wills, and to regulate the pursuit of those interests in such a manner as to preserve moral order, to secure the general welfare. (558)

I will come back to this model of federal government a little later in the context of James, who, in his 1909 work *A Pluralistic Universe*, deploys it in his formulation of pragmatic pluralism by suggesting that "The pluralistic world is thus more like a federal republic than like an empire or a kingdom" (*WJ2* 776). But I want to suggest here that what unites Jamesian pluralism with its post-Revolutionary and post-Civil War antecedents is the acknowledgment of forms of crisis and an attempt to manage them. At the end of the eighteenth century, and again in 1865, a federated pluralism was offered as a means of stabilizing the nation after the upheaval of the imperial and sectarian fissures; at the end of the nineteenth century, James articulated a form of pluralism that was concerned not only with questions of philosophical inquiry, but also deployed as a means of negotiating, through a principle of careful moderation, the extremes of a burgeoning and diversifying economy and culture in which national identity was in danger of turning into a dynamic process of negotiation without stable content. Henry James's well-known account in *The American Scene* of his visit to the Yiddish Quarter in New York generates a kind of sublime terror in which the potential of radical instability threatens the logic of the melting-pot metaphor. "What meaning," James asks, "in the presence of such impressions, can continue to attach to such a term as 'American' character? — what type, as the result of such a prodigious amalgam, such a hotch-potch of racial ingredients, is to be conceived as shaping itself?"[29] The specter of ontological instability is raised here through James's inability to regard diversity as foundational to national identity — *e pluribus unum* appears to be a fractured narrative, one that cannot be brought into coherent shape. James E. Block has characterized the last decades of the nineteenth century as ones of "complex role differentiation and social stratification" held together by organizations that imposed a "common ethos fostered by interconnection and interdependence" to guard against the sense of dispossession felt so keenly by Henry James.[30] For his brother William, the genteel liberal intellectual, a discourse of pluralism provided a model by which difference could be asserted in the face of this dominant homogenizing economy, while at the same time securing that economy, so essential for the future well-being of the nation, from the perils of unfettered heterogeneity. If Madison retreats from the Pandora's box of provisionality and indeterminacy that he had started to open, this chapter argues that William James, similarly, resists a pluralism of radical contingency for something that is instead keen to retain the possibilities of structured difference. As articulate as James is in advocating the virtues of pluralism against the dominant (and dominating) narratives of idealism, monism, or absolutism, he is unwilling to turn his back on the benefits of coherence and unity as they pertain to a healthy selfhood and an institutional position in which intellectual work might be most effectively accomplished.

Unity and the Dangers of Heterogeneity

In an influential reading of late nineteenth-century American literary culture, Amy Kaplan identifies what she regards as its characteristic antagonism to forms of unregulated difference. Realism, she argues, of the kind theorized by the novelist William Dean Howells, insisted upon a transparently shared reality. Famously, Howells had asserted in his 1887 essay, "Civilization, Barbarism, Romance and Reality" that "Men are more like than unlike one another: let us make them know one another better, that they may be all humbled and strengthened with a sense of their fraternity." Realism as an aesthetic strategy served also as a social cohesive, and its practitioners were those who refused "to paint the marvellous and impossible for the vulgar many, or to sentimentalize and falsify the actual for the vulgar few."[31] Neither elitist nor brashly populist, Howells's vision of the responsible writer aimed at representing "the face of common humanity" (118), such that literary worth was determined by an ideal of "truth," that we, perhaps with good reason, now find naively humanist, but which was nevertheless central to his criteria of judgment and evaluation. "If the book is true to what men and women know of one another's souls," Howells writes (in "Realism: The Moral Issue," another essay of 1887), "it will be true enough" (101). Realism, in other words, is animated by a desire to efface social difference by asserting what Kaplan calls an "aesthetic of the common."[32] In a nation transformed by increasing immigration and multiple dialects, realism was imagined as a "common language" that could contain plurality by refraining from jarring readers with "the shock of otherness" (23). Howells's wish to establish the realist novel as a source of cultural authority needs to be seen as a response to what T. J. Jackson Lears has noted as the fin-de-siècle's fear of middle-class "weightlessness" and "unreality," an anxiety about diminished status and solidity that provoked a reassertion of forms of stabilizing literary capital.[33] Howellsian realism participates in this retrenchment of bourgeois significance. In practice, of course, such a position was dependent upon banishing forms of diversity that could not fit easily into fiction's middle-class co-ordinates. (Howells's figure of the German communist Lindau in his novel *The Hazard of New Fortunes* [1890] is a good example of this move: radically destabilizing the bourgeois politics of the book, Lindau is marked as foreign by the typographical representation of his idiomatic use of English, and his death during a labor strike conveniently removes him from the narrative.)[34] For the turn-of-the-century realist reader and writer, social difference, Kaplan argues, becomes inseparable from social conflict. As a response to a world in which social diversity was considered threatening, realism gestures toward genuine inclusiveness (Howells's "common humanity") but quickly settles for the comfort of the familiar. Late Victorians' (mis)understanding of social reality as ordered, stable, and homogenous required the suppression of those incarnations of difference that resisted the middle-class narrative of assimilation.

William James's notion of a pluralistic universe offers us a competing model to this one, and represents a significant intervention in ways of imagining diversity, both philosophically and within the much-debated parameters of national self-definition. It is a conception of the relationship between the one and the many that "unstiffens" (to borrow James's word to describe the methodology of pragmatism) the inexorable trajectory of the national motto, while at the same time retaining a sense of boundary or of limit that ensures epistemological and, to extend the argument, institutional shape and structure. Rather than interpret the discourse of unregulated difference as a menace to social and political order, as is the case with much of the nativist rhetoric of the period and, as we have seen, subsequently, I am interested here in the ways in which Jamesian diversity is placed within a productive, and unresolvable, tension between the attractions of alterity and the imperatives of definition. James's desire to chart a course that could embrace both positions locates him at some distance from the fearful rhetoric of immigrant diversity common at the end of the nineteenth century. The celebrated social reformer and pioneering photographer Jacob Riis described New York's "Other Half" of urban poor in 1890 as "this queer conglomerate mass of heterogeneous elements" in which "the native stock is in no way involved."[35] Henry James similarly regarded the arrival of immigrants at Ellis Island as the perpetual "introduction of fresh . . . foreign matter into our heterogeneous system," a process that left him questioning "the sanctity of his American consciousness."[36]

Such a lack of ontological stability has long been regarded as one characteristic of the crowd: before crowd psychology even emerged as a scientific and anthropological discourse, conventional tropes evoked this sense of an evacuated self. Rendered as oceans, swarms, seas, streams, and masses that mob and throng and pack, the crowd, Mary Esteve has suggested, "obtains a pure, anonymous power or affect," one that is constituted through an aggregation of persons that, in turn, dissolves all common signifiers of interpretation.[37] Gustave Le Bon's *Psychologie des foules* (1895; translated and published in English as *The Crowd* the following year) expressed alarm at what its author perceived to be the unreflective power of society's collective will. Le Bon advocated instead the emergence of a commanding figure who might exert order and direction over the masses, the "instinctive need for all beings forming a crowd to obey a leader."[38] The solitary figure of authority, making sense of the more inchoate impulses of the crowd, is a version (perhaps with a sharper political edge) of the romantic self-fashioned intellectual; indeed the American sociologist Edward Ross argued in his 1897 essay "The Mob Mind" that "We must hold always to a sage Emersonian individualism, that . . . shall brace men to stand against the rush of the mass."[39] For Walt Whitman in *Democratic Vistas* (1871), it was the responsibility and privilege of the perceiving consciousness to draw significance from man, who, "viewed in a lump, displeases, and is a constant puzzle and affront to the merely educated classes."[40] "Merely" here is indicative of Whitman's disdain for the conventional arbiters of cultural capital. Instead he suggests that only the "rare, cosmical, artist-mind" (943) possessing "kosmic intellect" (973) is able to discern meaning in the multitude. As suggested earlier, Whitman's vantage point of elevated distinction runs the risk of reducing difference to undifferentiated wholeness. The question of how to organize variety becomes one of positioning for Whitman. For Jacob Riis, the common signifier that matters is the racial one: heterogeneity results in the dissolution of the Anglo-Saxon "native stock" that is a marker, for him, of normative nationality.

William James also regarded heterogeneity as threatening. In his Edinburgh Gifford Lectures, published in 1902 as *The Varieties of Religious Experience*, he warns that a "heterogeneous personality" signals "an incompletely unified moral and intellectual constitution." Random variety, in other words, is deleterious to the possibility of (self-)definition. James is clear to distinguish between "an inner constitution which is harmonious and well balanced" and one displaying a "discordancy of which the consequences may be inconvenient in the extreme" (*WJ2* 156). A vocabulary of stability and rupture is here located in the realm of ontology, but it also resonates with the possibility of its translation into the constitution of a *national* character similarly fearful of discord. For James there are degrees of heterogeneity, the more pronounced of which become increasingly disabling to the self. "There are persons," he writes, "whose existence is little more than a series of zigzags, as now one tendency and now another gets the upper hand. Their spirit wars with their flesh, they wish for incompatibles, wayward impulses interrupt their most deliberate plans, and their lives are one long drama of repentance and of effort to repair misdemeanours and mistakes" (*WJ2* 157). Deliberation and intent are overwhelmed by the randomness of synaptic firings, to the extent that here is an economy of the mind that, if allowed to operate without constraint, takes one to the verge of insanity: "'The dégénéré supérieur' is simply a man of sensibility in many directions, who finds more difficulty than is common in keeping his spiritual house in order and running his furrow straight, because his feelings and impulses are too keen and too discrepant mutually." Ontological stability is achieved, James writes, only "in the straightening out and unifying" of the "diversified temptations" and "comparative chaos within us" (*WJ2* 158). Uncontrolled plurality, then, implies surrender to forces greater than one's self, forces that Riis identified as racial and ethnic otherness and that James internalizes as proliferating sensations and desires.

The Varieties of Religious Experience represents in many ways James's most resolute commitment to a cosmopolitan pluralism that, he assures us, never runs the risk of spiralling out of control into dislocated randomness. Protestant ideas exist alongside the latest scientific theories, the more unconventional spiritualities of the transcendentalists and the mind-cure movement, passages of Hindu and Buddhist thought, and accounts of Tolstoy's gospel of social religion. The text creates the conditions by which multiple discourses are encouraged to intersect and communicate. Read and admired as a study of comparative religions, it is also concerned to model possibilities of social formation, to propose an argument for the structural multiplicity of human relations. James imagines a pluralistic space of competing and complementary systems. "The experiences which we have been studying," he writes, "plainly show the universe to be a more many-sided affair than any sect, even the scientific sect, allows for. . . , And why, after all, may not the world be so complex as to consist of many interpenetrating spheres of reality, which we can approach in alternation by using different conceptions and assuming different attitudes?" (*WJ2* 116). James proposes the idea that religious differences are the result not just of varied systems of thought but also of a more fundamental, and almost unthinkable, structural diversity within a cosmos that contains a range of different but "interpenetrating" spiritualities. In the concluding lecture he asks: "is the existence of so many religious types and sects and creeds regrettable?" (*WJ2* 436). In a rapidly secularizing culture in which the claims of an organizing institutional religion have long been surpassed, is it possible for faith to exist on coherent grounds? His answer is both unequivocal and neatly balanced:

> The divine can mean no single quality, it must mean a group of qualities, by being champions of which in alternation, different men may all find worthy missions. Each attitude being a syllable in human nature's total message, it takes the whole of us to spell the meaning out completely . . . We must frankly recognize the fact that we live in partial systems, and that parts are not interchangeable in the spiritual life. (*WJ*2 437)

To be collectively articulate, James suggests, requires the individual voicing of separate syllables, such that the unity of the "total message" can only come into being through the distinct and distinctive elements of its diverse parts. "Partial systems" remain unique and non-transferable but nevertheless all contribute to a final coherence that remains central. Plurality and totality co-exist; indeed plurality is the means by which James is able to imagine a united utterance. *The Varieties of Religious Experience* offers a powerful argument for the multiplicity of human experience, but the book still retains a notion of an organizing core, whether that be the possibility of a complete spelling out of meaning or, as here, the identification of the coherent vessel to which the diversity of a post-theological civilization contributes: "in *our Father's house* are many mansions, and each of us must discover for himself the kind of religion and the amount of saintship which best comports with what he believes to be his powers and feels to be his truest mission and vocation" (*WJ*2 340; my emphasis).

Even when he is most confident in the vitality of pluralism to resist the appropriative imperatives of monism, as in *Varieties*, James is reluctant to abandon the idea of structure (and of authority) altogether. As Charlene Seigfried has characterized it, James attempts to negotiate a position that allows for the "ordering of the diversity of experience without slighting variety."[41] Given this delicate balancing-act, it is curious how critics have tended to emphasize James's image as a philosophical populist who marries the best of liberal politics with a suspicion of expository cant and obscurantism. This has led, I suggest, to a serious misrepresentation of his role as a late-Victorian intellectual. He has been read, taught and interpreted as an all-American philosopher in an Emersonian vein, one whose benign image is synonymous with home-grown democratic ideals and the rights of the underdog. Writing in 1935 during the Great Depression, James's first major biographer, Ralph Barton Perry, was keen to endorse his subject's reformist credentials: James's impulse was "invariably to side . . . with the Boers and the Irish against England, with the Filipinos against the United States, with religion or psychical research against science, with privates or laymen against officers, with the disreputable against the respectable, with heresy against orthodoxy, with youth against age, or with the new against the old."[42]

More recently, and typical of this model, is Frank Lentricchia's praise of James as the founder of an indigenous left intellectual tradition. Lentricchia rightly recognizes the social embeddedness of intellectual work, its ability to enact and influence change, and James's philosophy, he proposes, insists upon thought as a mode of action: "All intellectuals play social roles, whether they like it or not, James believed, because interpretation is always a form of intervention, a factor in social change or in social conservation."[43] It becomes apparent from his essay, though, that Lentricchia favors the former of these final two potentials: "social change" is more suited to his idea of James than is the more problematic "social conservation." Like those of some Old Testament prophet, James's words, Lentricchia writes, are "emancipatory." To counter a perceived invasion of America by the forces of European poststructuralism, he asserts that William "would lead us out of suffocating and tyrannous theorizations" (22). Bluntly equating "theory" with the perspective of ordering omniscience, Lentricchia judges that, for James, "the site of theory turns out to be the totalitarian site of imposition where all local situations are coerced into conformity" (7–8). James's intellectual vocation is to evaluate between "a heterogeneous space of dispersed histories, . . . a cacophony of stories" (10) that do not cohere into an overarching explanation. The choice of "heterogeneous" here is significant in its failure to notice James's less comfortable understanding of the word. Indeed Lentricchia's heterogeneity is distinctly and proudly of a New World stripe, perhaps unexpectedly echoing Theodore Roosevelt's suspicion of the cosmopolitan sensibility referred to earlier: James's is a voice "that refuses the elocutionary lessons of cosmopolitan finishing schools. His unfinished (and unfinishable) text of history, authorized by no single author, is the text of American history as it ought to be" (11). More recently still, Jonathan Levin has read James as a key figure in an Emersonian genealogy of process and transition, the "projection of an imagination feeling its way through the world" and suspicious of abstractions and collective structures.[44] And in a stronger political vein, David Kadlec offers an account of James that locates his antifoundationalism within a wider discourse of radical American anarchism that continues to emphasize individualism and nonconformity as the dominant modes of his thought.[45]

Such a sustained interest in James tends to invoke pluralism as just another example of this democratic spirit, rather than to engage with it as a quite particular and more circumscribed theoretical intervention. James's concern with the dilemma of "The One and the Many," as he titled a chapter of his posthumously published *Some Problems of Philosophy* (1911), involved not only philosophical, but also linguistic, civic and, as I want to argue here, institutional implications. To ask the question, "Does reality exist distributively? Or collectively? — in the shape of *eaches, everys, anys, eithers*? or only in the shape of an *all* or *whole*?" (*WJ*2 1040), is to recognize the importance of vocabulary choices in the construction and projection of identity. It is also to be acutely aware of the tension in American social formation between individual dispersal and national unification; and to be aware of the vexed issue of where the intellectual might best be placed to articulate and embody a federated reality. What are the common or shared points of institutional contact? And what role does an intellectual have in describing and legislating for a culture where the common denominators of institutional or ideological support might no longer be tenable? The relations between unity and multiplicity, reflection and action, connectedness and autonomy, as we've seen, structure American political philosophy from at least the revolutionary period onward. James's oscillation between these polarities is partly due to the fact that he wanted to have it both ways. Louis Menand has described his "aversion to making up his mind," and indeed at the level of biography James's career is marked by indecision and false starts.[46] Yet a wider problem of intellectual history is also hinted at in this judgment, one that recognizes James's location at the intersection of antagonistic traditions. His ambivalence toward the pressing question of unity and multiplicity exhibits a desire to combine an embrace of modern plurality with a residual Victorian attachment to shared moral and cultural codes.

When James argued, in his 1906 lectures on pragmatism, that belief is conditioned by "temperament" giving "man a stronger bias than any of his more strictly objective premises" (*WJ*2 489), dogmas of theology are replaced by the varieties of personal inclination. Yet this abandonment of external authority does not leave James liberated from the seductions of structure, for a society in which individual desires solely determine action is one that James also finds unworkable. Tempering the Emersonian absoluteness of his individualism, James recognizes that acknowledged alterity is essential to the smooth running of the social body: "In our world, the wishes of the individual are only one condition. Other individuals are there with other wishes and they must be propitiated first" (*WJ*2 614). In other words, the purity of absolute variety must nevertheless negotiate modes of cohabitation that might require forms of alliance or combination. Elsewhere James notes how the success of any "social organism" is brought about by "the co-operation of many independent persons" who have a precursive faith in one another" (*WJ*1 474). "Precursive" here suggests an anticipated consensus, an already shared project of common endeavor that works to counter the irreducible randomness of isolated selves. The desire to feel "at home," a phrase James uses in *A Pluralistic Universe* to describe the quest for intellectual agreement, reverberates through a philosophy that has little time for the entrenched battles, the "technical verbiage" (*WJ2* 639), of academic discourse. To claim that "Common men find themselves inheriting their beliefs, they know not how. They jump into them with both feet, and stand there" (*WJ2* 636), suggests that the relationship between collective identity and an individual self is more entwined than declarations of James's radical antifoundationalism might lead us to believe. Inheritance provides a structure, of an intellectual, ideological, or institutional kind, that mitigates the dangers of atomized plurality. While it is an attempt to conceptualize philosophically a respect for particularities and difference, pluralism does not equate this with a celebration of the infinitely diverse. Diversity is located within a notion of unity, one that, in *A Pluralistic Universe*, James famously imagines as "strung-along": "This world *may*, in the last resort, be a block universe, but on the other hand it *may* be a universe only strung-along, not rounded in and closed" (*WJ2* 779). The reluctance to be dogmatic here is characteristically Jamesian; the philosopher entertains more than one possibility. However there is a sense that the second option (beginning with "on the other hand") is the one given intellectual priority; it is the choice we are left with most recently after the sentence closes. "Strung-along" has the effect of suggesting both proximity and connection, *and* a degree of liberal autonomy that remains unfettered. Existence is not "rounded in and closed," in the manner of the "block universe," but neither is it so entirely without structure as to be radically contingent.

"Foreignness" and the Comforts of Habitual Intellectual Space

Negotiating the twin imperatives of local autonomy and commonality (the "strung along" universe) sees James oscillating between optimism that such a marriage of incompatibles might be possible and, as we shall see, a textual ambivalence that reveals uncertainty as to its likelihood. That the ideal of unity-in-variety is a precarious one is suggested by Judith Green's assessment of the current landscape of multicultural pluralism, in which she praises the "preference (or at least tolerance) for variety, multiplicity, dynamism, and jazz-like fusions instead of (or at least in alternation with) purity, unity, simplicity, and stability."[47] The qualifying parentheses in such a formulation indicate the residual force that commonality has over the energetic freedoms of what Green calls "critical pluralism." "Or at least," in both cases, infers a compromise that reduces the boundlessness of pluralist innovation. In contradistinction to the seamless teleology of the *e pluribus unum* motto, Green casts plurality and unity as simultaneously viable impulses that co-exist competitively and, it seems, without resolution.[48]

The lure of absolute openness causes James to consider the nature and parameters of limits, to wonder, in other words, about the relationship between
unmediated plurality and those structures that provide us with forms of meaning. In this regard, Walt Whitman becomes something of a test case, and,
characteristically, James's response to the poet is far from consistent. In his
lecture "On a Certain Blindness in Human Beings" (first published in 1899),
James quotes Whitman at length (from his poem "Crossing Brooklyn Ferry"
and from a letter to his friend Pete Doyle), establishing him as someone who
"abolishes the usual human distinctions" in his guise as "a sort of ideal tramp, a
rider on omnibus-tops and ferry-boats." According to conventional parameters
of judgment ("considered either practically or academically"), Whitman is "a
worthless unproductive being." Yet James regards his poetry as "a succession of
interjections on an immense scale. He felt the human crowd as rapturously as
Wordsworth felt the mountains, felt it as an overpoweringly significant presence,
simply to absorb one's mind in which should be business sufficient and worthy
to fill the days of a serious man" (*WJ1* 851). What James presents us with here
is a familiar valorization of the romantic seer, one whose intellect is positioned
above the concerns of the masses and yet porous enough to incorporate all to
itself.[49] The impulse is assimilative, absorptive, and leaves nothing outside of its
totalizing reach. Our blindness, James argues, lies in our inability to silence "the
clamor of our own practical interests," where the limitations of those interests
prevent us from being able "to attain to any breadth of insight." The vocabulary
of expansion and incorporation here is deployed to characterize a persona immune to the anxieties that attend pluralism; difficult questions of inclusion and
exclusion fail to register with a consciousness not "stuffed with abstract conceptions, and glib with verbalities and verbosities" (*WJ1* 856).

Whitman's appearance in the later *Varieties of Religious Experience* presents
us with a more sober assessment that takes into account some of the implications of what James calls the poet's "quasi-pathological" optimism (*WJ2* 82). The
skeptical tone is worth quoting at some length:

> Walt Whitman owes his importance in literature to the systematic expulsion from
> his writings of all contractile elements. The only sentiments he allowed himself to
> express were of the expansive order; and he expressed these in the first person, not as
> your mere monstrously conceited individual might so express them, but vicariously
> for all men, so that a passionate and mystic ontological emotion suffuses his words,
> and ends by persuading the reader that men and women, life and death, and all
> things are divinely good.
>
> Thus it has come about that many persons to-day regard Walt Whitman as the

restorer of the eternal natural religion. He has infected them with his own love of comrades, with his own gladness that he and they exist. Societies are actually formed for his cult, a periodical organ exists for its propagation, in which the lines of orthodoxy and heterodoxy are already beginning to be drawn[.] (*WJ2* 83–84)

The tone and choice of vocabulary in the passage work to signify suspicion of Whitman's expansive impulse, in which differences and discriminations of all kinds are eliminated in the transcendent unity of the "divinely good." The telling irony, of course, is that, infected by the poet's optimism, Whitman's followers have institutionalized him in print (the reference is to Horace Traubel's monthly journal *The Conservator* [1890–1919]); as a result, "contractile elements" of membership and exclusion have started to attach themselves to his figure. Whitmanian inclusiveness, then, cannot sustain its vision of collective wholeness, being prone to an inevitable disintegration into claims of partiality and ownership. If Whitman's vision "has a touch of bravado and an affected twist" (*WJ2* 85), as James goes on to suggest, its exaggerations are precisely of a kind that exert the violence of monist totality. Where "On a Certain Blindness in Human Beings" had celebrated the unfettered perspective, now James recognizes the necessary—but also undermining—strategy by which transcendence is made to fit institutional shapes for it to have tangible meaning.

Lying behind James's oscillating discussion of Whitman is the desire to establish a philosophical position that both resists the incorporative urge of transcendence *and* avoids being overwhelmed by diversity. "Habit," and the kinds of regulative behavior that it inculcates, becomes a key term in James's desire to maintain the possibility of structured thought in the face of endlessly proliferating difference. David Hume's notion of "custom or habit"—the means by which principles of causation are imagined—looms in the background of James's thinking here. Hume's skepticism about the evidential nature of cause and effect (that it is unreasonable to conclude, "merely because one event, in one instance, precedes another, that therefore the one is the cause, the other the effect")[50] is pragmatically alleviated by his recognition of the usefulness of customary responses to particular phenomena: "after the constant conjunction of two objects, heat and flame, for instance, weight and solidity, we are determined by custom alone to expect the one from the appearance of the other" (121). James, in his discussion of Hume and causality in *Some Problems of Philosophy*, refers to the Scottish philosopher's desire to show that our "pseudo-idea of connection . . . is nothing but the misinterpretation of a mental custom" (*WJ2* 1083), but he fails to acknowledge the genuine epistemological work that custom plays for Hume. James criticizes him for positing an atomized mental (and, by extension, material) arena: "Hume's assumption that any factor of reality must be separable, leads to his preposterous view, that no relation can be real . . . Nothing, in short, belongs with anything else" (*WJ2* 1084). In fact, Hume's attachment to custom is more important than James's remarks here suggest, and point, as we will see, to James's own concern with the habitual. While Hume may indeed insist upon an epistemology in which two "events" cannot be linked through a principle of causality, causality itself is the necessary fiction that we construct, through the customary observation of a combination of instances that seem to have the same outcome. "All inferences from experience," he writes, "therefore, are effects of custom, not of reasoning."[51] Moreover, it is custom that provides the possibility for existence. In language that anticipates James's vocabulary of pragmatism, Hume asserts:

> Custom, then, is the great guide of human life. It is that principle alone, which renders our experience useful to us, and makes us expect, for the future, a similar train of events with those which have appeared in the past. Without the influence of custom, we should be entirely ignorant of every matter of fact, beyond what is immediately present to the memory and senses. We should never know how to adjust means to ends, or to employ our natural powers in the production of any effect. There would be an end at once of all action, as well as the chief part of speculation. (122–23)

This is a very different understanding of human possibility than the one James assigns to Hume in *Some Problems of Philosophy*. It is as if James is unable, or unwilling, to recognize the affinities that his own thinking on habit has with his philosophical predecessor.

Hume's focus on usefulness and adjustment, on effectiveness and action, clearly finds echoes in James's work. In *The Meaning of Truth* James suggests that intellectual accomplishment is achieved through the establishment of paths of consistency that enable ideas to take root and develop: "And are not both our need of such consistency and our pleasure in it conceivable as outcomes of the natural fact that we are beings that do develop mental habits—habit itself proving adaptively beneficial in an environment where the same objects, or the same kinds of objects, recur and follow 'law'?" (*WJ2* 878). "Habit" provides what Renee Tursi has usefully characterized as "footholds in the morass of the unknowable by emptying experience of its uncanniness. Only then do thoughts truly feel sufficient and at home."[52] James's wish to feel "at home," in the context of both rising immigration *to* and imperial expansion *by* the United States, at times underwrites a vision of social and economic stasis that reminds us of his inevitably class-bound contours. In a famous passage from his *Principles of*

Psychology, James regards the cultivation of habit as society's "most precious conservative agent":

> It alone is what keeps us all within the bounds of ordinance, and saves the children of fortune form the envious uprisings of the poor. It alone prevents the hardest and most repulsive walks of life from being deserted by those brought up to tread therein. It keeps the fisherman and the deck-hand at sea through the winter; it holds the miner in his darkness, and nails the countryman to his log-cabin and his lonely farm through all the months of snow; it protects us from invasion by the natives of the desert and the frozen zone . . . It keeps the different strata from mixing. (*WJ1* 145)

Here, then, habit is opposed to an earlier transcendental vista of ceaseless flux (for example, Emerson's characterization of power that "resides in the moment of transition from a past to a new state, in the shooting of the gulf, in the darting to an aim" [*CWE* 2: 269]) and to fin-de-siècle aestheticism's privileging of heightened states of awareness (e.g., Walter Pater's fear in his "Conclusion to *The Renaissance*" that habit forms a "thick wall of personality").[53] Instead William James's habitual structures—of thought, of social taxonomy, of racial and ethnic identity (those "natives of the desert and the frozen zone")—aim to prevent the eruption of reckless foreign and unassimilable impulses, while acknowledging the inevitability of habit's provisional status. Santayana's reading of this aspect of James's pragmatism is concise: "the law is a description *a posteriori* of the habit things have chosen to acquire, and which they may possibly throw off altogether."[54] As Tursi suggests, "Habit offered James's own mental faculties a way to keep his hands on the reins,"[55] even if the resulting picture, as the references to fishermen and deck-hands make clear, smacks of an elitist refusal to acknowledge the very real material differences surrounding the modes of habit practiced by working-class and genteel intellectual Americans. Geoffrey Hill, in a characteristically astute and nuanced reading of Emerson, judges that James's writing, confined by its professional and disciplinary contexts, resembles "strenuous case-work and, running parallel to it, a languid literary sensibility and condescending 'taste.'"[56] In comparison to the Concord writer, William James is finally unable to confront the "basic hermeneutical fact" which, Hill suggests, is acknowledged by Emerson in an early journal entry: "There is every degree of remoteness from the line of things in the line of words" (495–96). James is "finally estranged from [his] own deepest intelligence by a failure to recognize the existence of such an *aporia*" (496).

Hill is right to note the class-bound and institutional parameters that inform (or, in Hill's reading, constrict) the possibilities of James's intelligence. Yet it is important to recognize that against what he calls in *A Pluralistic Universe* "a background of foreignness" that instills "a general habit of wariness" (*WJ2* 644), James's appeal to a normative (and nonabsolute) common ground, where habit might be established, offsets what Michael Trask, in his astute study of modernist class and sexuality calls, "the problem that foreignness poses to the stability and order of thought."[57] The vocabulary of "foreignness" and "intimacy" that James deploys here reverberates with the demographic challenges of incorporation and assimilation that the nation faced. He writes that an all-encompassing philosophy is impossible, the "attempt to define nature so that no one's business is left out, so that no one lies outside the door saying 'Where do *I* come in?' is sure in advance to fail." Inclusiveness that allows one to feel "at home," then, is not guaranteed, and the threshold of philosophical inquiry, like that of immigrant access, is one that by necessity filters and excludes. For James, though, this exclusion is not permanent, for he goes on to maintain that one day access might be granted to what (or who) is currently denied entrance: "The most a philosophy can hope for is not to lock out any interest forever. No matter what door it closes, it must leave other doors open for the interests which it neglects" (*WJ2* 644). This uneasy withdrawal into a form of liberal possibility that, despite the presence of closed doors, offers the reassurance of other ones still left open for the excluded or hitherto marginalized, is revealing. It expresses James's uncertainty when caught between the requirements of structure and those of pragmatist diversity. While it is the latter quality that has continued to determine James's position within the intellectual history of the United States, the importance he simultaneously ascribed to philosophical and institutional containers that gave shape and coherence to intellectual work has been underestimated. The emphasis James places on "intimacy" makes possible "a coherent world, and not an incarnate incoherence"; principles of "continuity, contiguity, or concatenation" (*WJ2* 778) inform a pluralistic vision that depends on consensus to ward off the ever-present dangers to a society of a proliferating, "foreign" threat. As responsive members of that society, James argues that thought is best generated and developed when it is organized and directed within agreed co-ordinates. As Michael Trask has suggested, James sought "to embrace desire and the contingency it allowed and to delimit or to channel that desire in ways that maintained social, civil, and economic order."[58]

It should, I hope, be apparent by now that the variety of William James I am presenting here differs fundamentally from the figure recuperated by Richard Rorty, who, in the wake of the "linguistic turn" in literary and philosophical studies, argues that James, and pragmatism more generally, abandons anything akin to epistemological or material reality. For pragmatists, Rorty suggests, "there are no constraints on conversation save conversational ones—no wholesale constraints derived from the nature of objects, or the mind, or of language, but only those retail constraints provided by the remarks of our fellow inquirers."[59] Within a shared community like this, anything seems to be possible because resistances are "retail" ones, an adjective I connect to the *Oxford English Dictionary*'s definitions "petty" and "trivial." Without tangible opposition, Rortyian pragmatism can indulge in the free-play of inventiveness and possibility. Pluralism, with its connotations of plenitude and abundance, tends to elide this difficult issue of limits. Just how pluralistic does a society wish to be? And at what point does a philosophy and politics of radical pluralism render the coherent functioning of such a society impossible? In coining the term "interactive universalism" to recuperate a Habermasian sense of social consensus that, at the same time, recognizes the diversity of lived experience, Seyla Benhabib has posited the need to acknowledge "the plurality of modes of being human, and differences among humans, without endorsing all these pluralities and differences as morally and politically valid."[60] Acknowledging difference, then, becomes the starting-point for any discussion of political philosophy, but not at the expense of those democratic institutions and practices that might require the enforcement of limits and exclusions to operate successfully. As Amanda Anderson has interpreted Benhabib's position, "politics involves consolidating autonomy for the greatest collectivity,"[61] a challenge that echoes William James's own sense of that we "bear the burden of reconciling metaphysical unity with phenomenal diversity" (*WJ*2 651). For James, reconciliation works to make modern diversity less terrifying without taking refuge in the utopia of unregulated all-inclusivity; instead, it foregrounds interests (or partisanship) as inevitable and necessary, such that pluralism is defined as much by what it excludes as by what it incorporates.

The case of W. E. B. Du Bois is instructive in this regard, for the pragmatist ethos of flux that he inherits from James is intersected by a sense of racial identity that pulls against the prospect of proliferating indeterminacy. For Du Bois, the tense marriage of individual rights and collective belonging is focused through a pragmatic understanding of race that locates him neither as a romantic essentialist nor as a poststructuralist *avant la lettre*. For example, in *Dusk of Dawn* (1940), a combination of autobiography and sociological commentary, Du Bois constructs a debate between his narrator figure and a fictional white interlocutor, Van Dieman. As the conversation turns to the question of racial categorisation and the kinds of geometries that might be said to contain and classify distinctions of bloodline, the narrator refutes the myth of racial purity, at which point Van Dieman asks: "What then becomes of all your argument if there are no races and we are all so horribly mixed as you maliciously charge?"

The narrator responds in a manner that exemplifies Du Bois's unwillingness to abandon categories of collective identity:

> Oh, my friend, can you not see that I am laughing at you? Do you suppose this world of men is simply a great layer cake with superimposed slices of inferior and superior races, interlaid with mud? No, no. Human beings are infinite in variety, and when they are agglutinated in groups, great and small, the groups differ as though they, too, had integrating souls. But they have not. The soul is still individual if it is free. Race is a cultural, sometimes an historical fact. And all that I really have been trying to say is that a certain group that I know and to which I belong . . . , bears in its bosom just now the spiritual hope of this land because of the persons who compose it and not by divine command.[62]

While stressing here the politically charged correlation of freedom and individuality, Du Bois nevertheless chooses to see that individuality expressed in broader social structures. It is a racial identity that is genuinely pragmatic rather than essentialist, formed by, among other things, geographical location, economic conditioning and political struggle. To view this collective self as homogenous and eternally coherent ("by divine command") was to fail "to recognize the Universal in the Particular," Du Bois wrote in 1921, resulting in "the menace of all group exclusiveness and segregation" (1194). In his influential account of the African-American intellectual tradition, Ross Posnock allies Du Bois with William James, noting James's contention that pragmatism is "an attitude of orientation that stands for no particular results" and approving of Du Bois's instantiation of this in his "creative revisionary practice."[63] To negotiate between pragmatic self-determination of this kind and the parameters of a racial identity that generated political action was the challenge that Du Bois's writing set for itself. In the concluding paragraph of the central chapter of *Dusk of Dawn*, "The Concept of Race," he writes:

> This was the race concept which has dominated my life, and the history of which I have attempted to make the leading theme of this book. It has as I have tried to show all sorts of illogical trends and irreconcilable tendencies. Perhaps it is wrong to speak of it at all as "a concept" rather than as a group of contradictory forces, facts, and tendencies. At any rate, I hope I have made its meaning to me clear.[64]

This passage is nervously poised between an acknowledgment of racial identity as an organizing rubric for Du Bois's life and work, and a sense that the concept itself—even the idea of it *as* a concept—is riven with contradictions and ambiguities. The tentative nature of Du Bois's vocabulary ("I have attempted," "I have tried," "Perhaps it is wrong") illustrates his reluctance to grant a secure hermeneutics to race, yet the force of "At any rate" in the final sentence seems to insist on returning to race as the category whose definition provokes his work.

That James regarded these judgments as matters of, and for, intellectual endeavor is clear. Negotiating a way through the complexities of modern society required both a skilled interpreter and a framework within which such guidance might be fostered. In *A Pluralistic Universe* he quotes Hegel approvingly that the work of the intellect "is to divest the objective world of its strangeness, and to make us more at home in it" (*WJ2* 634). Hegel might seem a strange candidate for James's commendation, for the German philosopher is more usually the target for his critique of intellectual work that sets out to establish comprehensive systems of understanding that negate the possibility of contingency and revision.[65] Systematic thinking of this kind, James suggests, is often accompanied by a stylistic lexicon that resorts to "over-technicality and consequent dreariness" (*WJ2* 637), "verbiage" (*WJ2* 639) that both deadens the likelihood of effective communication and fails to embody what he regards as the vibrant, active role of thought and its expression. Tired word choices become synonymous with ossified philosophy; it is the responsibility of the philosopher-intellectual to articulate a language that provides a structure of meaning, however contingent and provisional, by which the uncanny and the foreign can become habitual and familiar.

In a well-known 1898 letter to his wife Alice, James describes the effects of the Adirondack Mountains on him during a sleepless night's camping. I want to quote the experience at some length:

> The influences of Nature, the wholesomeness of the people round me, . . . the thought of you and the children, dear Harry on the wave [his brother Henry James], the problem of the Edinburgh lectures [James was in the early stages of planning his Gifford series], all fermented within me till it became a regular Walpurgis night. I spent a good deal of it in the woods, where the streaming moonlight lit up things in a magical checkered play, and it seemed as if the gods of all the nature-mythologies were holding an indescribable meeting in my breast with the moral gods of the inner life . . . The intense *significance* of some sort, of the whole scene, if only one could *tell* the significance; the intense human remoteness of its inner life, and yet the intense *appeal* of it; its everlasting freshness and its immemorial antiquity and decay; its utter Americanism, and every sort of patriotic suggestiveness, and you, and my relation to you part and parcel of it all, and beaten up with it so that memory and sensation all whirled inexplicably together; it was indeed worth coming for, and worth repeating year by year, if repetition could only procure what in its nature I suppose must be all unplanned for and unexpected. It was one of the happiest lonesome nights of

my existence, and I understand now what a poet is. He is a person who can feel the immense complexity of influences that I felt and make some partial tracks in them for verbal statement. In point of fact I can't find a single word for all that significance, & don't know what it was significant of, so there it remains, a mere boulder of *impression*. Doubtless in more ways that [*sic*] one though, things in the Edinboro' lectures will be traceable to it.[66]

The Emersonian cadences in this passage are striking, with its emphasis on a mystical "Nature" whose intensely affective impact triggers a confluence of ideas and offers the possibility of expanded and expansive thinking. The scene is invested with the kind of national distinctiveness that we also find in Emerson's more exceptionalist strains; patriotism is, significantly, located at home, embodied in landscape, family and friendship, rather than through the exertions of an increasingly imperial United States. Metaphysical affect and what James calls the "moral" (which I take to mean here the "intellectual") sense meet in a manner that is undoubtedly significant, but as is clear from the letter, the *nature* of that significance never quite comes into focus. Habit becomes one possible option by which interpretation might be reached—the experience is "worth repeating year by year"—except James is worried that routine might negate the singularity of the scene's "magical checkered play." The compromise that habit necessarily enforces is apparent here; the potential uncanniness of spontaneity might need to be sacrificed for the sake of a readable world.

In response to this anxiety, James turns in admiration to the privileged figure of the poet, regarded by Emerson as "the sayer, the namer" who "is a sovereign, and stands on the centre" (*CWE* 3: 7). James's model of the romantic eye is one similarly endowed with intellectual authority and affective range, yet it differs from its Emersonian predecessor in its more modest sense of the poet's communicative effectiveness. Only "partial tracks" of "verbal statement" are possible, yet any kind of articulation still seems to depend on the seer-like qualities of the superior mind. Later that summer, James, addressing the Philosophical Union at Berkeley, extended to philosophers the role he had assigned to the poet. Both, he claimed in "Philosophical Conceptions and Practical Results," are "path-finders," able to "find words for and express" "what everyone can know in the bone and marrow of him." Taking his rhetorical cue from the unexplored "Eden" of his West Coast surroundings, James imagines his thinkers as "blazes made by the axe of the human intellect on the trees of the otherwise trackless forest of human experience. They give you somewhere to go from. They give you a direction and a place to reach." As pioneers in the mapping of civilization, James's intellectuals provide the co-ordinates that enable the kinds of social and cultural structures grounding human endeavor to take shape. They "give a sort of ownership" and, persevering with his landscape analogy, ensure that the forest "is no longer a place to merely get lost in and never return." The uncanny space is thus transformed into a habitable, habitual one; the "marking and fixing function" that the philosopher-poet undertakes inscribes a set of parameters that work to contain plurality within their structures of meaning (*WJ1* 1078).

Some of those structures of meaning were provided within educational establishments forced to respond to the changing demographics of modernity. The nature and position of American intellectuals underwent a massive reorientation toward the end of the nineteenth century, in response in part to the development of corporate capitalism and to a crisis of identity and authority among the middle classes. Anxiety over the effect that democracy—understood as a quantitative number rather than a political principle—might have on cultural and intellectual matters was expressed in 1868 by E. L. Godkin, editor of the *Nation*. "Numbers in politics must always and should always be a strong argument," he judged, yet in "matters intellectual and aesthetic" the demands of popularity risked being "fatal to excellence and to originality." Godkin hoped that locating intellectual work within institutional structures would both allay the disruptive influence of "mere numbers" as well as "infus[e] something like discipline and order into the most undisciplined and disorderly host in the world—the thoughtful classes of the US."[67] Professional institutions, as one cultural historian has remarked, were "a way to insure . . . that each emerging 'audience' would find its 'proper' guide."[68] Intellectuals established new sources and kinds of authority in a rapidly diversifying public sphere. The rise of the university, which began to take on its modern form in the United States in the 1870s, was indispensable in restructuring knowledge and locating intellectuals in a position of professional power. New schools such as Cornell University (1868) and Johns Hopkins University (1876) were founded in part to meet this need for a national basis for intellectual life amid the post–Civil War crises of individual, civic, and economic authority that had led to social unrest on many levels. As Thomas Bender has shown, one specific result was an erosion of public culture in urban environments as mass immigration and a developing mass culture disrupted intellectual communities traditionally based within the city. Confronted by the twin threat of a heterogeneous populace and a homogenous culture, intellectuals reformed within university departments to manage and guide in expert fashion the social, cultural, and economic systems of the nation. The university promised to restore to them an authority based on new methods of analysis and complex, specialized languages, what Bender calls "disciplinary professionalism."[69]

The move toward intellectual specialization and the emergence of a system of academic disciplines transformed the idea of public culture. No longer concerned with reaching a shared audience (the academic equivalent of Howells's commonality), "each new disciplinary profession developed its own conceptual basis" (10). In ways that are now thoroughly familiar to our contemporary academic climate, intellectual work began to be judged by disciplinary peers rather than a wider public. In the mid-eighteenth century, Bender argues, a Habermasian public sphere had operated across the diversity of American social spaces. This is not to assert a uniformity of culture, yet "while a real distinction must be made between learned and popular traditions, the two could be bridged. Elite culture depended upon and extended popular culture." In other words, in this earlier period it was possible for intellectuals to "speak to the pace of local thought" (11) in a manner that assumed a common community. Yet as I have been suggesting, this intellectual community was vulnerable to the redefinition of the public sphere inaugurated by the massive economic and demographic transformations of the nineteenth century. The dissemination of knowledge increasingly operated within the parameters of academic disciplines that were often perceived to be distant from, and increasingly disbelieving of, a shared public culture. These disciplines were able to develop precise and specialized protocols of intellectual work that provided reassurance at a time when the authority of the intellectual in the public sphere appeared particularly fragile. This is not to say that professionalized disciplines became socially irresponsible. But it changes, or at least offers an alternative definition of, the term "public intellectual," where what is understood by the word "public" in that phrase might be thought to have contracted considerably. Bender quotes Alfred North Whitehead's astute comment that "Each profession makes progress, but it is progress in its own groove . . . People have lives outside of their profession or their business. But the point is the restraint of serious thought within a groove. The remainder of life is treated superficially" (13–14).

Within Harvard, the intellectual home of William James for much of his career, the onset of disciplinary specialization had provoked a fierce debate about the best way to educate America's young minds. In 1908 Irving Babbitt, at the time of James's tenure an assistant professor of French, published *Literature and the American College*, a book that he characterized as "Essays in Defense of the Humanities." Babbitt was a forceful proponent of a humanistic education that sought to steer clear both of the perceived subjective excesses of romanticism and the scientific impulses of philology. He opposed the gradual introduction at Harvard, from the 1880s onward, of an elective system of education that allowed students to pick and choose their own courses. For Babbitt, such a move pandered to what he called "the democratic absurdity of asserting that all studies are, and by rights should be, free and equal."[70] Instead of the individualist ethos of an elective education, he argued for "a sense of measure," an organizing structure that encouraged intellectual exploration without underwriting the abandonment of what he felt to be the necessary frameworks within which such exploration could be undertaken:

> In one sense the purpose of the college is not to encourage the democratic spirit, but on the contrary to check the drift toward a pure democracy. If our definition of humanism has any value, what is needed is not democracy alone, nor again an unmixed aristocracy, but a blending of the two—an aristocratic and selective democracy. (80)

There are significant affinities here, I think, with that "strung-along" model of existence that James would advocate the following year. Within academia, forms of diversity can be countenanced under a general rubric that promotes and protects difference, without succumbing to the abandonment of structure, what Babbitt calls "pure democracy." How to maintain pluralism within the context of discriminating coherence is something that preoccupies both men.

With some justification Babbitt is regarded now as a cultural conservative. His celebration of a guided and guiding humanism does not play well in an intellectual and educational culture rightly suspicious of the normative agendas that lie behind such benign intentions. Yet, I would suggest that there are still things to be learnt from a man who lamented an academic age that "hopes to accomplish its main ends by the appointment of committees" (116) and worried that doctoral degrees might result in a narrowing of professional competence and intellectual range. ("We must be men before being entomologists," he warned [107].) William James's status as public intellectual was defined against this same process of intellectual specialization. Never attending graduate school, James, as Carrie Bramen has suggested, in many ways personified the Victorian "oratory and rhetoric" idea of the professor, the Arnoldian notion of believers in the moral and spiritual force of education. Critical both of academic narrowness and the homogenizing tendencies of professional graduate study, James theorizes plurality through the inevitable, and for him necessary, confines of conditions.

In his 1907 travel book *The American Scene*, Henry James spends several pages eulogizing the virtues of the country club, an institution in which, he marvels, "the flame of Democracy burns whitest and steadiest and most floods the subject."[71] This bizarre acclamation is earned because of Henry's sense that the country club is able to incorporate the widest imaginable configuration of "the Family," whose "latent multiplications" apparently pose no problem for it. However, what at first appears to be an indiscriminate permeability is immediately qualified by a more sober realization. "Even the most inclusive social scheme,"

Henry writes, "must in a large community always stop somewhere" (240). Invoking the necessity of limits articulates the idea of structure as the means by which social interaction of the kind Henry admires here can continue.

William James has recourse to a similar imperative in his writing on the university. An infinitely porous intellectual space is one that not only perpetuates the market ethos of academic specialization, but also endangers the possibility of genuine intellectual work. Within an academic culture, limits are necessary to protect intellectual autonomy, where eccentricities and dissenting points of view can be safely cultivated and encouraged. As we saw in chapter 1, James had praised what he called the "solitary sons" of Harvard, its intellectual eccentrics and vagrants: "our undisciplinables" represent "our proudest product." "Inner Harvard" offers an equilibrium of independence and connection, what he succinctly calls "an atomistic constitution," that fosters an ideal of community serving James as the model of a pluralistic universe. Embracing a multiplicity of "vital ideals," Harvard nevertheless "makes a scale of value among them" (*WJ2* 1128). Both the rigidity of an over-professionalized intellectual space and the disparate randomness of academic disconnection are rejected in favor of a more modest structure of sheltered autonomy.[72]

Such a model comes to characterize James's sense of philosophical and, by extension, political thinking. Pluralism, which is so central to both, challenges the universalist claims of most prior philosophical traditions. James insists that each philosophy can provide only a limited and partial view: "No philosophy can ever be anything but a summary sketch, a picture of the world in abridgement, a foreshortened bird's-eye view of the perspective of events" (*WJ2* 633). There are, he writes, only "partial knowers." Pluralism, then, flaunts its own limits. To underscore this point, James invokes the category of the "residuum," a space of excess that differentiates the pluralistic universe from its all-inclusive monistic other. He refers to this concept of incompleteness as the "ever not quite" of our attempts at system-building: "Things are 'with' one another in many ways, but nothing includes everything, or dominates over everything. The word 'and' trails along after every sentence. Something always escapes. 'Ever not quite' has to be said of the best attempts made anywhere in the universe at attaining all-inclusiveness" (*WJ2* 776). A sentence in which a connective supplants a full-stop is the grammatical corollary of the pluralistic universe.[73] It enables an intellectual maneuver that recognizes connection while also preserving autonomy: "each part of the world," he writes, "is in some ways connected, in some other ways not connected with its other parts" (*WJ2* 666).

In 1888 the socialist utopian Edward Bellamy had imagined an American future in which the "residuum" was a thing of the past: his novel *Looking Back-*

ward depicted a Boston in the year 2000 in which society operated at a level of inclusive perfection. The guide to this coherent world exclaims: "A solution which leaves an unaccounted-for residuum is no solution at all; and our solution of the problem of human society would have been none at all had it left the lame, the sick, and the blind outside with the beasts, to fare as they might."[74] Bellamy's model of a future America is, using James's terminology, monist; it incorporates all in a vision of social harmony. For a utopian imagination such as Bellamy's, one can understand the impulse that requires the elimination of those extraneous elements that obstruct the attainment of future perfection. In this regard, James's philosophy is profoundly anti-utopian in that it refuses to countenance the enclosed stability upon which utopia depends. The lack of a residuum, for James, is tantamount to abandoning acts of interpretative discrimination. Instead, James prescribes a form of unity that contains hierarchies that have been determined both by our inability to achieve a Whitmanian embrace *and* our decision to set limits. As James writes, "it is we who project order into the world by selecting objects and tracing relations . . . We carve out order by leaving the disorderly parts out" (*WJ*2 634). That principles of selection require a notion of hierarchy is also clear: "An order must be made; and in that order the higher side of things must dominate" (*WJ*2 645).

James's call here for the establishment of priorities as a way to sustain intellectual work is also, of course, an assertion of intellectual leadership. In the same way that, for the writers of *The Federalist Papers*, the threat of disparate factionalism could be eased by a constitution that invested political authority in representative figures (those described by Madison as "a chosen body of citizens, whose wisdom may best discern the true interest of their country"),[75] James's advocacy of discriminating hierarchical forms, however provisional, implies a claim for intellectual privilege that inevitably betrays his class-bound moorings. Despite the political attractions of Frank Lentricchia's pioneering democrat, or even of David Kadlec's radical anarchist, James occupies the position of a gentleman reformer whose idea of modest hierarchy is always in danger of slipping into cultural elitism. Cornel West has perhaps articulated most harshly this view, accusing pragmatists like James of "pandering to middle class pieties," blind to "the plight of the wretched of the earth, namely, the majority of humanity who own no property or wealth, participate in no democratic arrangements, and whose individualities are crushed by hard labor and harsh living conditions."[76] The passage from James quoted earlier describing "the fisherman and the deckhand" would seem to bear out such a critique. Yet, we would be wise to temper our political outrage with an acknowledgment that James's conception of pluralism is typical of what Bramen regards as a more widespread end-of-century crisis management. It depends on an Arnoldian notion of intellectual calling to articulate and sustain shared beliefs during times of upheaval. The challenge for James is how to imagine democratic models of collectivity that would allow the most autonomy for individual expression, while also circumscribing individual liberty within a sense of civic community. The choice of the federal republic as the predominant trope of the pluralistic universe is not arbitrary. In *The Metaphysical Club*, Louis Menand argues that James's conjoining of the pluralist world to the model of the federal republic is "probably just a figure of speech, an American (in fact, an Irish-American) tweaking his British listeners [the lectures that became *A Pluralistic Universe* were given at Oxford]."[77] To my mind, this rather underplays the historical resonances that are inevitably attached to it, as well as James's keen sense of the need for intellectuals to keep up with, and respond to, the challenges of modernity. If the relationship of the intellectual to a wider public sphere is no longer immediate or available, as Bender argues, then the recasting of the role of cultural authority requires a new shape in which it can best function. As I have suggested here, federated thought is both inclusive and structured; it recognizes its contingency yet still insists on the right to enact discriminations; it finds solace in the construction of habitual patterns that are nevertheless open to revision; and it connects ideas without fusing them together. When this taxonomy of mental work is extended to characterize ideal forms of learning (the "inner Harvard") and, further, a model for the American body politic in the grip of modernity's force, the wider implications of its use become apparent. *A Pluralistic Universe* ends with James issuing a call to intellectual arms. Insisting that "philosophy and reality, theory and action, work in the same circle indefinitely" (*WJ2* 780), he pleads for "some of the younger members of this learned audience to lay this hint to heart" by finding their intellectual orientation "from the *particulars of life*" (*WJ2* 781). James's vision of pluralism, in its multiple instantiations, represents his own response to such particularity.

5

AESTHETICS AND
INSTITUTIONS

Writing from London in 1915 to his one-time Harvard student Horace Kallen, and with the First World War in brutal progress, George Santayana articulated an exile's suspicion of nationality. Kallen had delivered an address, "Nationality and the Jewish State in the Great War," the previous year, and Santayana's letter was a response to its appearance in *The Menorah Journal*, one of the leading publications for Jewish intellectuals. Nationality, Santayana writes,

> seems to be behind the restlessness, ambition, and obduracy that brought the war about, behind the endurance and zeal of the combatants, and also before their eyes (in every camp) in so far as they see anything at all before them to aim at. . . . If ninetenths of a man's individuality are his nationality, nationality must cover a good deal that is common to all men, and much that is common to very few. And I hardly see how nationality, in this moral and inward sense, is to find political expression. Such national movements as the Italian, Balkan, or Irish are movements to establish what you call nationhood; so is Zioniosm, I suppose. Yet you hardly look to seeing the various nationalities in the U.S. establish special governments; I am not sure (I am so ignorant) whether the Pale is a district so preponderantly Jewish that a Jewish local government could be hoped for there. In these cases Nationality would have to be a voluntary and hazy thing: the degree to which anyone possessed it, the intensity and scope of his nationalism would be impossible to fix.[1]

Spanish-born, Harvard-educated and, from 1912 until his death in 1952, permanently resident in Europe, Santayana exhibited the kind of cosmopolitan reluctance to subscribe to affiliations of nationality or religion that would ensure his permanent sense of dislocation from both the Catholicism of his European ancestry and, as he would famously characterize it, the "genteel" New England Puritanism of the United States. In his letter to Kallen, Santayana acknowledges nationality's role in self-definition, yet he is keen to distinguish, somewhat awkwardly, between an expression of nationality that is "moral and inward" and its translation into political expression, that is to say its institutionalization into structures of adherence and control. The United States, he suggests, offers a good example of where the diversity of national identities has not resulted in the construction of a government or governments that reflect that. As we saw in chapter 4, the problem of how to reconcile transnational diversity with the political—and practical—expediency of national unity preoccupied William James, Santayana's colleague at Harvard. Whereas for James the idea of an "atomistic constitution" holds in productive tension the twin impulses of coherence and plurality, Santayana is more skeptical of declarations of unity that are based on assertions of shared national identity. He suggests instead that strength of national affiliation is difficult to assess, so that the formation of political structures would be entirely based upon something "voluntary and hazy," the "intensity and scope" of which would be "impossible to fix."

Of all the figures discussed in this book, Santayana could claim to be the most explicitly transnational in both his biographical narrative and his intellectual disposition. His own sense of national dislocation, accentuated by adolescent years moving between the Castile of his father and his mother's Boston, ensured that his philosophical and political outlook remained resolutely cosmopolitan, if, at times, also doubtful of the possibility of a widespread cosmopolitan conversation. His "complex allegiances," being "a child born in Spain of Spanish parents to be educated in Boston and to write in the English language,"[2] resulted in a double estrangement. Looking back on his formative years, Santayana writes of feeling "like a foreigner in Spain" where his "Yankee manners seemed outlandish" (6), yet also at such a remove from his acquired Americanness that he could "set out to say plausibly in English as many un-English things as possible" (7). In an anthology of writing that includes pieces by Santayana, collected under the rubric of "Conservative Critics of American Culture," the volume's editor identifies superfluity as the disposition common to his chosen authors, an alienation from the political, economic, and cultural motors that were driving the nation. While the credentials of Santayana's conservatism might be contested—indeed, as this chapter will show, his position of voluntary detachment often enabled a more wide-ranging critique than would have been possible for one more thoroughly interpellated within a culture — it is clear that Santayana's sense of exile became constitutive of his intellectual identity. In 1940, and living in Italy, he wrote that: "I have no American or English blood; I was not born in the United States; I have never become an American citizen; as soon as I was my own master I spent every free winter and almost every summer in Europe; I never married or kept house or expected to end my days in America. This sense of belonging elsewhere, or rather not belonging to where I lived, was nothing anomalous or unpleasant to me but, as it were, hereditary."[3]

His failure to belong to the normative American models of masculine citizenship — through birth, geographical location, or personal intimacy — suggests a figure whose relationship to what Ross Posnock calls "an ethic of compulsory heterosexuality" was marginal at best.[4] Posnock observes the resistancies to this compulsion that Santayana, along with Henry James and Howard Sturgis, attempted to articulate, what he calls "their effort to diffuse traditional gender polarities that define the masculine as the repudiation of the feminine" (200). Opposed to the ethical absolutism of "weedy intellectuals or self-inhibited Puritans," as Santayana would characterize the national orthodoxy of the United States, he offered in his volume of autobiography *Persons and Places* (1944) a vision of Whitmanian inclusiveness that sought to "see both sides and take neither, in order, ideally, to embrace both, to sing both, and love the different forms that the good and the beautiful wear to different creatures."[5] While this might seem to suggest a radical (or perhaps unquestioning) openness to alterity and pluralism that argues against Santayana's reputation as a detached ascetic, it becomes quickly apparent that "comprehensiveness in sympathy" of this kind does not preclude a keen awareness of criteria for moral evaluation. It "by no means implies," Santayana writes, "that good and evil are indistinguishable or dubious. Nature sets definite standards for every living being; the good and the beautiful could not exist otherwise; and the failure or lapse of natural perfection in each is an irreparable evil" (155–56).

Forms of Aesthetic and Political Legitimacy

This concern to imagine diversity without running the risk of degenerating into formlessness is, as we have seen, shared by William James. Santayana, though, is more explicit in his preoccupation with the idea of "form" both as an aesthetic category and as a structural necessity in the organization of a polity. The belief that aesthetic form might embody and express political values is central to his first book of prose, *The Sense of Beauty* (1896), in which he devotes a lengthy section to a consideration of how an idea of "the beautiful" can generate forms of civic solidarity in the face of social heterogeneity. Santayana is intent on developing a precise understanding of the geometries that multiplicity can, and indeed should take so as to be politically useful. The Arnoldian notion of a privatized articulation of "sweetness and light," in which aesthetic criteria contribute to individual self-cultivation, is re-imagined as a collective experience. Taste, instead of being the preserve of a cultured elite, instead generates, in the words of Hannah Arendt, "the political capacity that truly humanizes the beautiful and creates a culture."[6] As Russ Castronovo has explored, Santayana was just one of many turn-of-the-century academics and intellectuals who "stressed the importance of form" as a prerequisite for aesthetic appreciation; these theoretically minded figures existed alongside more practical "proponents of taste and culture who advocated parks with clear borders, public squares with symmetrical dimensions, and cultural performances that held audiences captive in their seats."[7] Castronovo details how aesthetics developed as an academic topic of study in the period and also became materially visible in the designs of city planners and architects who recognized the need to promote social cohesion through the kind of affective responses that tangible expressions of taste might trigger. The social reformer Jacob Riis, for instance, claimed that a correct conception of beauty was an indispensable tool in the formation of a stable national identity. "[A] good soil for citizenship to grow in," he writes, is aided by the construction of public spaces conducive to the sustenance of democracy liberated from institutional and political constriction:

> And, please God, the time is at hand. Here, set in its frame of swarming tenements, is a wide open space, some time, when enough official red tape can be unwound, to be a park, with flowers and grass and birds to gladden the hearts of those to whom such things have been as tales that are told, all these dreary years, and with a playground in which the children of yonder big school may roam at will, undismayed by landlord or policeman.[8]

In *The Sense of Beauty*, Santayana argues that any idea of form needs to acknowledge variety and combination; indeed it cannot be classified as such unless or until it contains within its shape strands of difference. "[A] moment's reflection," he writes, "will show us that unity cannot be absolute and be a form; a form is an aggregation, it must have elements, and the manner in which the elements are combined constitutes the character of the form. A perfectly simple perception, in which there was no consciousness of the distinction and relation of parts, would not be a perception of form; it would be a sensation." An opposition is drawn, then, between the unmediated quality of "sensation" and the implicated, relational structure of "form," and it is the latter's complexity, Santayana suggests, that works to generate, as we will see, possibilities of literary and political expression. It is only the "unattentive" who find value in the simplicity of sensation, those who "do not stop to survey the parts or to appreciate their relation, and consequently are insensible to the various charms of various unifications."[9] That final phrase—"various unifications"—perfectly encapsulates a geometry of coherence that seeks to contain form but not to curtail its diverse modes of articulation. Where "capacity for association is restricted," art becomes reduced to the monotony of the uniform, described as "the dryness, the crisp definiteness and hardness" of repetitious aesthetic practice. Santayana's example is the heroic couplet, the "compactness and inevitableness" of which "make it excellent for an epigram and adequate for a satire, but its perpetual snap and unvarying rhythm are thin for an epic, and impossible for a song" (70). From architecture, he cites the Greek colonnade as an instance of "perfect taste," which "is itself a limitation, not because it intentionally excludes any excellence, but because it impedes the wandering of the arts into those bypaths of caprice and grotesqueness in which, although at the sacrifice of formal beauty, interesting partial effects might still be discovered." In this, of course, Santayana is indebted to John Ruskin, and in a 1928 letter to the aesthetician Thomas Munro he explicitly aligned himself with Ruskin's generation, whose sense of the importance of beauty as an aesthetic category was, he lamented, no longer felt in the present age: "You must remember that we were not very much later than Ruskin, Pater, Swinburne, and Matthew Arnold: our atmosphere was that of poets and persons touched with religious enthusiasm or religious madness. Beauty (which mustn't be mentioned now) was then a living presence, or an aching absence, day and night."[10] Ruskin's preference for the gothic style, as described in his famous "Nature of Gothic" chapter in the second volume of *The Stones of Venice* (1853), was determined by his sense that it enabled each individual builder to work according to his abilities, to produce an object of beauty that did not need to conform to the overexacting standards of perfection demanded by Greek architecture. "The principle admirableness of the Gothic schools of architecture," he wrote, lies in the fact that they "receive the results of the labour of inferior minds; and out of fragments full of imperfection, and betraying that imperfection in every touch, indulgently raise up a stately and unaccusable whole."[11]

As with Ruskin, Santayana extends such a conception of aesthetics, in which purity of form is regarded as a failure of artistic execution, into the realm of the political, for beauty, he judges, "often accounts for a great deal in our moral and practical attitude" to social structuring (71). Democracy is as much an aesthetic category as it is a political one—one of its key "ingredients" being the articulation of an idea of beauty that illustrates "that effect of multiplicity in uniformity" which Santayana regards as constitutive of successful art. As a politics of democracy becomes more widely accepted and adopted, he suggests, our sense of the concept undergoes a transformation from one of utilitarian adoption ("prized at first as a means to happiness and as an instrument of good government") to innate, aesthetic value, a paradoxical vision of pure form that is defined by its diversities ("it was beginning to seem good in itself, in fact, the only intrinsically right and perfect arrangement"). The "essential right" of democracy "is something purely aesthetic" (72). While aesthetics can be deployed to underwrite and sustain a polity, Santayana suggests that beauty itself (or its absence) does not provide the basis for revolutionary action. Instead it works to normalize political systems *after* their emergence, creating the conditions in which the upheavals of revolution might be forgotten in favor of a narrative of consecration that helps to stabilize social forms. The "utilitarian scheme" of the French Revolution, for instance, was endorsed by the belief in democracy's beautiful justness, a quality of affect which was able, retrospectively, to elide the excesses of *la Terreur*: "The practical value of the arrangement, on which, of course, it is entirely dependent for its origin and authority, was forgotten, and men were ready to sacrifice their welfare to their sense of propriety; that is, they allowed an aesthetic good to outweigh a practical one" (72). As Castronovo notes, "International aesthetics mop up after the revolution so that its leveling seems less terrible."[12]

In the United States, Santayana was prepared to view Walt Whitman as the embodiment of the kind of variegated democracy that he theorizes here. As we'll see, Whitman remains an intellectual touchstone for Santayana, and his judgments on the poet are far from consistent, but *The Sense of Beauty* presents a figure who is celebrated for his perfect fusing of the political and the aesthetic. "Never, perhaps, has the charm of uniformity in multiplicity been felt so completely and so exclusively," he asserts.[13] There is a rugged masculinity about Whitman's lines, eschewing genteel rhythms and subjects, that appeals to Santayana's coded sexuality: Whitman writes "not flowers but leaves of grass, not music but drum-taps, not composition but aggregation, not the hero but the average man, not the crisis but the vulgarest moment" (72–73). The appealing bohemianism that lies behind this evaluation of the poet's worth as a writer does not, though, imply that a poetics of democracy is without form. "Aggregation" is not so much opposed to "composition" as a radical rethinking of it; it is a more vital understanding of art's responsibilities to articulate a United States transformed by the political, economic, and cultural forces of modernity. To underscore this point, Santayana is clear to draw a distinction between multiplicity and what he calls the "indeterminate," a quality that is "obscure and uncertain in its effect, and if used, as in many arts it often is, to convey a meaning, must fail to do so unequivocally." Indeterminacy prevents the articulation of meaning—it is "fatal to . . . expressiveness"—for "no precision of meaning can be reached without a precision of style." Multiplicity can only be politically and aesthetically effective if it is orchestrated within a structure—political democracy and Whitman's free-verse aesthetics—that marries precision with generosity of embrace. Significantly Emerson is produced by Santayana as an example of indeterminacy's occlusions, for "significant fragments are collected, and no system, no total thought, [is] constructed out of them" (91). We saw in chapter 1 that Emerson's embrace of the aphoristic fragment best encapsulates the kind of epistemological work that he wants language to perform; for Santayana, at this point in his career more attuned to the possibilities of philosophical system-building, such a strategy runs the risk of appearing inchoate rather than intellectually nimble. Balancing clarity of expression with variety is the challenge Santayana poses to all artists; for the writer, "the use of language as an instrument of thought" requires a careful attention to structure so as to avoid the "easy" descent "from ambiguity to meaninglessness" (92).

Santayana's concern to describe the developing structures of political and artistic expression might be said to reach its peak with the publication of the five-volume *The Life of Reason: Or the Phases of Human Progress* (1905–6). A dense, often contradictory expression of its author's moral philosophy, the work nevertheless set out its intent with hubristic clarity. In the general introduction, Santayana declares that "The Life of Reason is . . . neither a mere means not a mere incident in human progress; it is the total and embodied progress itself, in which the pleasures of sense are included in so far as they can be intelligently deployed and pursued."[14] The book represents, then, the elucidation of "progress" as the driving force behind human evolution, an idea that is to be understood both as a question of politics and, he suggests here, one of affect, where art's function in daily life is recognized as a marker of advance. Yet the emergence of civilization is far from being a utopian teleology of perfectibility, for Santayana suggests that the civilized are few in number and that the retention of humankind's "animal nature" is a necessary bulwark against extinction: "Mankind can never, without perishing, surrender its animal nature, its need to eat and drink, its sexual method of reproduction, its vision of nature, its faculty of speech, its arts of music, poetry and building. Particular races cannot subsist if they renounce their savage instincts, but die, like wild animals, in captivity." Diversity exists alongside what are, for Santayana, the essential continuities of human nature across time and space that survive "amid a continual fluctuation of its embodiments." Such fluctuations generate forms of differentiation that place in doubt our ability to communicate with each other: "spiritual unity" may run "like sap, from the common root to every uttermost flower," yet "at each forking . . . the branches part company, and what happens in one is no direct concern of the others." Progress understood as proliferation, then, might not be conducive to the kind of widespread cosmopolitan conversation that Margaret Fuller, for instance, advocated; in fact, Santayana is explicit about the isolationism that his model seems to suggest. "The products of one age and nation," he writes, "may well be unintelligible to another." Transmission of the more sophisticated components of a culture is only effected by a small number: "the highest things are communicable to the fewest persons, and yet, among these few, are the most perfectly communicable."[15]

The second volume of *The Life of Reason*, *Reason in Society*, is an analysis of various forms of social construction, from the tribal to the emergence of modern systems of government and the idea of "civilization," and of the relationship between society's massed ranks and its intellectual elite. The variety of experience that civilization can offer runs the risk of becoming a seductive lure that facilitates the growth of egotism: a drama in which the protagonist "calls himself I and speaks all the soliloquies" (150). To prevent a cacophony of noise, and the social incoherence that would follow, Santayana moves to privilege an idea of the "natural leader," our subordination to whom entails "no loss of liberty" but, instead, the possibility of "availing ourselves of the best instrument obtainable to accomplish our ends." Intellectual authority, the existence of an elite, is a necessary element of society's variety for Santayana, for whom "there is no greater stupidity or meanness than to take uniformity for an ideal." In a properly variegated society the "great man" is "exalted" for the superior skills he is able to exert over those subordinate to him; moreover, our "universal interest in whatever is extraordinary" is fed by the magnetic pull of these figures of cultural authority. The conundrum facing Santayana is how to reconcile his commitment to democracy (as evidenced in *The Sense of Beauty*) with the legitimacy he grants to the "distinguished" individual (130).

Reason in Society works its way around this problem by effecting a careful weighing up of the contending merits of aristocratic and democratic forms of government. Santayana's conception of democracy is of a system that must contain an idea of "eminence" as something which is "naturally representative," that is to say that democratic societies embody their political character by demonstrating coherently-functioning hierarchies of skill and influence. To be representatively democratic is to acknowledge qualitative aspects of difference, but within a system that finds harmony through the expression of diversity:

Eminence is synthetic and represents what it synthesizes. An eminence not representative would not constitute excellence, but merely extravagance or notoriety. Excellence in anything, whether thought, action, or feeling, consists in representation, in standing for many diffuse constituents reduced to harmony, so that the upshot of the experience concerned is mirrored and regarded with justice to all extant interests and speaking in their total behalf.

This conception of the representative thinker echoes, of course, Emerson's reading of intellectual authority as both hierarchical and embodying, as I discussed in chapter 2. The performative elements of eloquence, when not articulated in the service of a politics of embodiment, become for Santayana distorted and eccentric affectations—"extravagance" of this kind places the intellect outside the realm of representative significance. The passage also highlights for us once more a version of the *e pluribus unum* paradigm in its concern to celebrate a carefully situated diversity, whereby the figure of representative excellence authorizes and facilitates the narrative of curative coherence, "standing for many diffuse constituents reduced to harmony." Aristocracy, although more comfortable with the idea of hierarchy, risks exhibiting the kind of extravagancies against which Santayana warns here, where the decline into "a conventional and baseless authority" in which the "government reverts to the primeval robber; the church stands in the way of all wisdom" impedes the production of representative forms of intellectual identity. In such circumstances, assertions of democracy "allow some new organization, more representative of actual interests, to replace the old encumbrances and tyrannies" (142). Santayana treads, then, a careful line between an exhausted, corrupt aristocracy and a democratic polity that would be wise to resist the temptations of social leveling, in which those "highly elaborate ways of living and thinking" that distinguish and differentiate individuals are negated in favor of a politics of equality. The resulting social vision horrifies him: "Imagine those aristocratic influences removed, and would any head be lifted above a dead level of infinite dullness and vulgarity? Would mankind be anything but a trivial, sensuous, superstitious, custom-ridden herd? . . . Such a headless people has the mind of a worm and the claws of a dragon" (145). Under a tyranny of equality, "The only freeman in [such a society] would be one whose ideal was to be an average man."

Between these two conditions Santayana is prepared to imagine a more discriminating model of democracy in which the presence of an intellectual aristocracy might work to alleviate what he perceives to be those deadening effects of uniform equality. The "benefits of civilisation" should be "integrated in eminent men, whose influence in turn should direct and temper the general life." In the face of turn-of-the-century anxieties about intellectual legitimacy and the standardization of knowledge, Santayana reasserts the authority of exceptional figures able to direct society in what he calls, borrowing from Plato, a "timocracy": men of eminence "would formulate religion, cultivate the arts and sciences, provide for government and all public conveniences, and inspire patriotism by their discourse and example" (146). A timocracy, he writes, "would therefore seem to unite the advantages of all forms of government and to avoid their respective abuses" (147).

The Life of Reason deploys the voice of what Henry Levinson has described as an "intellectual statesman" to chart humankind's structures of development.[16] Its lofty ambition to explicate the idea of reason in terms of institutions and practices displays a comprehensive vision which, Levinson suggests, marks an endpoint in Santayana's attitude to the role that intellectual work in general—and philosophy in particular—could play in questions of social organization and governance. His resignation from Harvard and departure from the United States in 1912, his view of the cultural impact of the First World War as a bystander in England, and his skepticism about the professionalization of his discipline, all contributed to a growing conviction that thought needed to demonstrate a less portentous sense of its own significance. Aligned neither with the generation of William James and John Dewey who regarded it as intrinsic to the role of philosophy to adjudicate on questions of social policy, nor with "the new philosophical technicians" (58) whose university-ensconced sense of the subject removed it completely from wider significance, Santayana's writing, as Levinson demonstrates, became attuned to the possibilities of play and performance that worked to undermine the claims of the monumentalizing intellect. In *Soliloquies in England and Later Soliloquies* (1922), he focuses on the figure of "Hermes the Interpreter," the mediator between cultures, peoples and realms, the Greek god who "does not preach, who does not threaten, who does not lay new, absurd, or morose commands on our befuddled souls" but instead creates conditions of intellectual and affective unmasking.[17] Olympian distance is replaced by the stance of a deity who finds that "the confused rumble of civilization is pleasant to his senses, like sweet vapour rising from the evening sacrifice" (261). Whereas *The Life of Reason* chose to place structures of human thought within a narrative of progress, Santayana finds Hermes appealing through his willed resistance to the urges of intellectual clarification that only distort or impose meaning. He satirizes philosophers (or "rustics," as he calls them) who "think that any language but theirs is gibberish" and "are sorry for the stranger who can speak only an unintelligible language, and are sure he will be damned unless the truth is preached to him speedily by some impertinent missionary from their own country" (263). Interpretation as conversion, whereby language and the ideas it expresses are standardized according to the criteria of the interpreter, is countered by Hermes, Santayana argues, who replaces missionary zeal with lively playfulness, mediating between peoples so that mutual comprehension might be achieved: "He interprets us to the gods, and they accept us; he interprets us to one another, and we perceive that the foreigner, too, spoke a plain language" (263–64). As chapter 4 noted, the question of foreignness within the body politic preoccupied William James as a problem of proximity, of philosophical and social intimacy. Hermes performs the role of recasting difference as shared communicability, a cosmopolitanism that transcends the "false preconceptions" (264) of social duty.

Egotism and Exceptionalism

Santayana's move away from the intellectual authority of system-building to a suspicion that such endeavors perpetuated mythologies of uniformity and coherence is nowhere more clearly seen than in one of his most polemical works, *Egotism in German Philosophy*, published in 1916. The date is, of course, significant, for the book participates in a transatlantic debate over the relationship that the English-speaking world should have with Germany and its culture at a crucial moment. Santayana's one-time colleague in the philosophy department at Harvard, Hugo Münsterberg, had emerged during this period as the key translator of German ideas to the United States, and vice versa, "the true 'pontifex' between both countries," as Adolf von Harnack, the German academic theologian, labeled him.[18] Münsterberg's earlier works of transatlantic observation, such as *American Traits from the Point of View of a German* (1901) and *Die Amerikaner* (1904), had attempted to apply the developing theories of social psychology to the American scene, and, in the case of the latter title, to correct what Münsterberg considered to be an erroneous German perception that U.S. society was dominated by a rampant and selfish commercialism. As Matthew Hale notes, the outbreak of hostilities in 1914 galvanized German academic opinion in the service of defending and explaining an idea of *Kultur* abroad. Propagandists and pamphleteers "painted a picture of a united and regenerated German people, defending the Kantian principles of duty and transcendent values against the half-civilized Russians and the shopkeeper English" (171). Münsterberg entered the fray with a series of essays and books that attempted to make the case for his provoked and misunderstood homeland; in particular *The War and America* (1914) refuted a number of specific charges of German aggression and claimed that the conflict would regenerate an enervated civilization by serving as "a positive creator of better and higher forms of the life of mankind."[19] By recasting the war as a battle for German ideals of civilized intellect, Münsterberg hoped to lift the level of debate beyond that of the *Realpolitik* of imperial confrontation so that the issue could become one of philosophical disposition. Santayana's relations with Münsterberg, his academic senior at Harvard, had always been cordial if not warm. There is no evidence that he had read his former colleague's wartime writings, yet it is tempting to regard *Egotism in German Philosophy*, with its concern to unravel the relationship between national identity and philosophical thought, as a response to Münsterberg's consistent advocacy of German *Wissenschaft*.

Santayana's criticism is directed at the philosophical teleologies of Hegel and Fichte that assert a schema of German national identity "called by the plan of Providence to occupy the supreme place in the history of the universe" (21). Such an exceptionalist vision, he argues, determines the way in which structures of knowledge are envisaged — "the infinite and endlessly various" is replaced by "a closed plot like a drama in which one nation (the very one to which these philosophers belong) has the central place and the chief role" (21–22). The "indefeasible and divine" spirit of the organizing mind, Santayana suggests, transforms the diversity of nature so that it conforms "more tightly to the moral interests of the thinker" (22). Moreover, this narrative of constructed coherence is driven not by individuals but by "nations and institutions" under a secularized Protestantism of convention that sanctions "social and patriotic zeal" (23). The preface to the book makes explicit the wider geopolitical ramifications of this kind of philosophical self-aggrandisement, for its "glorified and dogged egotism," Santayana proclaims, is now "evident to the whole world"; its adherents "shared and justified prophetically that spirit of uncompromising self-assertion and metaphysical conceit which the German nation is now reducing to action" (7). *Egotism in German Philosophy*, then, attributes the upheavals of the war to a failure in thinking. Hegel, Santayana's chief antagonist in the book, authorizes a politics of exceptionalism that streamlines plurality into an enforced vision of coherence. Against this, Goethe is held up as a model of intellectual openness:

> He [Goethe] did not even arrange the phases of his experience (as he did those of Faust) in an order supposed to be a progress, although, as the commentators on *Faust* inform us, not a progress in mere goodness. Hegel might have *understood* all these moral attitudes, and described them in a way not meant to appear satirical; but he would have criticised and demolished them, and declared them obsolete — all but the one at which he happened to stop.

Hegel's systematic structuring of experience into a narrative of inexorable progression denies complexity in its adherence to a teleological objective. Goethe, whose cosmopolitanism we have already noted in chapter 3, and whose ability to "greet the variety of things" as "a traveler, a connoisseur, a philanderer" earns Santayana's favour here (45–46), embodies both a catholicity of interest and a refusal — even when, as in *Faust*, there is a *telos* to be achieved — to equate progression with advance.

Santayana had argued this point as early as 1905 in *Reason in Common Sense*, where he suggested that "The possibility of essential progress is bound up with the tragic possibility that progress and human life should some day end together."[20] Under the pressure of war, Santayana's critique of philosophical idealism is extended into a powerful condemnation of national self-regard. The "absolute egotism" of Goethe and Emerson, he wrote, nevertheless "felt the swarming universal life" and "had not thought of dragooning it all, as sectarians and nationalists would, into vindicating some particular creed or nation."[21] At the heart of all this lay Santayana's worry that transcendentalism *in extremis*, "made ultimate" as he phrases it (167), refuses to see the alterity of a world that cannot be brought under the control of a perceiving mind without hubristic distortion. Opposed to this kind of intellectual grandiosity, Santayana suggests provisional coherence as the best that we can manage, in the hope that it creates an appreciation for difference unseduced by narratives of mastery:

> Our whole life is a compromise, an incipient loose harmony between the passions of the soul and the forces of nature, forces which likewise generate and protect the souls of other creatures, endowing them with powers of expression and self-assertion comparable with our own, and with aims no less sweet and worthy in their own eyes; so that the quick and honest mind cannot but practise courtesy in the universe, exercising its will without vehemence or forced assurance, judging with serenity, and in everything discarding the word absolute as the most false and the most odious of words. (168)

Recalling in his autobiography his surprise at the poor reception *Egotism in German Philosophy* received by British critics, Santayana acknowledged that he had run the risk of potentially "debasing criticism into propaganda," of producing "philosophical inconsistency caused by political animus." To counter this, he is keen, at least retrospectively, to insist that wider principles were at stake in the book than a specific fixation on the wartime foe. "[T]he egotism I attacked," he writes, "was far from being exclusively German, but was present in them and in the Americans whenever they turned their national ideal into something cosmic and eschatological, and felt themselves to be the chosen people. That if they did so they were themselves neither good philosophers nor good Christians was one of the things they needed to hear."[22] While there is something a little disingenuous about this statement—*Egotism* is only by implication a commentary on other instances of national self-aggrandizement—it does nevertheless allow us to consider the terms of Santayana's resistance to an American exceptionalist tradition and, more specifically, its Emersonian incarnation.

From an early age Santayana had a strong sense of himself as a foreigner within the home of America's intellectual elite, a new England that, as Robert Dawidoff noted, was in the process of "branching out and dying off," a twin-movement that would generate for him his now axiomatic vision of an enervated genteel culture surrounded by the aggressive accumulations of corporate capitalism.[23] Santayana's habitual stance in the face of such bifurcation was profound ambivalence, unwilling to wish nostalgically, like Henry Adams, for a return to a simpler organicism or to condemn outright the modernizing energies of turn-of-the-century America. His attraction to the United States was predicated upon the benefits that distance from it were able to afford him. *Geographical* distance was certainly an important factor in this, and his voluntary removal to Europe in 1911 granted Santayana the kind of detachment that enabled him to see his adopted home more clearly—and more fairly. In addition to transformed spatial perspectives, though, Europe enabled Santayana to excavate with even greater forensic attention the structures of consent and rebellion that constitute American political mythology. Distance creates the conditions of intellectual inquiry that are less beholden to what Paul Giles has characterized as the naturalizing tendencies of national narratives. "The relationship between literature and national identity," he writes, "is not symbiotic or natural, but, at its extreme circumference, highly paradoxical, involving the backward projection of epistemological limits from a vantage point beyond their boundaries."[24] Santayana is located in exactly this kind of discursive geography. As this chapter goes on to discuss, his already-existing biographical marginality is re-enforced by residence in Europe, a set of circumstances that assists in Santayana's project to interrogate the shibboleths of America's ideological foundations by defamiliarizing their assumed coherencies.

Santayana's landmark 1911 Berkeley lecture "The Genteel Tradition in American Philosophy," his farewell jeremiad to the United States, constructed a narrative of increasingly diluted thinking, from the paralyzing rigors and clarities of Calvinist colonial America to the liberal sentimentality of post-Puritan genteel culture. "The nation became numerous," Santayana suggests, "it ceased to be either ecstatic or distressful; the high social morality which on the whole it preserved took another color; people remained honest and helpful out of good sense and good will rather than out of scrupulous adherence to any fixed principles."[25] Calvinism, with its insistence on the redemption of an elect and the unavoidability of original sin, had given way under the process of enlight-enment liberalization to a belated romanticism, centered on Emerson and his fellow transcendentalists, characterized by its tendency to be "self-indulgent" and to display a mind "like an old music-box, full of tender echoes and quaint fancies." Santayana is keen to locate Emerson outside of such "morbid" and "tin-kling" thought. Alongside Hawthorne and Poe, the Concord writer is judged as one who "could not retail the genteel tradition"—where "retail" works doubly to mean narrate *and* sell—because he is "too keen, too perceptive, and too in-dependent." Yet, even Emerson does not escape his philosophical and historical fate, for his independence of mind has a tendency, Santayana claims, to turn in on itself. Emerson's instinctive disposition to internalize is combined with his culture's lack of substance ("life offered . . . little digestible material"), resulting in a self-scrutiny that is judged to be both superficial and narrowly academic. Em-erson "read transcendentally, not historically, to learn what he himself felt, not what others might have felt before him. And to feed on books, for a philosopher or a poet, is still to starve. Books can help him to acquire form, or to avoid pit-falls; they cannot supply him with substance, if he is to have any" (40). Emerson's own claims for originality (e.g., "Instantly, when the mind itself wakes, all books, all past acts are forgotten" [*CWE* 11: 508]) are discarded in a reading that accuses him of an inevitable over-intellectualization.

Santayana's sense of the limitations of Emerson's thought for an increasingly complex and modernizing America had been present from the beginning of his engagement with the nation's philosophical tradition. "The Optimism of Ralph Waldo Emerson," an undergraduate essay from 1886 submitted in an unsuccess-ful bid to win Harvard's Bowdoin prize, was daring in its youthful critique of one of the college's most famous alumnus. As in the "Genteel Tradition" lecture twenty-five years later, Santayana hones in on inadequacies that he perceives to be present in Emerson's intellectual repertoire. He notes that Emerson's dis-cursive habit is to pass "easily from all points of view to that of the intellect; and to this fact, more than anything else, we owe his optimism." The transition from the potentially conflicted world of experience to that of reflection gener-ates, Santayana claims, Emersonian "truth": "In some contemplative hour, it [a fact] detaches itself from the life like a ripe fruit, to become a thought of the mind. Instantly it is raised, transfigured; the corruptible has put on incorrup-tion." The "adhesive, inert form" of material substance is able to "astonish us by soaring from our body into the empyrean."[26] Yet, as Santayana points out here, the shift to transcendence is harder to achieve with some realities than it is with others. "Not every event or person pleases by being remote," he judges, citing as evidence the fact that "wars and persecutions, famine and leprosy, are easily less transfigured than the fear of dogs and ferules" (77). We may be faced with a plethora of horrors, but Santayana describes how, for Emerson, such calamities can be translated into transcendence during "some contemplative hour" when we detach ourselves "from the life like a rip fruit, to become a thought of the mind": "Henceforth it is an object of beauty, however base its origin or neighborhood" (76). This transition from the material and embodied to the spiritual and transcendent has resulted in an optimism that is characterized by its affective detachment: Emerson's temperament and personality is at a "distance from the working day world; he speaks from afar off. His writing is concrete and poetic; but for one who takes such delight in mentioning miscellaneous objects, he leaves on the reader's mind a sense of strange unreality" (81). As Henry Levinson has noted, "Emersonian optimism is something that has to be shown or exemplified biographically, not vindicated metaphysically or epistemologically."[27] In this early piece, Santayana positions his subject as socially marginal, where such marginality accounts for Emerson's ability to discover a sense of (spiritual) beauty that is inevitably overlooked by those who pursue communal lives, those who labour under "social cares and ambitions." Such a stance of intellectual disaffiliation, of a kind addressed in chapter 1, results in what we might call a philosophy of disposition rather than one encoded in empirical thought: Emerson's optimism, Santayana judges, "is not so much a doctrine as a tendency: a quick eye for beauty, a turning aside from pain and sorrow, a mystical elevation of spirit."[28] For the young Harvard undergraduate, this first skirmish with the intellectual inheritance of American transcendentalism, and especially Emerson's modeling of the role of social critic therein, is unable to reconcile the attractions of a perspective that can identify the "beauty and excellence of things" with a simultaneous inability to acknowledge that "troublesome feelings" might be difficult to overcome (84). Intellectual detachment may be of benefit to society through the possession of unencumbered vision, but, as Santayana reads Emerson here, it runs the risk of succumbing to the impulse to mark as retrograde any and all social forms.

The significance of this undergraduate submission for a university prize lies, I suggest, in its establishment of the tensions that would go on to structure Santayana's sense of intellectual work—both its ambitions and the shapes it needs to take to be effective. While, as we've seen, elsewhere he is clear to criticize philosophical projects that aim at systematization, Emerson's failure to generate any kind of discursive coherence results in the absence of a space, however provisional it might be, in which words can work productively. For Santayana, a philosophy founded on a vision of optimistic advance, when aligned with social convention and political protocols, results in myopic thinking and the gradual establishment of those narratives of providential (self-)assertion that come to characterize American exceptionalism. Dawidoff is correct to note that the genteel tradition is not, for Santayana, a uniquely American phenomenon; the conditions of its generation are not nationally circumscribed. However, the United States offers Santayana, at the moment of his departure from it, an exemplary test-case for examining the political implications of a philosophy both central to American identity and, he judges, incompatible with its modernity. Dawidoff writes that "The genteel tradition privileged the vain attempt to reduce nature to a situation in which human deserts and luck correspond with, let alone confirm, right human conduct and reward."[29] While "vain" suggests incompetence and hubris in the face of modernity, it also slightly underplays the degree to which the genteel tradition worked to mold powerful personal and, by extension, national ideologies of progress and freedom.

As is well known, Santayana proposes two potential alternatives to the genteel mode in American intellectual thought, embodied in the figures of Walt Whitman and William James. As in his earlier reading of the poet in *The Sense of Beauty*, Whitman in "The Genteel Tradition" is celebrated for a democratic impulse that recognizes diversity within the body politic, the sense the "the various sights, moods, and emotions are given each one vote; they are all declared to be all free and equal, and the innumerable commonplace moments of life are suffered to speak like the others."[30] Yet, Santayana concludes that Whitman's "Bohemian" sensibility is ineffective as a genuine challenge to the genteel tradition because it lacks that quality of discrimination that converts indeterminacy into composition. Whitman, he asserts, "reduced his imagination to a passive sensorium for the registering of impressions . . . no element of construction remained in it, and therefore no element of penetration" (48). The demotic force that Whitman embraced in his poetry, and which ran so powerfully counter to the bourgeois niceties of the genteel tradition, is nevertheless too adolescent to be politically useful, evincing a "disintegrating" rebelliousness that cannot imagine purposive social structures.[31] More effective by far, Santayana thought, was William James, whose philosophy of pragmatism presented America with a methodology for intellectual work that avoided the false turns of Emersonian self-aggrandizement and Whitmanian rebelliousness. As I want to go on to explore here, though, Santayana also regards James as too firmly wedded to an ideal of American identity that celebrates democracy as a political given enshrined in its foundational text, so that the contingency of pragmatic thought is continually at risk of codification into forms of national self-evidence.

"The Genteel Tradition" is generous in its reading of William James. Whereas Whitman is finally deemed inadequate to the task of reorienting American thought, Santayana regards Jamesian pragmatism as offering the most plausible resistance to those schooled in the orthodoxies of social gentility. Indeed, it is precisely James's openness to the unorthodox and unconventional that marks, for Santayana, his credentials: he "gave a sincerely respectful hearing to sentimentalists, mystics, spiritualists, wizards, cranks, quacks, and impostors . . . He thought, with his usual modesty, that any of these might have something to teach him" and thereby became "the friend and helper" of America's "spiritually disinherited."[32] Opposed to the kind of transcendent egotism that, as we have seen, would earn Santayana's sharpest critique during the First World War, James's pragmatism is valuable because of its explicit acknowledgment of contingency, in which the relationship between mind and world is in a continual state of negotiation: "Intelligence has its roots and its issue in the context of events; it is one kind of practical adjustment, an experimental act, a form of vital tension." Pragmatism runs counter to the arid technicalities of what James calls "intellectualism," a quality which for Santayana is visible in the development of professionalized university-located thought, and which enshrines "[i]deas and rules that may have been occasionally useful" into immutable concepts. The pragmatic mind asserts that "all creeds and theories and all form precepts [must] sink in the estimation of the pragmatist to a local and temporary grammar of action" (50). In what is by now a familiar account of James's philosophy, pragmatism unseats the certainty of "transcendental logic" and its "deliberate morality" in favor of "the variety, the unspeakable variety, of possible life" (55). Yet there is a moment of qualification in all this that gestures toward a more ambivalent reading of James and the possibility of liberation from the genteel tradition. Pragmatism — or the "new theology" — is significant, Santayana suggests, because it is fundamentally disruptive. Disabusing us of the comforts of lazy thinking, it "has broken the spell" of orthodox systems of knowledge and "enticed faith in a new direction." Of significance, though, is the admission that pragmatic thought might not be strong enough to defeat gentility; it represents the best challenge currently available to conventional thought, but the genteel tradition nevertheless might be too well-protected within social hierarchies to come under threat of genuine dissolution: "The genteel tradition cannot be dislodged by these insurrections; there are circles to which it is still congenial, and where it will be preserved" (53). Santayana's farewell address to the United States, then, points to embryonic structures of thought that have the potential to overcome the forces of genteel orthodoxy. Yet, the lecture is far from convinced that intellectual congeniality—thinking that has become "slightly becalmed" (37)—can be entirely overcome. Indeed in Santayana's later writing, William James becomes a more problematic figure whose credentials to drive an American intellectual tradition able to cope with the dizzying pace of modernity are much less clear.

Writing in the second volume of his autobiography (first published in 1947), Santayana reflected on America's imperial adventures in the Philippines at the end of the nineteenth century. "In the autumn of 1898" he met with James and his fellow Harvard philosopher George Herbert Palmer where conversation inevitably turned to the war. Santayana writes that "James was terribly distressed" and "felt that he had lost his country." "What could be a more shameless betrayal of American principles?" he recalls James lamenting, "What could be a plainer symptom of greed, ambition, corruption, and imperialism?"[33] James's sense of indignation is not, however, shared by Santayana, and in a complex paragraph he tries to set out both his specific response to the Philippines case and his view of historical processes more generally:

> As for me, I couldn't help resenting the schoolmaster's manner of the American government, walking switch in hand into a neighbour's garden to settle the children's quarrels there, and to make himself master of the place. Yet that has been the way of the world from the beginning of time, and if anything could be reasonably complained of, it was the manner of the intrusion rather than the fact of it. For me, the tragedy lay in Spanish weakness rather than in American prepotency: Uncle Sam would have continued to regard all men as free and equal, if all other men had looked as strong as himself. Yet Spanish weakness comes only of Quixotic frailty, due to a tragic and comic disproportion between the spirit and the flesh. The resources of the country and people would not be materially contemptible if they were wisely husbanded, and devoted to developing at home, under native inspiration, an austere, passionate and intelligent life for the soul. The Spanish empire overseas was glorious enough, and the end, harshly as it grazed against my family memories, seemed to me almost a relief. I am not one of those who dream of a Spanish America subject in future to the influence of the mother country. Let Spanish America, I say, and let English America, be as original as they can; what is best in Spain, as what is best in England, cannot migrate. (402–3)

Santayana's Spanish identity generates his disquiet at America's intervention in the Philippines, and he mocks the punitive and pedagogical imperative of empire encapsulated in the trope of a scene of instruction—the schoolmaster subduing his unruly pupils. However, national pride is tempered by an awareness of the inevitability of the imperial narrative, imagined as hubristic expansion followed by decline and diminishment. Santayana had read his Gibbon, and this notion of a process that operates transhistorically prevents him from sympathizing with the force of William James's sense of national dispossession. Certainly, the specifics of the Philippines example offend him, but the outcome of the story fails to surprise him. The paragraph is more concerned to consider the reasons for Spanish decline than to condemn American might, although the claim that U.S. principles of democratic equality are set aside once exploitable weakness is identified elsewhere points, as we will see, to Santayana's skepticism about the continuing validity of the nation's foundational vocabulary and documents. Spain's failure to concentrate on the development of a strong home-grown identity, its "Quixotic frailty" no match for the rising American imperialist machine, accounts for its defeated international ambitions. The "relief" with which Santayana "almost" greets Spain's imperial demise suggests the exhaustion of that particular national narrative. While he acknowledges that a Spanish-speaking New World geography is here to stay, Santayana wishes it to develop according to its own logic, somehow disconnected from the European imperial center. Spanish, and indeed English, national traits, he judges, cannot be productively transplanted into other territories. There is much that is problematic about this, especially when viewed through the lens of current transnational theory that disputes the possibility of coherent and impermeable borders, yet Santayana's intent here is to puncture the exceptionalist hubris of extra-territorial adventure. "Every thesis had its antithesis" (402), Santayana imagines George Palmer thinking, in response to James's despair, and this statement neatly captures what he regards as the fallacy of either celebrating or resenting imperial ambition.

William James is a more divided figure in these autobiographical pages, and Santayana's reading of him more critical. He is willing to acknowledge James's unorthodox romantic sensibility — "his independent, radical, naturalistic temper," "his American sense of being born just into a world to be rediscovered." Yet this by-now very standard characterization of its subject's New World democratic credentials is significantly undermined in the next sentence, where Santayana retracts the judgment he has just offered. "But he was really far from free," he claims, "held back by old instincts, subject to old delusions, restless, spasmodic, self-interrupted: as if some impetuous bird kept flying aloft, but always stopped in mid-air, pulled back with a jerk by an invisible wire tethering him to a peg in the ground" (401). Those "congenial" circles of genteel tradition that Santayana had recognized as still exerting their force ensure that James is unable to escape the circumstances of his intellectual and cultural history. Santayana's reading is a powerful counterweight to the impulse to celebrate James within a decontextualized space of American radicalism. As the previous chapter sought to explore, James's work was performed under the conditions of self-division that Santayana describes here, in which independence and institutionalization, form and freedom, frequently constituted the antinomies around which his thinking oscillated. The conventional side of James was most visible, Santayana judged, in his adherence to an idea of American exceptionalism located in the Declaration of Independence. James was wedded to an idea, and an ideal, of America that, Santayana thought, was implausibly naïve. Of the Philippines campaign, he asked:

> Why was William James so much upset by an event that the victims of it could take so calmly? Because he held a false moralistic view of history, attributing events to the conscious motives and free will of individuals; whereas individuals, especially in governments, are creatures of circumstance and slaves to vested interests. These interests may be more or less noble, romantic, or sordid, but they inevitably entangle and subjugate men of action . . . Catastrophes come when some dominant institution, swollen like a soap-bubble and still standing without foundations, suddenly crumbles at the touch of what might seem a word or an idea, but is really some stronger material force. This force is partly that of changing circumstances, partly that of changing passions; but passions are themselves physical impulses, maturing in their season, and often epidemic, like contagious diseases. . . . [Y]et the over-ruling tradition in [James] was literary and theological, and he cried disconsolately that he had lost his country, when his country, just beginning to play its part in the history of the world, appeared to ignore an ideal that he had innocently expected would always guide it, because this ideal had been eloquently expressed in the Declaration of Independence. (403–4)

Santayana's indictment of James focuses precisely on the latter's inability to forego the ideological comforts of America's foundational text. James's reliance on the "moralistic" and "theological" frameworks provided by that document has resulted in a fallaciously optimistic privileging of individual agency as the driving force of historical transformation. James overlooks, Santayana believed, the degree to which assertions of singularity are already located within structures of thought that determine the possible directions that the self can take. The vocabulary of the Declaration is, then, inadequate to explain away the complex motives of an event such as the Spanish-American War, but James's sense of national dispossession is linked to his patriotic attachment to those very words as they confront the new patriotism of imperial expansion:

> [T]he Declaration of Independence was a piece of literature, a salad of illusions. Admiration for the noble savage, for the ancient Romans (whose republic was founded

on slavery and war), mixed with the quietistic maxims of the Sermon on the Mount, may inspire a Rousseau but it cannot guide a government. The American Colonies were rehearsing independence and were ready for it; that was what gave the declaration of independence timeliness and political weight. In 1898 the United States were rehearsing domination over tropical America and were ready to organise and to legalise it; it served their commercial and military and their imaginative passions. Such antecedents and such facilities made intervention sooner or later inevitable. Domination was the implicit aim, whatever might be the language or even the thoughts of individuals. William James had lost his country; his country was in good health and just reaching the age of puberty. He had merely lost his way in its physiological history. (404)

This is an astonishingly unsentimental view of an American sacred cow, a view that was perhaps more readily available for a thinker whose own relationship to the United States had always been structured around the polarities of compromise and self-preservation. By contrast, James's position is judged to be nostalgically impotent in the face of *Realpolitik*'s manipulations, characterized by Santayana as "the impulses of young, ambitious, enterprising America" that "may ignore or even insult all that I most prize, but [which] please me nevertheless for their honest enthusiasm and vitality" (404–5). American democratic individualism, at least as it is articulated through the Declaration, becomes further evidence of the intellectual inertia Santayana characterizes as constitutive of the genteel tradition. His distance from the United States, along with his refusal to participate in the standard rites of patriotic expression (either Spanish or American), enable the sober observations of empire that we read here.[34] Richard Rorty wrote that Santayana "saw us [the United States] as one more great empire in the long parade" and that "his genial hope was that we might enjoy the imperium while we held it."[35] While this, perhaps, overstates Santayana's relaxed understanding of empire, it nevertheless reflects a very real difference in intellectual disposition from that of the liberal New England mind as it is represented by James. James is, finally, too conventionally American to sustain Santayana's interest. "I trusted his heart but I didn't respect his judgment," he writes (401), as James's desire to invest in an ideal of democratic politics failed to see the manifold ways in which such a political philosophy was always already available to the kinds of manipulation that, in the instance of the 1898 war, so horrified him.

Perhaps Santayana's most nuanced reckoning of the ideological structures maintaining the American national imaginary is to be found in his chapter on "English Liberty in America" in *Character and Opinion in the United States* (1920). The book's "Preface" makes clear the context of expatriation that structures Santayana's assessments of America's intellectual history. He is unapologetic about "preserving the tone and attitude of a detached observer," one who tries "to understand [the United States], as a family friend may who has a different temperament."[36] Such an unaffiliated stance generates the complex transatlantic narrative that "English Liberty" charts, in which contrasting principles of indebtedness and singularity configure Santayana's analysis of American political culture. In his autobiography, as we have seen, when thinking back on the Spanish-American war Santayana felt that the most distinctive national characteristics were immune to migration, and that this fact accounted for the ultimate failure of all imperial projects. "English Liberty," published twenty-seven years earlier, seems initially at least to rehearse that position, for the opening paragraph conceives of the transatlantic space as one of mutual separation in which attempts to circulate ideas and cultures across the ocean are ultimately unsuccessful. The Atlantic, "although it has favoured a mixed emigration and cheap intercourse," has "cut off America so effectually that all the people there, even those of Latin origin, have become curiously different from any kind of European" (192). Instead, contact with the New World results in the acquisition of defiantly transformed characteristics: "everything has changed its accent, spirit, and value," for "the scale and speed of life have made everything strangely un-English" (193). However, rather than developing an argument that celebrates American exceptionalism, the essay quickly changes direction to consider the significance of at least one form of transatlantic transplantation that, Santayana judges, has been effective. "[T]he spirit of free co-operation," of "free individuality" has found in the United States "a more favourable atmosphere in which to manifest its true nature," he writes, such that its "wholly English" character, corrupted on home soil by "entanglement in custom and privilege" (194), is able to thrive and "deserves to be called English always, to whatever countries it may spread." The kind of "social servitude" that, in England, undermines the possibilities of individuality is "reduced to a minimum" in the United States (195), so that a society of voluntary co-operation is more able to prosper. Amid the ethnic and racial plurality of American modernity—"the unkempt polyglot peoples that turn to the new world"—Santayana chooses to imagine "the essence of Americanism" as a kind of optimistic, energetic fusion of self-determination and productive social encounter (196).

The essay then proceeds to take us in a new direction, where, in a very Emersonian sense, the position that Santayana has enunciated thus far becomes prone to interrogation and revision. The model of social and political harmony that he has described is reformulated as an "unstable convention" (197), to the extent that it depends upon a careful policing and vigilance for its perpetuation:

It implies a rather unimaginative optimistic assumption that at bottom all men's interests are similar and compatible, and a rather heroic public spirit — such that no special interest, in so far as it has to be overruled, shall rebel and try to maintain itself absolutely. In America hitherto these conditions happen to have been actually fulfilled in an unusual measure. Interests have been very similar — to exploit business opportunities and organise public services useful to all; and these similar interests have been also compatible and harmonious. (197–98)

This is an early incarnation, of course, of Louis Hartz's 1955 analysis of the monopoly of liberalism within cold war American culture, as discussed in chapter 1. Santayana's reading emphasizes the success with which the United States manages to inculcate structures of stability in the face of "special interest." "[M]inorities," he writes, "can dismiss their special plans without sorrow, and cheerfully follow the crowd down another road" (198): the diverse masses are channeled in authorized directions rather than being allowed to congregate in threatening form. This disciplinary aspect to American society needs to be acknowledged, Santayana thinks, in the face of the country's exceptionalist rhetoric of liberty: "Although it has always thought of itself in an eminent sense the land of freedom, even when it was covered with slaves, there is no country in which people live under more overpowering compulsions" (209). Even those attributes that have been naturalized as singularly American are compulsorily enforced, a condition that induces a degree of psychological pressure in the citizen. Indeed failure to conform results in the kind of alienation that might be said to characterize Santayana's own relationship to his adopted country: "You must wave, you must cheer, you must push with the irresistible crowd; otherwise you feel like a traitor, a soulless outcast, a deserted ship high and dry on the shore" (211). Liberty of this kind takes the sheen off those articulations of absolute, self-regulated freedom that voice the American national imaginary. Santayana's reading of transatlantic principles of independence and community depends upon the recognition that, even in the renewing environment of the United States, liberty needs to be a contingent, impure characteristic for it to have any purchase in the running of social structures. He returns to his earlier excoriation of German thinkers — those "apologists of absolute will" (215) who find incarnation in a "fanatic, a poet, a doctrinaire, a dilettante" (216) — to establish a pattern of political revolution that mandates freedom as an unwavering principle but quickly degenerates into forms of inflexible policing. "Every new heresy professed to be orthodoxy itself, purified and restored," he writes. "Such was the aspiration even of the American declaration of independence and the American constitution: cast-iron documents, if only the spirit of co-operative English liberty had not been there to expand, embosom, soften, or transform them" (217–18). Revolutions that lack this tempering force—he cites the French and Russian examples—summon "every man to become free in exactly their own fashion, or have his head cut off" (218). There is undoubtedly a political conservatism at work here, for behind his words lies a profound skepticism about the long-term benefits of revolution. Yet Santayana's stance might be more properly characterized as pragmatically astute in terms of its ability to see through the rhetorical layering that distorts and exaggerates newborn political structures. Emerson's polarized struggle between freedom and fate is recast here as a politics of compromise, one that is prepared to acknowledge that "[a]ll the declarations of independence in the world will not render anybody really independent" (228–29). While the impulses engendered by the desire for "[a]bsolute liberty" are valuable—Santayana cites "inspiration, free intelligence, uncompromising conviction" (230)—they fail to create the conditions of social harmony that "Reason and the principle of English liberty" provide. Toward the end of the essay, he develops an elaborate simile to describe the contours of this more moderate, undemonstrative polity. The work of English liberty

> is accordingly like those cathedrals at which many successive ages have laboured, each in its own style. We may regret, sometimes, that some one design could not have been carried out in its purity, and yet all these secular accretions have a wonderful eloquence; a common piety and love of beauty have inspired them; age has fused them and softened their incongruities; and an inexpressible magic seems to hang about the composite pile, as if God and man breathed deeply within it. It is a harmony woven out of accidents, like every work of time and nature, and all the more profound and fertile because no mind could have designed it. Some such natural structure, formed and reformed by circumstances, is the requisite matrix and home for every moral being. (231)

Santayana's Catholic faith had long since lapsed but, as Irving Singer has noted, there remained, "as a constant from beginning to end," an "appreciation of the myths and rituals of Catholicism that could embellish everyday experience."[37] His configuration here of religious space (the cathedral) to signify a workable social structure brings together the registers of politics and aesthetics that this chapter has been concerned to explore. It offers an image of a hybrid yet harmonizing form that has developed through accretion rather than insistence. Such a building proudly displays its incongruities as components of the narrative of its existence, its "accidents" part of the fabric that gives it shape. Santayana's belief in the *Realpolitik* of negotiated diversity rather than in enforced ideologies of national coherence ensures that he avoids the disappointment that William

James felt over America's betrayal of its values in the Philippines. James's failure at that moment, Santayana implies, was to forget his pragmatic principles, to hold instead to a philosophy of immutable exceptionalism unsustainable within the lived experience of global politics. It is a sober lesson that continues to be learned.

After George Santayana's death in 1952, Wallace Stevens, who had known him at Harvard, composed a commemorative poem, "To an Old Philosopher in Rome," that eulogizes its subject as he awaits the end of his life. Its moving final two stanzas read:

> It is a kind of total grandeur at the end,
> With every visible thing enlarged and yet
> No more than a bed, a chair and the moving nuns,
> The immensest theatre, the pillared porch.
> The book and candle in your ambered room,
>
> Total grandeur of a total edifice,
> Chosen by an inquisitor of structures
> For himself. He stops upon the threshold,
> As if the design of all his words takes form
> And frame from thinking and is realized.[38]

Stevens offers us a very different kind of architectural space to the proud plurality of Santayana's cathedral. The philosopher's final home, a room at the Convent of the Blue Nuns in Rome, is sparse and minimal, yet it is transfigured into a location of Emersonian transcendence that, for Stevens, signifies the "grandeur" and immensity of Santayana's mental geography. The "inquisitor of structures" chooses for himself a space of simplicity in which to range over the terrains of philosophy, intellectual history and literary criticism, determined to remain unseduced by their affective pull. In a final affirmation of thinking, the "design" of Santayana's words—both their pattern and their intent—takes shape allowing the words to circulate and take flight while he waits "upon the threshold" of death.

CODA: THE SCENE OF
INSTRUCTION

In his influential analysis of the development of an American republic of letters, *The Golden Day* (1926), Lewis Mumford constructs a revisionist literary
history in which New England's writers expressed the desire "to prefigure in the
imagination a culture which should grow out of and refine the experiences the
transplanted European encountered on the new soil."[1] Central to this national
canon of the literary avant-garde was Emerson, who Mumford was keen to
rescue from accusations of dilettantish idealism, claiming that "it has been mis-
construed" that "he lived in a perpetual cloud-world." While acknowledging that
Emerson had indeed at times withdrawn from the "hurly-burly of American
life," Mumford argued that this was a strategic positioning: "it was a withdrawal
of water into a reservoir, or of grain into a bin, so that they might be available
later" (100). Emerson's antisocial inclinations therefore needed to be understood
as part of a larger dialectic that incorporated the "thoroughly socialized existence
of the New England town" (118) as a check on the excesses of individualism,
thereby enabling a politics of self-reliance to function creatively within public
life. Mumford felt that the balance between mind and environment, between
self and society that resulted would prove to be a most useful model for a United
States in need of cultural renewal in the early decades of the twentieth century:

> The mission of creative thought is to gather into it all the living sources of its day, all
> that is vital in the practical life, all that is intelligible in science, all that is relevant in

the social heritage and, recasting these things into new forms and symbols, to react upon the blind drift of convention and habit and routine. Life flourishes only in this alternating rhythm of dream and deed: when one appears without the other, we can look forward to a shrinkage, a lapse, a devitalization. Idealism is a bad name for this mission; it is just as correct to call it realism; since it is part of the natural history of the human mind. (166)

Mumford saw no tension between the tangible materiality of Emerson's existence and the possibility of intellectual work that could refresh and redefine his culture. "Emerson rethought life," he asserted, "and in the mind he coined new shapes and images and institutions" in which, and through which, thought could best be articulated (99).

Mumford's concern to imagine a location in which ideas are able to prosper is evident in an early short story published in *The Forum* magazine in 1914, in which he depicts a scene of pedagogical encounter that proves to be disorienting for the tale's central character, Jarvis, a lecturer in Latin. Already worried about declining standards and increased student power, "Jarvis was wont to lament at faculty conferences that there was a 'tendency fraught with the greatest danger' to allow untrained youths to elect their studies—none of which ever, by any chance, proved to be a discipline."[2] The reversal of the conventional—and, for Jarvis, appropriate—shape of the pedagogical transaction generates a wider concern about national vitality, for if the work of intellectual exchange is mishandled at this early stage, the implications are potentially severe. "The absence of discipline caused nations to become soft," the narrative voice, firmly ventriloquizing Jarvis's thoughts, asserts. Intellectual rigor is allied with national self-sufficiency and well-being. Its absence "increased the discontent of the masses; was a source of sundry evils in our Public Life; and perhaps in some measure could be connected with the disgraceful sophomore beer-drinking contest." As this sequence of anxieties makes clear, Mumford encourages the reader not to take his central character entirely seriously. Jarvis both over-dramatizes the decline in standards he laments witnessing and over-values his own status as their intellectual guardian: "For twenty years Jarvis had taught Latin with a full recognition of the immense value of himself and his subject, and of the important part both played in creating a Stable Commonwealth" in the face of "these Sadly Shifting Times" (13). Jarvis's self-satisfaction is undermined by a classroom unwilling to accept the disciplinary authority of the institution. His students were "always questioning, always urging, always disturbing. Theirs was such an *infringing* attitude to life." One in particular, "an aggressive little fellow," "informed Jarvis, with an irritating confidence, that *he* was a Vitalist, and he wanted to know how Latin aided Life? He appealed fiercely to Jarvis to answer whether the energy wasted on the Humanities of yesterday could not better be spent on the Humanity of today" (14). Mumford wryly describes here a moment of intellectual rebellion, where the parameters of acceptable pedagogy have been exceeded, *infringed*, by the student's questioning of their relevance. Jarvis is left stunned by this confrontation, and in a move that seems to echo a Thoreauvian turn, we read that he "stumbled to the porch; he seized a spade; and he went forth into the garden and began to dig" (14–15). The final image of the story presents a character exiled from his intellectual world, putting all of his efforts instead into manual labor as a still unsullied alternative to the debased world of academia.

Mumford's tale whimsically explores the consequences of knowledge that is deemed to be no longer vital, of professional pedagogy that is unable to connect with young minds, and of questions that disrupt the ordered transmission of conventional thought. The solace found in the natural world is deliberately anti-intellectual, a retreat from the life of the mind until, perhaps, a different way of asking what thinking is for can be approached. Jarvis may never return to the classroom, but Mumford's story allows us to turn our attention, in conclusion, to the conditions in which scenes of instruction are most propitious. In Stanley Cavell, a present-day New England intellectual (at least by institutional affiliation, if not by birth), we have a figure whose work has been centrally concerned to examine the impact of an Emersonian tradition of thinking on larger structures of American identity, to attend to the ways in which Emerson's exercises in articulated thought might still lead us out of the dead-ends of habit and routine. Cavell makes a radical claim about the status of Emerson and Thoreau within American intellectual culture. Both writers, he argues, have been repressed as philosophers, as thinkers, a condition that causes America to remain disconnected from its foundations and thus not to know itself. Moreover, founding figures, Cavell writes, "may themselves be victimized by what they originate. I take such matters to be in play in the way Emerson and Thoreau write in and from obscurity, as if to obscure themselves is the way to gain the kind of standing they require of their fellow citizens."[3] The culture's repression of its thinkers is compounded by the disposition of those thinkers to enact forms of hermeneutical self-repression, an unwillingness to give up easy or programmatic answers to difficult questions that makes Emerson and Thoreau problematic figures within the conventional academy. While both are "philosophers of direction, orientation, tirelessly prompting us to be on our way, endlessly asking us where we stand, what it is we face,"[4] their writing evolves through strategies of indirection and revision, their texts, as we have seen, structured by false starts, restarts and contradiction. As Richard Eldridge remarks, "Their writing enacts a sense of *seeking* to be on the way out of present straits and toward happiness, freedom, and self-reliance. As things stand, our getting on the way is enabled, but also inhibited, by imperfect present conditions."[5] A culture of conformity creates the environment in which new thought is most required, but that very same environment makes its appearance all the more difficult to accomplish.

In *In Quest of the Ordinary* Cavell singles out George Santayana — and specifically Santayana's "Genteel Tradition" address at Stanford University in 1911 — as representing one of the "more decisive . . . moments in the history of what I am calling the repression of Emerson in American philosophy":

> For some, Santayana will represent the last serious writer in America in whose work such a confrontation [of philosophy and poetry] was undertaken, for others, a warning that such an undertaking is doomed to posturing; if infectious for while, in the end ineffectual. I hope that both representations are wrong, but I will not argue against them now. What interests me here is that when, in "The Genteel Tradition," Santayana describes Emerson as "a cheery, childlike soul, impervious to the evidence of evil" he does not show (there or anywhere else I know that he mentions Emerson) any better understanding of Emerson's so-called optimism than, say, his contemporary H. L. Mencken shows of Nietzsche's so-called pessimism — he merely retails, beautifully, of course, but essentially without refinement, the most wholesale view there is of him.

Cavell exhibits here a typical reluctance to adjudicate between infelicitous and opposing critical responses to Santayana, neither of which, it is implied, does more than perpetuate the kinds of intellectual blindnesses that prevent productive thinking. Given his own commitment to exploring the relationship between philosophy and literature in ways that resist the confines of the disciplinary map, it is perhaps not surprising that Cavell might want to resist the idea that Santayana represents "the last" of such thinkers. More significant though is his critique of Santayana's own failures of reading, in which an Emerson of genteel optimism becomes enshrined within a culture that is no longer able, or willing, to see a writer whose work is "more treacherous because of its care to maintain a more genteel surface." Cavell accuses Santayana of an attractive but unrefined, or non-nuanced, reduction, one that has helped to perpetuate Emerson's (and, for that matter, Thoreau's) invisibility as serious and strenuous thinkers.

Cavell's reading, in itself, is a somewhat narrow rendition of Santayana's more unresolved, and therefore less complacent, response to Emerson's thought, as the previous chapter went some way to illustrating. Indeed Santayana's doubts about the value of institutional learning, and his disdain for the seductive claims of exceptionalism, suggest a mind more willing to test and revise ideas than

Cavell's comments might indicate. I am less concerned here, however, to contest Santayana's reputation than to focus more closely on the kind of Emerson that, Cavell argues, Santayana misses in his evaluation of the genteel tradition with its "incessant public celebrations."[6] Specifically, I am interested in the relationship that Cavell wants to establish between intellectual work and pedagogy: how are ideas conveyed? And what are the responsibilities of, and claims that can be made for, both teacher and pupil in the exchange of those ideas? Cavell wonders if the writing of Emerson and Thoreau is even teachable at all, according to conventionally understood forms of instruction. In this, he takes his cue from Emerson himself, who, in his "Divinity School Address" of 1838, speaks as a student in claiming that "Truly speaking, it is not instruction, but provocation, that I can receive from another soul" (*CWE* 1: 127),[7] and from Wittgenstein, who, as a teacher, voices the contention in *Philosophical Investigations* remark number 217 that "If I have exhausted the justifications I have reached bedrock, and my spade is turned. Then I am inclined to say: 'This is simply what I do.'"[8] By citing both of these statements, Cavell is alive to the possibility that the intellectual encounter that is being transacted might end in failure or disturbance. It demands of its participants an openness to both possibilities, such that the student's acquiescence in learning and the teacher's authority in instruction can no longer be taken for granted. As Michael Fischer has commented, "Emerson and Wittgenstein admit that the effectiveness of their teaching depends on the always unpredictable consent of their students or readers."[9]

As *Thinking America* has shown, the consensual conditions in which intellectual exchange can best be established preoccupied Emerson, Thoreau, Margaret Fuller, William James, and Santayana. Cavell's desire to establish a scene of instruction that, rather than being coerced into existence or regularized as routine, generates dialogic possibilities of conversation (in Fuller's terms), of slightly different angles of vision (in Emerson's), allows thinking to have an existence beyond its moment of articulation. It is born with an afterlife. "Suppose the issue," Cavell states, "is not to win an argument (that may come late in the day) but to manifest for the other another way . . . a shift in direction, as slight as a degree of the compass, but down the road making all the difference in the world."[10]

Pedagogical exchange consists neither in the compelling of agreement nor in the resolution of issues, but instead allows for future possibilities of transformation as yet unimaginable. To return to the conclusion of Wittgenstein's scene of instruction ("This is simply what I do"), Cavell reads this neither as arrogance nor as despair, but instead suggests that it might be taken as a statement of provisionality, with both minds always open to future and further engagement. "I do not, put otherwise, find that the case generalizes into a surmise, let alone a thesis, of scepticism," Cavell writes, "since the little myth of instruction strikes me as asking that we take crises or limits of learning case by case, asking ourselves how important it is that we agree, and how thoroughly, in various strains of our form or forms of life, and where we may, or can, or ought to, or must, tolerate differences, even perhaps be drawn to change *our* lives—or suffer the consequences."[11] This is an important revision of Wittgenstein's scenario, for, in its consideration of the relative values of acknowledged difference and claimed agreement, Cavell's gloss goes to the heart of an American problem of constitution. It embodies "the permanent crisis of a society that conceives of itself as based on consent," where the conditions of that consent might be enforced or even refused. In a society where differentials of power construct the shape of relationships among different constituencies of gender, race, ethnicity, and sexuality, the acquisition of identity—and therefore of the sense of belonging—often seems to entail careful protocols of instruction. William James's concern to yolk variety to a stabilizing, if flexible, structure is just one instance of this desire to contain and control diversity, to prevent its overflow into heterogeneous incoherence. Failures of belonging might, then, be regarded as failures to acquire the correct national narrative, where the scene of instruction is unable to generate the requisite lesson. For Cavell, however, *whose* failure this is remains an important and open question, especially given his engagement with Emerson's notion of self-reliance and its necessary resistance to society's expectations. Does the scene of instruction provide a genuine pedagogical encounter, or does the punitive threat that might accompany it, backed up by the institutional authority of school, university, or government, provoke Emersonian nonconformity that is misunderstood as an inability to learn? The student may articulate an identity that is, as yet, unassimilable. The scenario is therefore, as Cavell acknowledges, intensely political, "one in which the issue of the newcomer for society is whether to accept his or her efforts to imitate us" and, by extension, one in which the newcomer may choose which aspects of that society she or he wishes to imitate.[12] "Newcomer," as John Michael has remarked, is a significant choice of word here, invoking a variety of identities that includes not only children and immigrants but also dissenting intellectuals, those "who might attempt to bring a new perspective and sense of rectitude to public discourse."[13]

What an intellectual should consent to, and from where that consent might best be granted, have been central concerns of this book. Each of the figures it discusses has to negotiate the terms of his or her relationship to society, where the pressures of particular geographical location or historical circumstance bring to acute focus the parameters of that engagement. Cavell's scene of instruction is always, potentially, one in which the voices that are resistant to consent might not be heard—the child, the immigrant, the intellectual, all ignored because of the imperative to impose a coherent national identity. When Emerson, in "Self-Reliance," writes that "For nonconformity the world whips you with its displeasure," he describes a moment, from the teacher's point of view, of pedagogical failure and, from the student's, of imposed institutional authority. The lines that follow present, in concentrated form, many of the problems associated with intellectual activity bequeathed to those writers and thinkers participating in an Emersonian tradition. In its desire to enact effective judgment, in its anxiety to claim a position that is appropriately masculine in its legitimacy, in its concern about the populist sway of the mass media, in its suspicion of institutional centers of knowledge, and in its establishment of intellectual distinction as a marker of genuine aversive thought, the passage is an eloquent summation of the criteria that *Thinking America* has sought to investigate. Emerson deserves the last word:

And therefore a man must know how to estimate a sour face. The by-standers look askance on him in a public street or in the friend's parlor. If this aversion had its origin in contempt and resistance like his own he might well go home with a sad countenance; but the sour faces of the multitude, like their sweet faces, have no deep cause, but are put on and off as the wind blows and a newspaper directs. Yet is the discontent of the multitude more formidable than that of the senate and the college. It is easy enough for a firm man who knows the world to brook the rage of the cultivated classes. Their rage is decorous and prudent, for they are timid, as being very vulnerable themselves. But when to their feminine rage the indignation of the people is added, when the unintelligent brute force that lies at the bottom of society is made to growl and mow, it needs the habit of magnanimity and religion to treat it godlike as a trifle of no concernment. (*CWE* 2: 55–56)

NOTES

Introduction

The first epigraph to this chapter is from *Journal & Miscellaneous Notebooks* 5: 39; the second from "The Scholar," 1863, *Later Lectures of Ralph Waldo Emerson* 2: 310.

1. Friedrich Nietzsche, *On the Genealogy of Morals*, tr. Walter Kaufman (New York: Vintage Books, 1969), p. 16.

2. Paul Bové, "Mendacious Innocents, or, The Modern Genealogist as Conscientious Intellectual: Nietzsche, Foucault, Said," *boundary 2* 9.3 (1981): 359–88 (370).

3. Randall Jarrell, "The Intellectual in America," *A Sad Heart at the Supermarket: Essays and Fables* (London: Eyre & Spottiswoode, 1965), p. 18.

4. Pierre Bourdieu, "Universal Corporatism: The Role of Intellectuals in the Modern World," *Poetics Today* 12.4 (Winter 1991): 655–69 (656).

5. Pierre Bourdieu, "The Intellectual Field: A World Apart," *In Other Words: Essays Towards a Reflexive Sociology*, tr. Matthew Adamson (Stanford: Stanford University Press, 1990), p. 145.

6. Paul Giles, "Transnationalism and Classic American Literature," *PMLA* 118.1 (January 2003): 62–77 (73).

7. Zygmunt Bauman, *Legislators and Interpreters: On Modernity, Post-Modernity and Intellectuals* (Cambridge: Polity Press, 1987), p. 19.

8. In *Anti-Oedipus* (1972), Gilles Deleuze and Félix Guattari establish a tension between the security of a "despotic State" that polices its own coherence and "flows that are increasingly deterri-torialized" (London: Athlone Press, 1984), pp. 29, 218.

9. Bauman, *Legislators and Interpreters*, p. 22.

10. Stefan Collini, *Absent Minds: Intellectuals in Britain* (Oxford: Oxford University Press, 2006), p. 126.

11. Pierre Bourdieu, *The Rules of Art: Genesis and Structure of the Literary Field* (Stanford: Stanford University Press, 1995), p. 129.

12. Ross Posnock, "Assessing the Oppositional: Contemporary Intellectual Strategies," *American Literary History* 1 (1989): 147–71 (147).

13. Lawrence Buell, *Emerson* (Cambridge, Mass.: Harvard University Press, 2003), p. 287.

14. Peter S. Field, *Ralph Waldo Emerson: The Making of a Democratic Intellectual* (Lanham: Rowman & Littlefield, 2002), pp. 4–5.

15. Buell, *Emerson*, p. 58.

16. Field, *Ralph Waldo Emerson*, p. 40.

17. See, for example, David Robinson, "Grace and Works: Emerson's Essays in Theological Perspective," in Conrad Edick Wright, ed., *American Unitarianism, 1805–1865* (Boston: Northeastern University Press, 1989), pp. 121–42 and, more recently, Catherine Albanese, *A Republic of Mind and Spirit: A Cultural History of American Metaphysical Religion* (New Haven: Yale University Press, 2006), pp. 161–76.

18. William Ellery Channing, *Self-Culture* (1838) (Boston: James Munroe and Co., 1843), p. 24.

19. Joseph Stevens Buckminster, "The Dangers and Duties of the Men of Letters" (1809), in Lewis P. Simpson, ed., *The Federalist Literary Mind: Selections from 'The Monthly Anthology and Boston Review,' 1803–1811, Including Documents Relating to the Boston Athenaeum* (Baton Rouge: Louisiana State University Press, 1962), pp. 97, 99.

20. Richard Deming, *Listening on All Sides: Toward an Emersonian Ethics of Reading* (Stanford: Stanford University Press, 2007), p. 60.

21. Anita Haya Patterson, *From Emerson to King: Democracy, Race, and the Politics of Protest* (New York: Oxford University Press, 1997), p. 153.

22. W. E. B. Du Bois, "The Talented Tenth" (1903), *Writings* (New York: Library of America, 1984), p. 847. For a discussion of the relationship between "The Talented Tenth" and Emerson, see Shamoon Zamir, *Dark Voices: W. E. B. Du Bois and American Thought, 1883–1903* (Chicago: University of Chicago Press, 1995), pp. 65–6.

23. Quoted in Ralph Barton Perry, *The Thought and Character of William James*, 2 vols. (Boston: Little, Brown and Company, 1935), vol. 1, p. 51.

24. Caroline Dall, *Transcendentalism in New England: A Lecture* (Boston: Roberts Brothers, 1897).

25. William Dean Howells, ""The Man of Letters as a Man of Business," *Scribner's Magazine* 14 (1893): 429–45 (429).

26. Brander Matthews, "Literary Men and Public Affairs," *North American Review* 189 (January–June 1909): 527–38 (527, 528).

27. Elisa Tamarkin characterizes the Harvard pedagogy at mid-century as one of "aimlessness: this suggests the emerging shape of what we now know as Arnoldian humanism and its defense of the liberal arts but also the more fugitive ends of lounging, lazing, smoking, conversing, and doing as one pleased that gave the acquisition of knowledge at the college its particular manner" (*Anglophilia: Deference, Devotion, and Antebellum America* [Chicago: University of Chicago Press, 2008], p. 252).

28. James Ballowe, ed., *George Santayana's America: Essays on Literature and Culture* (Urbana: University of Illinois Press, 1969), p. 59.

29. Helen Lefkowitz Horowitz, *Campus Life: Undergraduate Cultures from the End of the Eighteenth Century to the Present* (New York: Alfred A. Knopf, 1987), p. 71.

30. Ballowe, ed., *George Santayana's America*, p. 64.

31. Walt Whitman, *Poetry and Prose* (New York: Library of America, 1982), p. 963.

32. George Santayana, *My Host the World* (London: The Cresset Press, 1953), p. 174.

1. Affiliation and Alienation

The epigraph to this chapter is from "The American Scholar," *Complete Works of Ralph Waldo Emerson* 1: 94.

1. For an account of Emerson's appropriation of the language of economic exchange, see Richard Grusin, " 'Put God in Your Debt': Emerson's Economy of Expenditure," *PMLA* 103.1 (1988): 35–44.

2. Rob Wilson, "Literary Vocation as Occupational Idealism: The Example of Emerson's 'American Scholar,' " *Cultural Critique* 15 (Spring 1990): 83–144 (93, 98). See also Simon Critchley's analysis of Romanticism's failure in general to assume political effectiveness in *Very Little . . . Almost Nothing: Death, Philosophy and Literature* (London: Routledge, 2004), pp. 105–10.

3. Herbert Marcuse, "The Affirmative Character of Culture" (1937), *Negations: Essays in Critical Theory*, tr. Jeremy J. Shapiro (London: Free Association Books, 1988), p. 95. By the mid-1970s Marcuse would revise this judgment, urging his fellow Marxists to reconsider their hostility to practices of inwardness and retreat: "the insistence on a private sphere may well serve as [a bulwark] against a society which administers all dimensions of human existence. Inwardness and subjectivity may well become the inner and outer space for the subversion of experience, for the emergence of another universe" (*The Aesthetic Dimension* [Boston: Beacon Press, 1977], p. 38).

4. Paul Jay, *Contingency Blues: The Search for Foundations in American Culture* (Minneapolis: University of Minnesota Press, 1997), p. 46. While I do not share Jay's critique of Emerson's inevitable turn to the transcendent ("The primacy of the specific and the local in Emerson is continually superseded by the primacy of Spirit" [9]), his book has been important in my own thinking on the relationship between intellectual work and practical action.

5. The temptation to read Emerson "transcendentally," as the exponent of Romantic individual genius, is further challenged in his 1868 essay "Quotation and Originality," where he asserts that "the debt is immense to past thought. None escapes it. The originals are not original. There is imitation, model and suggestion, to the very archangels, if we knew their history" (*CWE* 8: 180). Barbara Packer usefully describes Emerson's aesthetic as a "blend of larceny and self-confidence" ("Origin and Authority: Emerson and the Higher Criticism," in *Reconstructing American Literary History*, ed. Sacvan Bercovitch [Cambridge, Mass.: Harvard University Press, 1986], p. 91).

6. Stanley Cavell, *This New Yet Unapproachable America* (Albuquerque: Living Batch Press, 1989), p. 81.

7. Frank Lentricchia, *Criticism and Social Change* (Chicago: University of Chicago Press, 1983), pp. 2, 12.

8. Richard Poirier, *Poetry and Pragmatism* (London: Faber and Faber, 1992), p. 122.

9. Wai Chee Dimock, "Deep Time: American Literature and World History," *American Literary History* 13.4 (2001): 755–75 (770).

10. Pierre Bourdieu, "Universal Corporatism: The Role of Intellectuals in the Modern World," *Poetics Today*, 12.4 (Winter 1991): 655–69 (656).

11. Ross Posnock, *Color and Culture: Black Writers and the Making of the Modern Intellectual* (Cambridge, Mass.: Harvard University Press, 1998), pp. 54–5.

12. Ray Nichols, *Treason, Tradition, and the Intellectual: Julien Benda and Political Discourse* (Lawrence: Regents Press of Kansas, 1978), p. 13.

13. Quoted in Posnock, *Color and Culture*, p. 54.

14. Harvey J. Cormier, "Pragmatism, Politics, and the Corridor," *The Cambridge Companion to William James*, ed. Ruth Anna Putnam (Cambridge: Cambridge University Press, 1997), p. 354.

15. Edward W. Said, *The World, the Text, and the Critic* (Cambridge, Mass.: Harvard University Press, 1983), p. 10.

16. John McGowan, *Democracy's Children: Intellectuals and the Rise of Cultural Politics* (Ithaca: Cornell University Press, 2002), p. 16.

17. Edward W. Said, "Michael Walzer's *Exodus and Revolution*: A Canaanite Reading," *Blaming the Victims: Spurious Scholarship and the Palestinian Question*, ed. Edward W. Said and Christopher Hitchens (London: Verso, 1988), p. 178.

18. Edward W. Said, *Humanism and Democratic Criticism* (Basingstoke: Palgrave Macmillan, 2004), p. 141.

19. Edward W. Said, *Representations of the Intellectual* (London: Verso, 1994), p. 39.

20. Stefan Collini, *Absent Minds: Intellectuals in Britain* (Oxford: Oxford University Press, 2006), p. 61. For Collini's thoroughly convincing critique of Said's *Representations of the Intellectual*, see *ibid.*, pp. 427–32.

21. McGowan, *Democracy's Children*, p. 17.

22. Said, *Representations of the Intellectual*, pp. xiii–xiv.

23. Bourdieu, "Universal Corporatism," p. 660.

24. Pierre Bourdieu, "Are Intellectuals Out of Play?" *Sociology in Question*, tr. Richard Nice (London: Sage, 1993), p. 38.

25. Edward Shils, "Ideology and Civility," *The Intellectuals and the Powers: And Other Essays* (Chicago: University of Chicago Press, 1972), p. 57.

26. Cormier quotes James's assertion that, faced with an "aboriginal" state we become "absolutely dumb and evanescent," needing instead to find a substitution that is "peptonized and cooked for our consumption" ("Pragmatism, Politics, and the Corridor," p. 355).

27. John Michael, *Anxious Intellects: Academic Professionals, Public Intellectuals, and Enlightenment Values* (Durham: Duke University Press, 2000), p. 12 (my emphasis).

28. Richard Posner, *Public Intellectuals: A Study of Decline* (Cambridge, Mass.: Harvard University Press, 2002), p. 5.

29. Collini, *Absent Minds*, p. 63.

30. Said, *Representations of the Intellectual*, p. xv.

31. Edward Said, *Culture and Imperialism* (London: Vintage, 1994), p. 59.

32. Jonathan Arac, "Criticism Between Opposition and Counterpoint," in *Edward Said and the Work of the Critic: Speaking Truth to Power*, ed. Paul A. Bové (Durham: Duke University Press, 2000), p. 67.

33. Said, *Culture and Imperialism*, p. 15.

34. Thomas Wentworth Higginson, "The American Lecture-System," *Macmillan's Magazine* 18 (May–October 1868): 48–56 (48).

35. Buell, *Emerson*, p. 23.

36. Higginson, "The American Lecture-System," p. 53.

37. Mary Kupiec Cayton, "The Making of an American Prophet: Emerson, His Audiences, and the Rise of the Culture Industry in Nineteenth-Century America," *American Historical Review* 92.3 (June 1987), 597–620 (614–15). See also Donald M. Scott, "The Popular Lecture and the Creation of a Public in Mid-Nineteenth-Century America," *Journal of American History* 66 (1980): 791–809.

38. Francis Bacon, "Of Studies," *The Essays*, ed. John Pitcher (Harmondsworth: Penguin, 1987), p. 209.

39. Steven Mailloux, *Reception Histories: Rhetoric, Pragmatism, and American Cultural Politics* (Ithaca: Cornell University Press, 1998), p. 130.

40. Oliver Wendell Holmes, *Ralph Waldo Emerson* (Boston: Houghton Mifflin, 1884), p. 181.

41. James Russell Lowell, "Emerson the Lecturer," *The Recognition of Ralph Waldo Emerson*, ed. Milton R. Konvitz (Ann Arbor: University of Michigan Press, 1972), p. 45.

42. T. S. McMillin, *Our Preposterous Use of Literature: Emerson and the Nature of Reading* (Urbana: University of Illinois Press, 2000), p. 27.

43. Harold Bloom, *A Map of Misreading* (New York: Oxford University Press, 1975), p. 171.

44. Quoted in McMillin, *Our Preposterous Use of Literature*, pp. 23–4.

45. Cyrus R. K. Patell, *Negative Liberties: Morrison, Pynchon, and the Problem of Liberal Ideology* (Durham: Duke University Press, 2001), pp. xi–xii.

46. Philip Fisher, *Still the New World: American Literature in a Culture of Creative Destruction* (Cambridge, Mass.: Harvard University Press, 1999), p. 23.

47. Fisher, *Still the New World*, p. 50.

48. Louis Hartz, *The Liberal Tradition in America: An Interpretation of American Political Thought* (New York: Harcourt, Brace, 1955), p. 5.

49. F. O. Matthiessen, *American Renaissance: Art and Expression in the Age of Emerson and Whitman* (New York: Oxford University Press, 1968), p. xv.

50. David Shumway, *Creating American Civilization: A Genealogy of American Literature as an Academic Discipline* (Minneapolis: University of Minnesota Press, 1994), p. 260.

51. Paul Giles, "Transnationalism and Classic American Literature," *PMLA*, 118.1 (January 2003): 62–77 (72, 64). See also his *Transatlantic Insurrections: British Culture and the Formation of American Literature, 1730–1860* (Philadelphia: University of Pennsylvania Press, 2001).

52. For an excellent account of "transition" as it manifests itself in Emerson and the mod-

ernist tradition that follows him, see Jonathan Levin, *The Poetics of Transition: Emerson, Pragmatism and American Literary Modernism* (Durham: Duke University Press, 1999). See also David M. Robinson's essay, "Experience, Instinct, and Emerson's Philosophical Reorientation," which associates transition with Emerson's conversion of instinctual impulses into inspirational acts (*Emerson: Bicentennial Essays*, ed. Ronald A. Bosco and Joel Myerson [Boston: Massachusetts Historical Society, 2006], pp. 391–404).

53. See Gertrude Stein, *Lectures in America* (New York: Random House, 1935), p. 53.

54. Gilles Deleuze, *Nietzsche and Philosophy*, tr. Janis Tomlinson (New York: Columbia University Press, 1983), p. 31.

55. Philippe Lacoue-Labarthe and Jean-Luc Nancy, *The Literary Absolute* (Albany: State University of New York Press, 1988), p. 49.

56. Theodor Adorno, "The Essay as Form" ("Der Essay als Form," 1958), *New German Critique* 32 (1984): 151–71 (158). Adorno goes on to assert that the essay "takes the antisystematic impulse into its own procedure" (160).

57. Ralph Waldo Emerson, *The Poetry Notebooks of Ralph Waldo Emerson*, ed. Ralph H. Orth, Albert J. von Frank, Linda Allardt, and David W. Hill (Columbia: University of Missouri Press, 1986), p. 155.

58. Georges van den Abbeele, in his book *Travel as Metaphor: From Montaigne to Rousseau*, suggests that "the metaphor of travel . . . conjures up the image of the innovative mind that explores new ways of looking at things" ([Minneapolis: University of Minnesota Press, 1992], p. xiii).

59. Anne McClintock, "The Angel of Progress: Pitfalls of the Term 'Post-colonialism,'" *Social Text* 31–2 (1992): 84–98 (87).

60. See Aijaz Ahmad, "Postcolonialism: What's in a Name?" in *Later Imperial Culture*, ed. Roman de la Campa, E. Ann Kaplan, and Michael Sprinker (London: Verso, 1995), pp. 11–32.

61. Edward Watts, *Writing and Postcolonialism in the Early Republic* (Charlottesville: University Press of Virginia, 1998), p. 19. See also Marek Paryż, "Beyond the Traveler's Testimony: Emerson's *English Traits* and the Construction of Postcolonial Counter-Discourse" (*American Transcendental Quarterly* 20.3 [2006]: 565–90) for an account of the ways in which Emerson's postcoloniality is revealed in his subversion of the conventions of the travel writing genre.

62. Susan Castillo, "'The Best of Nations'? Race and Imperial Destinies in Emerson's *English Traits*," *The Yearbook of English Studies* 34 (2004): 100–11 (101).

63. Joel Myerson, ed., *Emerson and Thoreau: The Contemporary Reviews* (Cambridge: Cambridge University Press, 1992), p. 275.

64. Castillo, "'The Best of Nations'?" p. 101.

65. In the summer of 1852, Emerson consolidated his disparate journal entries on England into a new Notebook ED, before filling up further volumes (Journal DO and Journal GO).

66. See Reginald Horsman, *Race and Manifest Destiny: The Origins of American Racial Anglo-Saxonism* (Cambridge, Mass.: Harvard University Press, 1981).

67. Paul Giles has recently argued for the importance of recovering a conservative

Wordsworth in the narrative of Anglo-American cultural and political encounter (*Atlantic Republic: The American Tradition in English Literature* [Oxford: Oxford University Press, 2006], pp. 35–42).

68. Paryż, "Beyond the Traveler's Testimony," p. 576.

69. There are numerous references in Emerson's journal entries of the period that indicate his awareness of Ireland's political and economic situation. See, for example, *JMN* 10: 310, 539, 548.

70. Carolyn Soriso, *Fleshing Out America: Race, Gender, and the Politics of the Body in American Literature, 1833–1879* (Athens: University of Georgia Press, 2002), p. 130.

71. For more on Emerson and Knox, see Philip L. Nicoloff's *Emerson on Race & History: An Examination of "English Traits"* (New York: Columbia University Press, 1961), pp. 142–4.

72. Soriso, *Fleshing Out America*, pp. 136, 134.

73. Lawrence Buell, "Saving Emerson for Posterity," in Bosco and Myerson, eds., *Emerson*, pp. 38, 36.

74. Buell, *Emerson*, p. 51.

75. The editors of the journal print the entry thus: "↑Is↓ <T>the air of America <seems to be> loaded with imbecility, irresolution, dispersion↑?↓"

76. See, e.g., a letter to his brother William Emerson, June 2 1856 (*Letters* 5: 23).

77. For the abbreviated journal entry version of the speech, see *JMN* 10: 504–6.

78. Giles details the fluctuating response of Emerson to America's expansionist drive westwards and into Mexico ("Transnationalism," pp. 66–7).

79. See Richard Bridgman, "From Greenough to 'Nowhere': Emerson's *English Traits*," *New England Quarterly* 59.4 (1986): 469–85.

80. Emerson's therapeutics of warfare here, restoring "intellectual and moral vigor to these languid and dissipated populations" (*LL2* 327), anticipates William James's more explicit consideration of this topic in his "The Moral Equivalent of War" (1906).

81. In 1878, Emerson delivered a revised version of "Fortune of the Republic," the text of which is published in the 1903 Centenary Edition of his works. This later text removes most of the specific references to the Civil War, focusing instead on a call for those with "universal" legitimacy: "We want men of original perception and original action, who can open their eyes wider than to a nationality,—namely, to considerations of benefit to the human race" (*CWE* 11: 537).

82. Giles charts the relationship between the two men and notes that Clough's poem *Amours de Voyage* (1849) "might be described as a poem of negative Transcendentalism" in which a dialogue "between Neoplatonism and contingency, between idealist affinities and a more random sense of time and space" is played out (*Atlantic Republic*, p. 117).

2. Thought and Action

The epigraph to this chapter is from "Slavery in Massachusetts," *Political Writings* 135.

1. See Len Gougeon, *Virtue's Hero: Emerson, Antislavery, and Reform*, for an excellent

account tracing Emerson's engagement with events in Kansas (Athens: University of Georgia Press, 1990), ch. 7.

2. Jenine Abboushi Dallal, "American Imperialism UnManifest: Emerson's 'Inquest' and Cultural Regeneration," *American Literature* 73.1 (2001): 47–83 (49).

3. Dallal, "American Imperialism UnManifest," p. 54.

4. Thomas Wentworth Higginson, *The New Revolution: A Speech before the American Antislavery Society, at Their Annual Meeting in New York, May 12, 1857* (Boston: Wallcut, 1857), p. 8.

5. Ethan J. Kytle, "From Body Reform to Reforming the Body Politic: Transcendentalism and the Militant Antislavery Career of Thomas Wentworth Higginson," *American Nineteenth Century History* 8.3 (2007): 325–50 (337).

6. [Thomas Wentworth Higginson], "Physical Courage," *Atlantic Monthly* 13.2 (November 1858): 728–37 (736).

7. James Perrin Warren, *Culture of Eloquence: Oratory and Reform in Antebellum America* (University Park: Pennsylvania State University Press, 1999), p. 25.

8. Stanley Cavell, *The Senses of Walden* (Chicago: University of Chicago Press, 1992), pp. 53, 102.

9. Wai Chee Dimock, *Through Other Continents: American Literature Across Deep Time* (Princeton: Princeton University Press, 2006), p. 17.

10. Cavell, *Senses of Walden*, p. 8.

11. Samuel Weber, "A Touch of Translation: On Walter Benjamin's 'The Task of the Translator,'" *Nation, Language, and the Ethics of Translation*, ed. Sandra Bermann and Michael Wood (Princeton: Princeton University Press, 2005), p. 75.

12. Cavell, *Senses of Walden*, pp. 17, 7.

13. Stanley Cavell, "Emerson, Coleridge, Kant (Terms as Conditions)," *In Quest of the Ordinary: Lines of Skepticism and Romanticism* (Chicago: University of Chicago Press, 1988), p. 35.

14. Stanley Cavell, *Conditions Handsome and Unhandsome: The Constitution of Emersonian Perfectionism* (Chicago: University of Chicago Press, 1990), pp. xxxi–xxxii.

15. Particularly useful here is Maurice S. Lee's nuanced account of Emerson's shifting sympathy toward forms of political action (*Slavery, Philosophy, and American Literature* [Cambridge: Cambridge University Press, 2005], pp. 165–209). Lee suggests that Emerson's early statements advocated what he calls "passive patience" (173). For example, in an 1840 lecture, "Reforms," we find the following: "Though I sympathize with your sentiment and abhor the crime you assail yet I shall persist in wearing this robe, all loose and unbecoming as it is, of inaction, this wise passiveness until my hour comes when I can see how to act with truth as well as to refuse" (*EL* 3:266).

16. Jack Turner, "Performing Conscience: Thoreau, Political Action, and the Plea for John Brown," *Political Theory* 33.4 (2005): 448–71 (452).

17. Joseba Zulaika and William A. Douglass, *Terror and Taboo: The Foibles, Fables, and Faces of Terrorism* (New York: Routledge, 1996), pp. 31–2, 11.

18. Anthony Kubiak, *Stages of Terror: Terrorism, Ideology, and Coercion as Theatre His-

tory (Bloomington: Indiana University Press, 1991), p. 1. For useful accounts on the relationship between textuality and acts of terror, see also David E. Apter, "Political Violence in Analytical Perspective," in *The Legitimization of Violence*, ed. David E. Apter (New York: New York University Press, 1997), pp. 1–32 and Jeffrey A. Clymer, *America's Culture of Terrorism* (Chapel Hill: University of North Carolina Press, 2003).

19. Lewis Hyde, "Henry Thoreau, John Brown, and the Problem of Prophetic Action," *Raritan* 22.2 (2002): 125–44 (143).

20. On Thoreau's wide-ranging interest in language, see Michael West, *Transcendental Wordplay: America's Romantic Punsters and the Search for the Language of Nature* (Athens: Ohio University Press, 2000) and Philip F. Gura, *The Wisdom of Words: Language, Theology, and Literature in the New England Renaissance* (Middletown: Wesleyan University Press, 1981).

21. See David S. Reynolds, *John Brown, Abolitionist: The Man Who Killed Slavery, Sparked the Civil War, and Seeded Civil Rights* (New York: Alfred A. Knopf, 2005), pp. 206–38.

22. Stanley Cavell, *The Claim of Reason* (Oxford: Oxford University Press, 1979), p. 23.

23. Stanley Cavell, "Henry James Returns to America and to Shakespeare," *Philosophy the Day After Tomorrow* (Cambridge, Mass.: Harvard University Press, 2005), p. 107.

24. Stephen Mulhall, *Stanley Cavell: Philosophy's Recounting of the Ordinary* (Oxford: Blackwell, 1994), p. 275. Hannah Arendt argues that the principle of "consent" is central to American political activity, legitimating acts of civil disobedience: "A contract presupposes a plurality of at least two, and every association established and acting according to the principle of consent, based on mutual promise, presupposes a plurality that does not dissolve but is shaped into the form of a union — *e pluribus unum*" (*Crises of the Republic* [1972] [Harmondsworth: Penguin, 1973], p. 76).

25. Frank Lentricchia and Jody McAuliffe, *Crimes of Art and Terror* (Chicago: University of Chicago Press, 2003), pp. 2–3.

26. Michael Waltzer regards it as "the best single statement of the critical intellectual's creed" (*The Company of Critics: Social Criticism and Political Commitment in the Twentieth Century* [New York: Basic Books, 2002], p. 29), and Edward Said in his Reith Lectures confessed that "there is no doubt in my mind at least that the image of a real intellectual as conceived by Benda remains an attractive and a compelling one" (*Representations of the Intellectual* [London: Vintage, 1994], p. 6). As Stefan Collini notes, Benda's use of the word "clercs" in his title, as opposed to the more contemporary (and secular) "intellectuels," signifies his intent to legitimate "the withdrawn 'disinterested' thinker or scholar who from time to time acted in the public sphere in order to uphold eternal values of truth and justice" (*Absent Minds: Intellectuals in Britain* [Oxford: Oxford University Press, 2006], pp. 286–87).

27. Julien Benda, *The Betrayal of the Intellectuals*, tr. Richard Aldington (Boston: Beacon Press, 1955), pp. 30, 122.

28. The legal scholar Michael Mello draws a connection between Kaczynski and John Brown in his *The United States versus Theodore John Kaczynski: Ethics, Power, and the Invention of the Unabomber* (New York: Context, 1999), suggesting that Kaczynski's radical

environmentalism instills the same ethical dilemmas as Brown's unswerving commitment to the cause of abolition.

29. See Elizabeth D. Samet's *Willing Obedience: Citizens, Soldiers, and the Progress of Consent in America, 1776–1898* (Stanford: Stanford University Press, 2004) for a succinct account of Thoreau's conviction that "the citizen's education ought to culminate in the dissolution of government" (61). It is easy to see how Thoreau has been embraced by libertarian proponents of "small government" within current U.S. political culture. For example, the "Center for Small Government" (a political think-tank) cites Thoreau as one of its inspirations, and the "Thoreau Institute" is concerned with opposing government bureaucracy in environmental planning.

30. Matthew Arnold, "The Function of Criticism at the Present Time" (1865), *Selected Prose*, ed. P. J. Keating (Hammondsworth: Penguin Books, 1987), p. 142.

31. Benda, *Betrayal of the Intellectuals*, p. 153.

32. Turner, "Performing Conscience," p. 455.

33. Hannah Arendt, *The Human Condition* (1958) (Chicago: University of Chicago Press, 1998), pp. 14–15.

34. Arendt judges Thoreau's ineffectiveness as a political figure to lie in exactly this inability to translate a solipsistic concern for self-improvement into a wider, more publicly active agenda for social improvement: Thoreau "argued his case not on the ground of a *citizen's* moral relation to the law, but on the ground of individual conscience and conscience's moral obligation" (*Crises of the Republic*, p. 49). Thoreau's apparent solipsism — and therefore his failure as a political thinker — has become a critical commonplace: see, for example, George Hochfield, "Anti-Thoreau," *Sewanee Review* 96 (Summer 1988): 433–43; John Patrick Diggins, "Thoreau, Marx, and the 'Riddle' of Alienation," *Social Research* 39 (Winter 1972): 571–98; and Jane Bennett, *Thoreau's Nature* (Thousand Oaks, CA.: Sage, 1994).

35. Lewis A. Coser, *Men of Ideas: A Sociologist's View* (New York: Free Press, 1965), p. viii.

36. Eric Sundquist, *Home as Found: Authority and Geneaolgy in Nineteenth-Century American Literature* (Baltimore: Johns Hopkins University Press, 1979), p. 42.

37. Antonio Gramsci, *Selections from the Prison Notebooks of Antonio Gramsci* (1949), tr. and ed. Quintin Hoare and Geoffrey Nowell Smith (London: Lawrence and Wishart, 1971), pp. 7, 12.

38. Sam McGuire Worley, *Emerson, Thoreau, and the Role of the Cultural Critic* (Albany: State University of New York Press, 2001), p. 103.

39. See, for example, Allan Bloom, *The Closing of the American Mind: How Higher Education has Failed Democracy and Impoverished the Souls of Today's Students* (New York: Simon and Schuster, 1987) and Samuel P. Huntington, *The Clash of Civilizations and the Remaking of the World Order* (New York: Simon and Schuster, 1996) on the "right"; and Todd Gitlin, *The Twilight of Common Dreams* (New York: Henry Holt, 1995) and Christopher Norris, *Uncritical Theory: Postmodernism, Intellectuals, and the Gulf War* (Amherst: University of Massachusetts Press, 1992) on the "left."

40. George Konrad and Ivan Szelenyi, *The Intellectuals on the Road to Class Power*, tr. Andrew Arato and Richard E. Allen (New York: Harcourt Brace Jovanovitch, 1979), p. 22.

41. Max Horkheimer and Theodor Adorno, *Dialectic of Enlightenment*, tr. John Cumming (New York: Continuum, 1989).

42. William Lloyd Garrison, "The Tragedy at Harper's Ferry," *Liberator* October 28 1859, in William E. Cain, ed., *William Lloyd Garrison and the Fight against Slavery* (New York: St. Martin's Press, 1995), p. 154.

43. Joseph A. Conforti, *Imagining New England: Explorations of Regional Identity from the Pilgrims to the Mid-Twentieth Century* (Chapel Hill: University of North Carolina Press, 2001), p. 171. David Reynolds, in his *John Brown, Abolitionist*, supports the view that Brown's paternal ancestor arrived to America on the *Mayflower*, p. 19; Oswald Garrison Villard's 1910 biography, *John Brown, 1800–1859: A Biography Fifty Years After* (Boston: Houghton Mifflin, 1910), was the earliest to dispute this (p. 10).

44. Michael Meyer, "Thoreau's Rescue of John Brown from History," *Studies in the American Renaissance: 1980*, ed. Joel Myerson (Boston: Twayne, 1980), pp. 301–16. In contrast, Walter Harding claims that Thoreau could not have known about Pottawatomie because if he had, "he might never have endorsed him and might [even] have been convinced of his insanity" (*The Days of Henry Thoreau: A Biography*, rev. edn. (Princeton: Princeton University Press, 1993), p. 418. The conditionals in Harding's statement rather work to undermine its conviction.

45. Stephen B. Oates's *To Purge this Land with Blood* (New York: Harper & Row, 1970) still offers the best account of the competing readings of this episode.

46. Thomas Jefferson, *Writings* (New York: Library of America, 1984), p. 752. For a succinct account of Cromwell's fluctuating status in America, see Peter Karsten, "Cromwell in America," in *Images of Oliver Cromwell: Essays for and by Roger Howell, Jr.*, ed. R. C. Richardson (Manchester: Manchester University Press, 1993), pp. 207–21.

47. Anon., "Carlyle's Cromwell," *New Englander and Yale Review* 4.14 (April 1846): 211–29 (211).

48. Charles Lane, "Cromwell," *Dial* 3.4 (October 1842): 258–64 (259, 260).

49. While it is true to say that the use of Oliver Cromwell as a model for American potential was expounded more readily in New England (and the North more generally), a recent essay notes how the Roundhead/Cavalier opposition did not map securely onto the U.S. North/South fault line. See Robert B. Bonner, "Roundhead Cavaliers? The Context and Limits of a Confederate Racial Project," *Civil War History* 48.1 (2002): 34–59.

50. Wendell Phillips, *Speeches, Lectures, and Letters. First Series* (Boston: Lee & Shepard, 1894), p. 276. Stearns quoted in Charles E. Heller, *Portrait of an Abolitionist: A Biography of George Luther Stearns, 1809–1867* (Westport, Conn.: Greenwood Press, 1996), p. 78. F. B. Sanborn, *Recollections of Seventy Years*, 2 vols. (Boston: Richard G. Badger, 1909), vol. 1, p. 83. Theodore Roosevelt, in his 1900 biography of Cromwell, also draws parallels between English Republicanism and the American Civil War: "In the great American Civil War the masterspirits in the contest for union and freedom were actuated by a fervor as intense as, and even finer than, that which actuated the men of the Long Parliament" (*Oliver Cromwell* [London: Archibald Constable, 1900], p. 5).

51. Reynolds, *John Brown, Abolitionist*, p. 231. Joel T. Headley, *The Life of Oliver Cromwell* (1848) (New York: Charles Scribner, 1851), p. ix.

52. "Buncombe" is now more familiar as "bunkum"; the word derives from a county in North Carolina, whose congressman c. 1820 made an empty speech "for Buncombe" (*American Heritage Dictionary*).

53. Worley, *Emerson, Thoreau, and the Role of the Cultural Critic*, p. 116.

54. Worley, *Emerson, Thoreau, and the Role of the Cultural Critic*, p. 122.

55. In a recent account of the American trial system in American culture Robert A. Ferguson is right to remind us that Brown's eloquence did, in fact, draw heavily on established literary and generic conventions: "While Brown brought no special craft to these devices, he understood them well enough to enrich a capacity for self-dramatization" (*The Trial in American Life* [Chicago: University of Chicago Press, 2007], p. 129 and ch. 4 *passim*).

56. Stephen E. Whicher, *Freedom and Fate: An Inner Life of Ralph Waldo Emerson* (New York: A. S. Barnes, 1953). See Stanley Cavell, "Emerson's Constitutional Amending: Reading 'Fate,'" *Emerson's Transcendental Etudes*, ed. David Justin Hodge (Stanford: Stanford University Press, 2003), pp. 192–214; Pamela J. Schirmeister, *Less Legible Meanings: Between Poetry and Philosophy in the Work of Emerson* (Stanford: Stanford University Press, 2000), pp. 165–72.

57. The journal source for this exchange is to be found in *JMN* 13: 270.

58. Lee, *Slavery, Philosophy, and American Literature*, p. 205.

3. Conversation and Cosmopolitanism

The epigraph to this chapter is from "A Short Essay on Critics," *Dial* 1.1 (July 1840): 10.

1. Adam-Max Tuchinsky, "'Her Cause Against Herself': Margaret Fuller, Emersonian Democracy, and the Nineteenth-Century Public Intellectual," *American Nineteenth Century History* 5.1 (2004): 66–99 (83).

2. Yet, as his most recent biographer has noted, Horace Greeley was indispensable in the circulation of Emerson's ideas, praising his work in the *Tribune* and furnishing him with contacts in the New York publishing world (Robert C. Williams, *Horace Greeley: Champion of American Freedom* [New York: New York University Press, 2006], p. 82). Emerson received his first real attention from newspapers in New York, in February 1842, when Greeley promoted his course on "The Times" in the *Tribune*.

3. Gustavus Stadler, *Troubling Minds: The Cultural Politics of Genius in the United States 1840–1890* (Minneapolis: University of Minnesota Press, 2006), p. xxii.

4. Russell Jacoby, *The Last Intellectuals: American Culture in the Age of Academe* (New York: Basic Books, 1987), p. 235.

5. Margaret Fuller, Notebook 1836, bMS Am 1086(3), Margaret Fuller Papers, Houghton Library, Harvard University. Hereafter Fuller Papers.

6. The standard account of developments in U.S. newspaper publishing during the antebellum period is Frank Luther Mott's *American Journalism: A History of Newspapers in the United States through 250 Years, 1690–1940* (New York: The Macmillan Company, 1941), chs.

12–19. For an analysis of the impact of these changes on the growth of a "democratic market society," see Michael Schudson, *Discovering the News: A Social History of American Newspapers* (New York: Basic Books, 1978), ch. 1. Charles Capper notes that Dana, on visiting the less than salubrious offices of Horace Greeley's *Tribune* newspaper in 1849, complained that "Nowhere is the contrast between circumstances & influence greater" (*Margaret Fuller: An American Romantic Life: The Public Years* [New York: Oxford University Press, 2007], p. 197).

7. The most comprehensive reading of the *Dial*'s impact remains Joel Myerson's *The New England Transcendentalists and the* Dial: *A History of the Magazine and Its Contributors* (Rutherford, N.J.: Fairleigh Dickinson University Press, 1980).

8. Ralph Waldo Emerson, "The Editors to the Reader," *Dial* 1.1 (July 1840): 1–4 (2).

9. Fuller, "A Short Essay on Critics," p. 5.

10. Julie Ellison, *Delicate Subjects: Romanticism, Gender, and the Ethics of Understanding* (Ithaca: Cornell University Press, 1990), p. 256.

11. Capper, *Margaret Fuller: An American Romantic Life: The Public Years*, p. 7.

12. James Snead, "European Pedigrees/African Contagions: Nationality, Narrative, and Community in Tutuola, Achebe, and Reed," in Homi K. Bhabha, ed., *Nation and Narration* (London: Routledge, 1990), p. 245.

13. Ellison, *Delicate Subjects*, p. 260.

14. Christina Zwarg, "Reading before Marx: Margaret Fuller and the *New-York Tribune*," in James L. Machor, ed., *Readers in History: Nineteenth-Century American Literature and the Contexts of Response* (Baltimore: Johns Hopkins University Press 1993), pp. 228–58 (244).

15. Margaret Fuller, "Boston 20 September 1840," loose sheets inside Fuller's "Journal 1834," bMS Am 1086(4), Fuller Papers.

16. *Conversations* was published in two volumes and comprised the edited transcript of conversations Alcott had had with his pupils on the New Testament Gospels. Comments about conception and birth startled the moderate Unitarians of Boston, with Harvard's Andrews Norton judging the book to be "one third absurd, one third blasphemous, and one third obscene" (quoted in John Matteson, *Eden's Outcasts: The Story of Louisa May Alcott and Her Father* [New York: W. W. Norton & Company, 2007], p. 80).

17. Fuller, "Boston 20 September 1840," Fuller Papers.

18. Margaret Fuller, "Publishers and Authors. *Dolores* by Harro Harring," *New-York Daily Tribune* April 25 1846, in Judith Mattson Bean and Joel Myerson, eds., *Margaret Fuller, Critic: Writings from the New-York Tribune, 1844–1846* (New York: Columbia University Press, 2000), p. 351.

19. Benedict Anderson, *Imagined Communities: Reflections on the Origin and Spread of Nationalism* (London: Verso, 1983), p. 24. Anderson writes that "the newspaper reader, observing exact replicas of his own paper being consumed by his subway, barbershop, or residential neighbours, is continually reassured that the imagined world is visibly rooted in everyday life" (35–36).

20. Ronald J. Zboray, *A Fictive People: Antebellum Economic Development and the American Reading Public* (New York: Oxford University Press, 1993), pp. 12, 15, xvi.

21. James Russell Lowell, "Scotch the Snake, or Kill it?" *North American Review* 101.208 (July 1865): 190–205 (192–93).

22. Ferdinand Tönnies, *Community and Society*, tr. and ed. Charles P. Loomis (East Lansing: Michigan State University Press, 1957), p. 221.

23. Margaret Fuller, "Thom's Poems," *New-York Daily Tribune* (23 August 1845): 1.

24. Margaret Fuller, ["Review of Thomas Arnold, Introductory Lectures on Modern History"], *New-York Daily Tribune* (28 August 1845): 1.

25. Amanda Anderson, *The Way We Argue Now: A Study in the Cultures of Theory* (Princeton: Princeton University Press, 2006), p. 44.

26. Octavius Brooks Frothingham, *Transcendentalism in New England: A History* (1876) (New York: Harper & Brothers, 1959), p. 57.

27. Quoted in Charles Capper, *Margaret Fuller: An American Romantic Life: The Private Years* (New York: Oxford University Press, 1992), p. 129.

28. Francis Jeffrey, "German Genius and Taste: Goethe's Wilhelm Meister," *Edinburgh Review* 42 (1825). Reprinted in Francis Jeffrey, *Contributions to the "Edinburgh Review"* (New York: D. Appleton, 1866), pp. 104–20 (106).

29. George Bancroft, *Literary and Historical Miscellanies* (New York: Harper and Brothers, 1855), pp. 203–4.

30. For a full account of Goethe's status in *Representative Men*, see Gustaaf Van Cromphout, *Emerson's Modernity and the Example of Goethe* (Columbia: University of Missouri Press, 1990), pp. 98–115.

31. Margaret Fuller, undated journal fragment, bMS Am 1086(1), Fuller Papers. Still the only extended study of Fuller's engagement with Goethe is Frederick Augustus Braun, *Margaret Fuller and Goethe: The Development of a Remarkable Personality, Her Religion and Philosophy, and Her Relationship to Emerson, J.F. Clarke, and Transcendentalism* (New York: H. Holt, 1910). Perry Miller, in his edited collection *Margaret Fuller: American Romantic: A Selection from Her Writings and Correspondence* (Ithaca: Cornell University Press, 1963), suggests that Fuller was the first American thinker to realize the power of the German poet (pp. 77–78).

32. Quoted in Capper, *Margaret Fuller: An American Romantic Life: The Private Years*, p. 130.

33. Colleen Glenney Boggs, "Margaret Fuller's American Translation," *American Literature* 76.1 (2004): 31–58 (39). See also Arthur R. Schultz, "Margaret Fuller — Transcendentalist Interpreter of German Literature," in Joel Myerson, ed., *Critical Essays on Margaret Fuller* (Boston: G. K. Hall, 1980), pp. 195–208.

34. Margaret Fuller, "Menzel's View of Goethe," *Dial* 1.3 (January 1841): 340–47 (340, 347). Fuller's most extensive treatment of Goethe, a 41-page article in the July 1841 issue of the *Dial*, similarly acknowledged the German's worldly flaws, but viewed them as the inspiration for his creative projects ("Goethe," *Dial* 2.1 [July 1841]: 1–41).

35. Boggs, "Margaret Fuller's American Translation," p. 33.

36. Fuller, "Menzel's View of Goethe," p. 346.

37. Wai Chee Dimock, *Through Other Continents: American Literature Across Deep Time* (Princeton: Princeton University Press, 2006), p. 66.

38. Fuller, "Menzel's View of Goethe," p. 346.

39. Zwarg notes that Fuller resists "a hermeneutic deriving its authority from a struggle for mastery over meaning [which] has violent historical consequences" ("The Storied Facts of Margaret Fuller," *New England Quarterly* 69 (1996): 128–42 (133). For more on Fuller's polyvocality, see also Christina Zwarg, *Feminist Conversations: Fuller, Emerson, and the Play of Reading* (Ithaca: Cornell University Press, 1991), William W. Stowe, *Going Abroad: European Travel and Nineteenth-Century American Culture* (Princeton: Princeton University Press, 1994), pp. 102–24, and Annette Kolodny, "Inventing a Feminist Discourse: Rhetoric and Resistance in Margaret Fuller's Woman in the Nineteenth Century," *New Literary History* 25.2 (1994): 355–82.

40. The motto, taken from Milton's *History of Britain*, Book 3, faces the unpaginated front page of Fuller's translation of the Conversations.

41. Margaret Fuller, "Preface" to Fuller, ed., *Conversations with Goethe, from the German of Eckermann* (Boston: Hilliard, Gray, 1839), pp. vii–viii.

42. David Damrosch notes that "Eckermann's account both a portrait of the great man and the record of his inability to grasp his subject" (*What is World Literature?* [Princeton: Princeton University Press, 2003], p. 1).

43. Margaret Fuller, Reading journal B, March 1835, bMS Am 1086(1), Fuller Papers.

44. Margaret Fuller, "Bettine Brentano and her Friend Günderode," *Dial* 2.3 (January 1842): 313–57 (321).

45. Karen A. English, " 'Genuine Transcripts of Private Experience': Margaret Fuller and Translation," *American Transcendentalist Quarterly* 15.2 (June 2001): 131–47 (140–42).

46. Margaret Fuller, *Woman in the Nineteenth Century and Other Writings* (Oxford: Oxford University Press, 1994), p. 75.

47. Ralph Waldo Emerson, William Henry Channing, and James Freeman Clarke, eds., *Memoirs of Margaret Fuller Ossoli*, 2 vols. (Boston: Phillips, Sampson and Company, 1852), vol. 1, p. 14.

48. Eric Wilson, *Romantic Turbulence: Chaos, Ecology, and American Space* (New York: St. Martin's Press, 2000), ch. 1.

49. Johann Wolfgang von Goethe, *Scientific Studies, Goethe: The Collected Works*, vol. 12, tr. and ed. Douglas Miller (Princeton: Princeton University Press, 1988), p. 43.

50. S. M. Fuller, *Conversations with Goethe in the Last Years of His Life, Translated from the German of Eckermann* (Boston: Hilliard, Gray, and Company, 1839), p. 204.

51. See Damrosch, *What Is World Literature?* pp. 1–36.

52. Quoted in Stefan Hoesel-Uhlig, "Changing Fields: The Directions of Goethe's Weltliteratur," in Christopher Prendergast, ed., *Debating World Literature* (London: Verso, 2004), p. 38.

53. Azade Seyhan, *Writing Outside the Nation* (Princeton: Princeton University Press, 2001), pp. 93, 24.

54. J. Hillis Miller, "English Romanticism, American Romanticism: What's the Difference?" in *American Theory Now and Then* (London: Harvester Wheatsheaf, 1991), p. 219.

55. Damrosch, *What Is World Literature?* p. 285. Recently Franco Moretti has advocated the practice of what he calls "distant reading" as a route out of this impasse. Close reading of the kind practiced by Miller is, he judges, "a theological exercise": "what we really need is a pact with the devil: we know how to read texts, now let's learn how not to read them. Distant reading: where distance . . . is a condition of knowledge: It allows you to focus on units that are much smaller or much larger than the text: devices, themes, tropes — or genres and systems" ("Conjectures on World Literature," *New Left Review* 1 [January–February 2000]: 54–68 [57]). As a methodology for reading, Moretti's essay offers the possibility of comprehensive structural systems that extend across different national traditions, systems that work to dispense with the centrality of those traditions. Yet its explicit resistance to textual analysis runs counter to my concern here to resist the lure of such an Olympian view in favor of exploring the textual shape of moments of encounter and cultural exchange.

56. John Carlos Rowe, in a discussion of the term "postnational," notes that while it "calls attention to the negative heritage of . . . national practices . . . [it does not] assum[e] that . . . nationalism has disappeared (or will shortly do so)," for "even as we encourage such research and theoretical models on which it depends, we must be careful not to confuse our methods, models, and terminology with geopolitical realities" ("Nineteenth-Century United States Literary Culture and Transnationality," *PMLA* 118 [2003]: 78–89 [79, 80]).

57. Quoted in John Pizer, "Goethe's 'World Literature' Paradigm and Contemporary Cultural Globalization," *Comparative Literature* 52.3 (2000): 213–27 (217).

58. Homi Bhabha, *The Location of Culture* (London: Routledge, 1994), p. 147.

59. [Anon.], "Bryant's Poems," *The United States Magazine and Democratic Review* 6.22 (October 1839): 273–86 (283–4). For a full account of the relationship between "Young America" nationalism and the publishing industry of the period, see Edward L. Widmer, *Young America: The Flowering of Democracy in New York City* (New York: Oxford University Press, 1999).

60. Walt Whitman, "Death of Abraham Lincoln," *Specimen Days and Collect* (Philadelphia: David McKay, 1882–3), p. 314.

61. Karl Marx and Friedrich Engels, *The Communist Manifesto* (Oxford: Oxford University Press, 1998), pp. 6–7.

62. Friedrich Nietzsche, *Human, All Too Human*, tr. R. J. Hollingdale (New York: Cambridge University Press, 1986), p. 174.

63. Margaret Fuller, "American Literature, Its Position in the Present Time, and Prospects for the Future," in *Margaret Fuller: Essays on American Life and Letters*, ed. Joel Myerson (New Haven: College and University Press, 1978), p. 382.

64. Pascale Casanova, *The World Republic of Letters* (Cambridge, Mass.: Harvard University Press, 2004), p. 36.

65. Declan Kiberd, *Inventing Ireland* (London: Vintage Books, 1996), p. 646.

66. See also Wai Chee Dimock's essay "Literature for the Planet" (*PMLA* 116 [2001]: 173–88), where she takes issue with Benedict Anderson's equation of imagined communities

with nations, arguing, like Miller, that a literary "continuum extends across space and time, messing up territorial sovereignty and numerical chronology" (174). Instead we should consider "the entire planet as a unit of analysis" (175).

67. Bruce Robbins, "Cosmopolitanism and Boredom," *Theory & Event* 1.2 (1997), http://muse.jhu.edu/journals/theory_and_event/v001/1.2r_robbins.html. Accessed October 19, 2009.

68. Martha Nussbaum, "Patriotism and Cosmopolitanism," *For Love of Country: Debating the Limits of Patriotism*, ed. Joshua Cohen (Boston: Beacon Press, 1990), p. 7.

69. Quoted in Jessica Berman, *Modernist Fiction, Cosmopolitanism, and the Politics of Community* (Cambridge: Cambridge University Press, 2001), p. 29. Timothy Brennan's most extended critique of universalizing versions of cosmopolitanism is found in *At Home in the World: Cosmopolitanism Now* (Cambridge: Harvard University Press, 1997). More recently he has summed up his position by asserting that "the essence of cosmopolitanism . . . is a discourse of the universal that is inherently local—a locality that's always surreptitiously imperial." ("Cosmopolitanism and Internationalism," in Danielle Archibugi, ed., *Debating Cosmopolitics* [London: Verso, 2003], p. 45).

70. Kwame Anthony Appiah, *The Ethics of Identity* (Princeton: Princeton University Press, 2005), p. 214.

71. *The Letters of Margaret Fuller*, ed. Robert N. Hudspeth, 6 vols. (Ithaca: Cornell University Press, 1983–94), vol. 6, p. 193.

72. Fuller, "American Literature," p. 381.

73. Herman Melville, "Hawthorne and His Mosses" (1850), in Richard Ruland, ed., *The Native Muse: Theories of American Literature from Bradford to Whitman* (New York: E. P. Dutton & Co, 1976), p. 324.

74. Lawrence Buell, "Are We Post-American Studies?" in Marjorie Garber et al., eds., *Field Work: Sites in Literary and Cultural Studies* (New York: Routledge, 1996), p. 89.

75. Fuller, "American Literature," p. 381.

76. Paolo Gemme, *Domesticating Foreign Struggles: The Italian Risorgimento and Antebellum American Identity* (Athens: University of Georgia Press, 2005), p. 18. Gemme notes how American narratives of the Risorgimento often chose to elide the use made of the Roman empire as a republican archetype by the nation's founders: "Rome's republican phase was erased and its imperial one emphasized so that America could conceive of itself as the first realization of republicanism" (25–26).

77. Anon., "Pius the Ninth and the Revolutions in Rome," *North American Review* 74 (1852): 24–71 (34).

78. Margaret Fuller, *"These Sad But Glorious Days": Dispatches from Europe, 1846–1850*, ed. Larry J. Reynolds and Susan Belasco Smith (New Haven: Yale University Press, 1991), p. 132.

79. Giuseppe Mazzini to Margaret Fuller, December 1847, bMS Am 9086 (11), Fuller Papers. In an article in the London-based *People's Journal* in 1847, Mazzini had already elaborated on this view: "And as for the moralists, the philosophical writers, who would begin by transforming the inward man, they are undoubtedly right in theory; but the labouring

man, who works fourteen or sixteen hours a day for a bare subsistence, with no security for the morrow's existence but the labour of his hands, has not the time to read and reflect, if he knows how to read: he drinks and sleeps. It is very difficult to find the *ubi consistat* of the lever of Carlyle, Emerson, and all the noble minds which resemble them, to act on the Glasgow weaver, the *canut* of Lyon, or the Gallician serf" (*Thoughts Upon Democracy in Europe (1846–1847)*, ed. Salvo Mastellone [Firenze: Centro Editoriale Toscano, 2001], p. 7).

80. Bell Gale Chevigny, "To the Edges of Ideology: Margaret Fuller's Centrifugal Evolution," *American Quarterly* 38.2 (1986): 173–201 (182). See also Chevigny, "Mutual Interpretation: Margaret Fuller's Journeys in Italy," in Charles Capper and Cristina Giorcelli, eds., *Margaret Fuller: Transatlantic Crossings in a Revolutionary Age* (Madison: University of Wisconsin Press, 2007), pp. 99–123.

81. Fuller, *"These Sad But Glorious Days,"* p. 132.

82. Brigitte Bailey, "Representing Italy: Fuller, History Painting and the Popular Press," in Fritz Fleischmann, ed., *Margaret Fuller's Cultural Critique: Her Age and Legacy* (New York: Peter Lang, 2000), pp. 229–47 (230).

83. Quoted in Mason Wade, *Margaret Fuller: Whetstone of Genius* (New York: Viking, 1940), p. 139. Heidi Kolk writes astutely on Fuller's cultivation of her "prodigal daughter" persona, "a female outsider with no home to return to and no father to welcome her back with open arms" ("Tropes of Suffering and Postures of Authority in Margaret Fuller's European Travel Letters," *Biography* 28.3 [Summer 2005]: 377–413 [394]).

84. Fuller, *"These Sad But Glorious Days,"* p. 163.

85. George Berkeley, "Verses by the Author on the Prospect of Planting Arts and Learning in America," in *American Poetry: The Seventeenth and Eighteenth Centuries* (New York: Library of America, 2007), p. 346.

86. Fuller, *"These Sad But Glorious Days,"* p. 257.

87. Ellison, *Delicate Subjects*, p. 294.

88. Fuller, *Woman in the Nineteenth Century*, p. 115.

89. Fuller, *"These Sad But Glorious Days,"* p. 280.

90. Paolo Gemme is critical of what she calls Fuller's "aestheticizing" strategies, which work to downplay the political import of events in favor of supplying her readers with elements of touristic local color. This results, she argues, in "the reduction of foreign liberalism into visual entertainment for the American spectator" (*Domesticating Foreign Struggles*, 102). While Gemme is acute in identifying the strategies by which Fuller feels able to represent the scene of political upheaval, she is overly harsh in her contention that such instances "leave the contemporary reader with a nagging suspicion that Fuller half wished the revolution had never taken place, and Italy could be preserved as it best suited the American observer in search of curiosities" (104).

91. Fuller, *"These Sad but Glorious Days,"* p. 320.

92. Emerson had written in an 1828 journal entry that "Christianity . . . takes off the film that had got on the human eye" (*JMN* 3: 101), an allusion to Book XI of Milton's *Paradise Lost* in which "Michael from Adams eyes the Filme remov'd" (line 412).

93. Leslie E. Eckel, "Margaret Fuller's Conversational Journalism: New York, London, Rome," *Arizona Quarterly* 63.2 (Summer 2007): 27–48 (32).

4. Variety and Limits

1. Shamoon Zamir, *Dark Voices: W. E. B. Du Bois and American Thought, 1888–1903* (Chicago: University of Chicago Press, 1995), p. 12.

2. For standard accounts of this transition, see John Higham, *Strangers in the Land: Patterns of Nativism, 1860–1925* (New York: Atheneum, 1968), Alan Trachtenberg, *The Incorporation of America: Culture and Society in the Gilded Age* (New York: Hill and Wang, 1982), and Martin J. Sklar, *The Corporate Reconstruction of American Capitalism, 1890–1916* (New York: Cambridge University Press, 1988).

3. "He becomes an American by being received in the broad lap of our great *alma* mater. Here individuals of all nations are melted into a new race of men" (J. Hector St John de Crèvecoeur, *Letters from an American Farmer* [Oxford: Oxford University Press, 1997], p. 44).

4. Theodore Roosevelt, "True Americanism," *The Works of Theodore Roosevelt*, National Edition, vol. 13 (New York: Charles Scribner's Sons, 1926), p. 21.

5. William James to Henry Bowditch, 25 May 1900. Quoted in Linda Simon, *Genuine Reality: A Life of William James* (New York: Harcourt Brace and Company, 1998), p. 303. See also William James, "Governor Roosevelt's Oration," in *Essays, Comments, and Reviews* (Cambridge, Mass.: Harvard University Press, 1987), pp. 162–66. The first chapter of Jonathan M. Hansen's *The Lost Promise of Patriotism: Debating American Identity, 1890–1920* (Chicago: University of Chicago Press, 2003) astutely contrasts William James and Roosevelt in the context of their respective responses to U.S. imperialism and the cosmopolitan impulse.

6. Roosevelt, "True Americanism," p. 20.

7. Henry James, *Literary Criticism: Essays on Literature, American Writers, English Writers* (New York: Library of America, 1984), p. 664.

8. For a discussion of the genesis and development of the trope, see Philip Gleason, "The Melting Pot: Symbol of Fusion or Confusion?" *American Quarterly* 16.1 (1964): 20–46.

9. Israel Zangwill, *The Melting Pot: A Drama in Four Acts* (1908) (London: William Heinemann, 1914), pp. 184–85.

10. Marcus Klein, *Foreigners: The Making of American Literature 1900–1940* (Chicago: University of Chicago Press, 1981), p. 4.

11. J. R. Pole, *The Pursuit of Equality in American History* (Berkeley: University of California Press, 1993), p. 287.

12. Nina Baym, "Early Histories of American Literature: A Chapter in the Institution of New England," *American Literary History* 1.3 (1989): 459–88 (460).

13. Arthur M. Schlesinger, Jr., *The Disuniting of America: Reflections on a Multicultural Society* (1991) (New York: Norton, 1992), p. 16. For a more recent diagnosis of this kind, see Samuel P. Huntingdon, *Who Are We? The Challenges to America's National Identity* (New York: Simon and Schuster, 2004).

14. Francis Fukuyama, "The End of History?" *The National Interest* 16 (1989): 3–18.

15. More confident is Peter Salins's later (and unashamedly more populist) book *Assimilation, American Style* (New York: Basic Books, 1997), which embraces the teleology of the melting pot narrative as the "miracle" that "contradicts the ethnic particularism that is assimilationism's great enemy" (pp. 4, 107). For a succinct account of the cultural politics of Schlesinger's book, see Michael Bérubé, "Disuniting America Again," *The Journal of the Midwest Modern Language Association* 26.1 (1993): 31–46.

16. William Harris has tracked the possible classical sources of the phrase and their adaptation in seventeenth- and eighteenth-century public discourse. See W. C. Harris, *E Pluribus Unum: Nineteenth-Century American Literature and the Constitutional Paradox* (Iowa City: University of Iowa Press, 2005), pp. 195–208.

17. Jay Grossman, *Reconstituting the American Renaissance: Emerson, Whitman, and the Politics of Representation* (Durham: Duke University Press, 2003), p. 28.

18. Emerson would recycle this notebook passage in the final paragraph of his chapter on Goethe in *Representative Men*.

19. Arnold Henry Guyot, *The Earth and Man: Lectures on Comparative Physical Geography in its Relation to the History of Mankind* (1849) (London: Richard Bentley, 1850), pp. 83–84. Emerson possessed a copy of an 1851 reprint of Guyot's book; and Thoreau quotes from *The Earth and Man* at length in his essay "Walking" (1862), first developed in lecture form in 1851.

20. See Günter Leypoldt, *Cultural Authority in the Age of Whitman: Transatlantic Perspectives* (Edinburgh: Edinburgh University Press, 2009).

21. Guyot, *The Earth and Man*, p. 206.

22. John Stahl Patterson, "American Destiny," *Continental Monthly: Devoted to Literature & National Policy* 3.1 (1863): 79–99 (85).

23. Walt Whitman, *Complete Poetry and Collected Prose* (New York: Library of America, 1982), p. 1011.

24. Judith Butler, *Bodies That Matter: On the Discursive Limits of Sex* (New York: Routledge, 1993), p. 116. In *Studies in Classic American Literature*, D. H. Lawrence had written of Whitman's self as a "mush" and "hotch-potch . . . The individuality had leaked out of him" (London: Penguin Books, 1977), p. 173. Ali Behdad writes that Whitman's "aestheticization of national ideologies of expansion and commercialism, and his disavowal of racial and geographical divisions, unveil how mid-nineteenth-century liberal discourse represented the (hi)story of the nation in monumentalising terms, in such a way as to posit a unified and inclusive imagined community" (*A Forgetful Nation: On Immigration and Cultural Identity in the United States* [Durham: Duke University Press, 2005], p. 94).

25. George Santayana, "The Poetry of Barbarism," *Interpretations of Poetry and Religion* (1900) (New York: Charles Scribner's Sons, 1916), p. 180.

26. James Madison, Alexander Hamilton, and John Jay, *The Federalist Papers* (London: Penguin Books, 1987), p. 319.

27. Carrie Tirado Bramen, *The Uses of Variety: Modern Americanism and the Quest for National Distinctiveness* (Cambridge, Mass.: Harvard University Press, 2000), p. 13.

28. Charles Eliot Norton, "American Political Ideas," *North American Review* 101 (October 1865): 550–66 (555). For a discussion of Norton's understanding of national identity in the context of this essay, see James Turner, *The Liberal Education of Charles Eliot Norton* (Baltimore: Johns Hopkins University Press, 1999), pp. 202–5.

29. Henry James, *The American Scene* (1907) (New York: Penguin Books, 1994), p. 92.

30. James E. Block, *A Nation of Agents: The American Path to a Modern Self and Society* (Cambridge, Mass.: Harvard University Press, 2002), p. 493.

31. Edwin H. Cady, ed., *William Dean Howells as Critic* (London: Routledge and Kegan Paul, 1973), p. 115.

32. Amy Kaplan, *The Social Construction of American Realism* (Chicago: University of Chicago Press, 1988), p. 21.

33. See T. J. Jackson Lears, *No Place of Grace: Antimodernism and the Transformation of American Culture, 1880–1920* (New York: Pantheon Books, 1981), ch. 1.

34. For an astute recent discussion of the limitations of Howells's aesthetic, see Daniel G. Williams, *Ethnicity and Cultural Authority: From Arnold to Du Bois* (Edinburgh: Edinburgh University Press, 2006), pp. 88–103.

35. Jacob Riis, *How the Other Half Lives: Studies Among the Tenements of New York* (Boston: Bedford/St. Martin's, 1996), p. 73.

36. James, *The American Scene*, pp. 50, 66.

37. Mary Esteve, *The Aesthetics and Politics of the Crowd in American Literature* (Cambridge: Cambridge University Press, 2003), p. 6.

38. Gustave Le Bon, *The Crowd*, tr. anon. (London: T. Fisher Unwin, 1896), p. 133. William James reviewed the New York edition of the book. While suggesting that it "ought to be read by everyone who is interested in the problems which popular government presents," he was unconvinced by the alarmist tone of Le Bon's analysis (*Essays, Comments, and Reviews*, p. 533). For more on James and his analysis of crowd psychology, see George Cotkin, *William James: Public Philosopher* (Baltimore: Johns Hopkins University Press, 1990), pp. 132–36.

39. Edward Ross, "The Mob Mind," *Popular Science Monthly* 51 (1897): 390–98 (398).

40. Whitman, *Complete Poetry and Collected Prose*, p. 943.

41. Charlene Haddock Seigfried, *William James's Radical Reconstruction of Philosophy* (Albany: State University of New York Press, 1990), p. 70.

42. Ralph Barton Perry, *The Thought and Character of William James*, 2 vols. (Boston: Little, Brown, 1935), vol. 2, p. 281. I am indebted to Amy Kittelstrom's essay "Against Elitism: Studying William James in the Academic Age of the Underdog," for this reference (*William James Studies* 1.1 [Summer 2006], http://williamjamesstudies.press.uiuc.edu/1.1/kittelstrom .html. Accessed October 19, 2009.

43. Frank Lentricchia, "The Return of William James," *Cultural Critique* 4 (Fall 1986), pp. 5–31 (6). Bramen notes that, with the recent revival of pragmatism within literary and theoretical studies, James is associated with "the image of the frontiersman who liberates the American intellect from totalizing theories and oppressive wholes" (30). Lentricchia's most radical critique of the turn to (European) models of post-structuralism is to be found in *Criticism and Social Change* (Chicago: University of Chicago Press, 1983).

44. Jonathan Levin, *The Poetics of Transition: Emerson, Pragmatism, and American Literary Modernism* (Durham: Duke University Press, 1999), p. 65. James Bense offers a thoughtful account of the Emerson-James relationship that disrupts Levin's pragmatist genealogy ("At Odds with "De-Transcendentalizing Emerson": The Case of William James," *New England Quarterly* 79.3 [2006]: 355–86).

45. David Kadlec, *Mosaic Modernism: Anarchism, Pragmatism, Culture* (Baltimore: Johns Hopkins University Press, 2000), pp. 22–34.

46. Louis Menand, *The Metaphysical Club* (New York: Farrar, Straus and Giroux, 2001), p. 75.

47. Judith Green, "Educational Multiculturalism, Critical Pluralism, and Deep Democracy," in Cynthia Willett, ed., *Theorizing Multiculturalism: A Guide to the Current Debate* (Oxford: Blackwell, 1998), p. 436.

48. The difficulty of resolving the tension between unity and multiplicity that, I argue, is similarly characteristic of James's philosophy, contrasts with Jürgen Habermas's belief in the communicative reality of mutual understanding that reconciles the claims of diversity within an organizing whole. See "The Unity of Reason in the Diversity of its Voices," *Postmetaphysical Thinking: Philosophical Essays* (Cambridge: Polity Press, 1992), pp. 115–48.

49. William Harris, in his otherwise excellent account of James and political philosophy, reads this passage from "On a Certain Blindness" as a critique of intellectual "loafing," where the disconnection from material practicality leads to "a static, uniform world" (*E Pluribus Unum*, p. 182). While, as I have suggested, Whitman's politics — and poetics — are prone to this kind of criticism, my sense is that the tone of James's lines here is celebratory and affirmative.

50. David Hume, *An Enquiry Concerning Human Understanding* (1748), ed. Tom L. Beauchamp (Oxford: Oxford University Press, 1999), p. 120.

51. Hume, *An Enquiry*, p. 121.

52. Renee Tursi, "William James's Narrative of Habit," *Style* 33.1 (1999): 67–87 (74). Tursi's essay provides a comprehensive account of James's ideas on "habit" and pays particular attention to his anticipation of Freud's famous analysis of "the *Unheimlich*."

53. Walter Pater, *Essays on Literature and Art* (London: J. M. Dent & Sons, 1990), p. 45.

54. George Santayana, "The Genteel Tradition in American Philosophy" (1911), *The Genteel Tradition: Nine Essays by George Santayana*, ed. Douglas L. Wilson (Cambridge, Mass.: Harvard University Press, 1967), p. 58.

55. Tursi, "William James's Narrative of Habit," p. 82.

56. Geoffrey Hill, "Alienated Majesty: Ralph W. Emerson," *Collected Critical Writings*, ed. Kenneth Haynes (Oxford: Oxford University Press, 2008), p. 498.

57. Michael Trask, *Cruising Modernism: Class and Sexuality in American Literature and Social Thought* (Ithaca: Cornell University Press, 2003), p. 55.

58. Trask, *Cruising Modernism*, p. 58.

59. Richard Rorty, *Consequences of Pragmatism: Essays 1972–1980* (Minneapolis: University of Minnesota Press, 1982), p. 165. For an excellent account of Rorty's response to James,

see David C. Lamberth, *William James and the Metaphysics of Experience* (Cambridge: Cambridge University Press, 1999).

60. Seyla Benhabib, *Situating the Self: Gender, Community and Postmodernism in Contemporary Ethics* (New York: Routledge, 1992), p. 153. See also Andrew G. Fiala's essay "Toleration and Pragmatism," which takes a similarly skeptical position against undiscriminating "heterophilia" (*The Journal of Speculative Philosophy* 16.2 [2002]: 103–16).

61. Amanda Anderson, *The Way We Argue Now: A Study in the Cultures of Theory* (Princeton: Princeton University Press, 2006), p. 30.

62. W. E. B. Du Bois, *Writings* (New York: Library of America, 1986), pp. 665–6.

63. Ross Posnock, *Color and Culture: Black Writers and the Making of the Modern Intellectual* (Cambridge, Mass.: Harvard University Press, 1998), p. 114.

64. Du Bois, *Writings*, p. 651.

65. See the third lecture of James's *A Pluralistic Universe*, "Hegel and his Method," for a detailed analysis of Hegel's literary style and philosophical premises.

66. William James, *The Correspondence of William James*, ed. Ignas K. Skrupskelis and Elizabeth M. Berkeley, vol. 8 (Charlottesville: University Press of Virginia, 2000), pp. 390–91.

67. E. L. Godkin, "Organization of Culture" (1868), quoted in Leslie Butler, *Critical Americans: Victorian Intellectuals and Transatlantic Liberal Reform* (Chapel Hill: University of North Carolina Press, 2007), p. 166.

68. Thomas L. Haskell, *The Emergence of Professional Social Science: The American Social Science Association and the Nineteenth-Century Crisis of Authority* (1977; rpt. Baltimore: Johns Hopkins University Press, 2000), p. 63. Haskell describes the late nineteenth century construction and regulation of professional institutions as "part of a broad movement to establish or re-establish authority in the face of profoundly disruptive changes in habits of causal attribution, in the criteria of plausibility, in the relation of the man of knowledge to his clientele" (65).

69. Thomas Bender, *Intellect and Public Life: Essays on the Social History of Academic Intellectuals in the United States* (Baltimore: Johns Hopkins University Press, 1993), p. 6.

70. Irving Babbitt, *Literature and the American College* (Boston: Houghton, Mifflin and Company, 1908), p. 97.

71. James, *American Scene*, p. 238.

72. Steven Biel, in *Independent Intellectuals in the United States, 1910–1945*, writes persuasively of the development of, and resistance to, the professionalization of the intellect within universities at the turn of the century. The book's reading of James, however, rather overplays his antagonism to educational structures in suggesting that James and his fellow rebels set out to "make clear to their students that the next generation of American thinkers would be better off creating a place for itself outside the universities" (New York: New York University Press, 1992), p. 22.

73. See also Susan Manning's analysis of the function of James's connectives as providing essential vehicles for thought in *Fragments of Union: Making Connections in Scottish and American Writing* (London: Palgrave, 2002), pp. 266–68.

74. Edward Bellamy, *Looking Backward, 2000–1887* (New York: Penguin Books, 1986), p. 111.

75. Madison, Hamilton, and Jay, *The Federalist Papers*, p. 126.

76. Cornel West, *The American Evasion of Philosophy: A Genealogy of Pragmatism* (Madison: University of Wisconsin Press, 1989), pp. 66, 147–48.

77. Menand, *The Metaphysical Club*, p. 379.

5. Aesthetics and Institutions

1. George Santayana, *The Letters of George Santayana: 1910–1920*, ed. William G. Holzberger (Cambridge, Mass.: The MIT Press, 2002), pp. 224–25. Kallen's essay had argued for the coherence of American nationhood through "the liberation and harmonious coöperation of nationalities" ("Nationality and the Hyphenated American," *The Menorah Journal* 1.2 [April 1915]: 79–86 [81]).

2. George Santayana, "A Brief History of My Opinions" (1930), in Richard Colton Lyon, ed., *Santayana on America: Essays, Notes, and Letters on American Life, Literature, and Philosophy* (New York: Harcourt, Brace, & World, Inc, 1968), p. 3.

3. George Santayana, "Apologia Pro Mente Sua," in *The Philosophy of George Santayana*, ed. Paul Arthur Schlipp (Chicago: Northwestern University Press, 1940), pp. 495–605 (602). The anthology mentioned here is Robert M. Crunden, *The Superfluous Men: Conservative Critics of American Culture 1900–1945* (Wilmington: ISI Books, 1999).

4. Ross Posnock, *The Trial of Curiosity: Henry James, William James, and the Challenge of Modernity* (New York: Oxford University Press, 1991), p. 194.

5. George Santayana, *The Last Puritan* (New York: Charles Scribner's Sons, 1936), p. 600; George Santayana, *Persons and Places* (Cambridge, Mass.: The MIT Press, 1986), p. 155.

6. Hannah Arendt, *Between Past and Future: Six Exercises in Political Thought* (Cleveland: World Publishing, 1963), p. 224. For Arendt, aesthetics properly understood and expressed worked to articulate a political vision of democracy in the face of totalitarian challenges to it.

7. Russ Castronovo, *Beautiful Democracy: Aesthetics and Anarchy in a Global Era* (Chicago: University of Chicago Press, 2007), p. 17.

8. Jacob Riis, "The Tenement House Blight," *Atlantic Monthly* 83 (June 1899): 760–71 (762, 769).

9. George Santayana, *The Sense of Beauty: Being the Outlines of Aesthetic Theory* (1896) (Cambridge, Mass.: The MIT Press, 1988), p. 63.

10. George Santayana, *The Letters of George Santayana: 1928–1932*, ed. William G. Holzberger (Cambridge, Mass.: The MIT Press, 2003), p. 85.

11. John Ruskin, *The Stones of Venice: Volume 2, The Sea-Stories* (London: Smith, Elder, and Co., 1853), pp. 159–60.

12. Castronovo, *Beautiful Democracy*, p. 91. Santayana's response to the French Revolution was not always so politically disinterested. By the time of his final book he had come to regard it as "not liberal except verbally and by accident," the regrettable outcome of "the

whole tender school of Rousseau": "[P]olitically the Revolution led to nationalism, industrialism, and absolute democracy, intellectually it ended in romantic egotism" (*Dominations and Powers* [New York: Charles Scribner's Sons, 1951], pp. 224–25).

13. Santayana, *The Sense of Beauty*, p. 72.

14. George Santayana, *The Life of Reason*, in *The Works of George Santayana*, Triton Edition, 15 vols. (New York: Charles Scribner's Sons, 1936–40), vol. 3, p. 15.

15. George Santayana, *The Life of Reason* (London: Constable and Co., 1954), p. 84.

16. Henry Samuel Levinson, "Santayana's Contribution to American Religious Philosophy," *Journal of the American Academy of Religion* 52.1 (1984): 47–69 (57).

17. George Santayana, *Soliloquies in England and Later Soliloquies* (London: Constable and Co., 1922), p. 263.

18. Quoted in Matthew Hale, Jr., *Human Science and Social Order: Hugo Münsterberg and the Origins of Applied Psychology* (Philadelphia: Temple University Press, 1980), p. 88.

19. Hugo Münsterberg, *The War and America* (New York: D. Appleton & Co., 1914), p. 190. In this, Münsterberg echoes William James's sense of conflict as culturally energising in "The Moral of Equivalent of War" (1906), without, of course, James's sense of equivalence as the necessary surrogate for warfare. Münsterberg's other key wartime publications include: "Fair Play," *Boston Herald*, 5 August 1914, p. 12; *The Peace and America* (New York: D. Appleton & Co., 1915); and "The Impeachment of German-Americans," *New York Times*, 19 September 1915, sec. 4, p. 2.

20. Santayana, *Life of Reason*, p. 85.

21. Santayana, *Egotism in German Philosophy*, p. 49.

22. Santayana, *Persons and Places*, p. 505.

23. Robert Dawidoff, *The Genteel Tradition and the Sacred Rage: High Culture vs. Democracy in Adams, James and Santayana* (Chapel Hill: University of North Carolina Press, 1992), p. 145.

24. Paul Giles, *Virtual Americas: Transnational Fictions and the Transatlantic National Imaginary* (Durham: Duke University Press, 2002), p. 3.

25. George Santayana, "The Genteel Tradition in American Philosophy," *Santayana on America: Essays, Notes, and Letters on American Life, Literature, and Philosophy*, ed. Richard Colton Lyon (New York: Harcourt, Brace & World, Inc., 1968), p. 39.

26. James Ballowe, ed., *George Santayana's America: Essays on Literature and Culture* (Urbana: University of Illinois Press, 1967), p. 76.

27. Henry Samuel Levinson, *Santayana, Pragmatism, and the Spiritual Life* (Chapel Hill: University of North Carolina Press, 1992), p. 50.

28. Ballowe, ed., *George Santayana's America*, p. 83.

29. Dawidoff, *The Genteel Tradition and the Sacred Rage*, p. 181.

30. Santayana, "The Genteel Tradition," p. 47.

31. In "The Poetry of Barbarism" Santayana had rehearsed this more skeptical view of Whitman, aligning him with Robert Browning as a poet of "miscellaneous vehemence": "This abundance of detail without organisation, this wealth of perception without intelligence and of imagination without taste, makes the singularity of Whitman's genius"

(*Interpretations of Poetry and Religion* [1900] [Cambridge: The MIT Press, 1989], pp. 104, 111). Shira Wolosky has argued that the commitment to aesthetic formalism in Santayana's own poetry works to enforce a mode of cool detachment in his thought. She writes: "The configuration which emerges in Santayana's essays, as in his poetic writing, opposes form to history, to time, and is detached from nature as a distinct, alternative world." I suggest instead that his understanding of form is always bound to a sense of variety that recognizes fundamental differences without losing the aspiration for a collectively understood experience of life ("Santayana and Harvard Formalism," *Raritan* 18.4 [Spring 1999]: 51–67 [63]).

32. Santayana, "The Genteel Tradition," p. 49.

33. Santayana, *Persons and Places*, p. 402.

34. Santayana had rehearsed this position in two poems, "Spain in America" (1898) and "Young Sammy's First Wild Oats" (1900). In the latter, the transition from imperial Spain to an imperial United States is imagined as a natural cycle of advance and decline: "[A]ll [Spain] had to teach / She taught the younger world—her faith and speech," an America that "Comes from the north, with other hopes and fears" (George Santayana, *Poems* [New York: Charles Scribner's Sons, 1923], pp. 127, 128).

35. Richard Rorty, "Professionalized Philosophy and Transcendentalist Culture," *Georgia Review* 30 (1976): 757–69 (757).

36. George Santayana, *Character and Opinion in the United States: With Reminiscences of William James and Josiah Royce and Academic Life in America* (1920) (New York: Charles Scribner's Sons, 1922), pp. v, vi.

37. Irving Singer, *George Santayana, Literary Philosopher* (New Haven: Yale University Press, 2000), p. 48.

38. Wallace Stevens, *Collected Poems* (London: Faber and Faber, 1984), pp. 510–11.

Coda

1. Lewis Mumford, *The Golden Day: A Study in American Experience and Culture* (New York: Boni and Liveright, 1926), p. 278.

2. Lewis Mumford, "Fruit: A Story" (1914), *Findings and Keepings: Analects for an Autobiography* (London: Secker & Warburg, 1976), pp. 12–15 (12–13).

3. Stanley Cavell, *In Quest of the Ordinary: Lines of Skepticism and Romanticism* (Chicago: University of Chicago Press, 1994), p. 28.

4. Stanley Cavell, *The Senses of Walden: An Expanded Edition* (San Francisco: North Point Press, 1981), pp. 141–42.

5. Richard Eldridge, "Cavell on American Philosophy and the Idea of America," in *Stanley Cavell*, ed. Richard Eldridge (Cambridge: Cambridge University Press, 2003), pp. 172–89 (180).

6. Cavell, *In Quest of the Ordinary*, p. 34.

7. Cavell quotes this in *Conditions Handsome and Unhandsome: The Constitution of Emersonian Perfectionism* (Chicago: University of Chicago Press, 1990), pp. 37–38.

8. Quoted in Cavell, *Conditions Handsome and Unhandsome*, p. 70.

9. Michael Fischer, "Stanley Cavell and Criticizing the University from Within," *Philosophy and Literature* 30 (2006): 471–83 (474).

10. Cavell, *Conditions Handsome and Unhandsome*, p. 31.

11. Stanley Cavell, *Philosophy the Day After Tomorrow* (Cambridge, Mass.: Harvard University Press, 2005), p. 204.

12. Cavell, *Conditions Handsome and Unhandsome*, p. 76.

13. John Michael, "Liberal Justice and Particular Identity: Cavell, Emerson, Rawls," *Arizona Quarterly* 64.1 (2008): 27–47 (32).

INDEX

Dall, Caroline, 13
Dallal, Jenine Abboushi, 56
Damrosch, David, 109, 110
Dana, Richard Henry, 90–91
Dartmouth College, 10
Davis, Paulina Wright, 21
Dawidoff, Robert, 172, 175
Declaration of Independence, 179–80
Deleuze, Gilles, 39; and Félix Guattari, 5, 193n8
Deming, Richard, 9
Derrida, Jacques, 23
Dial, 76, 91–94, 106, 205n7
Dickens, Charles, 50
Dimock, Wai Chee, 59–60, 105, 208n66
double consciousness, 11–12, 24–25, 28
Dreyfus Affair, 6, 26
Du Bois, W. E. B., 11, 12, 126, 149–50

E Pluribus Unum, 101, 117, 130, 132, 135, 143, 167, 201n24, 212n16
Eckel, Leslie, 124
Eckerman, Johann Peter, 105
egotism, 171
Eldridge, Richard, 187–88
Ellison, Julie, 95, 97, 122
Emerson, Charles, 24
Emerson, Edward, 24
Emerson, Ralph Waldo: and action, 19–20; appropriations of, 34–36; Cavell on, 187–88; and the *Dial*, 92–3; and double consciousness, 11–12, 24–25, 28; and eloquence, 59; and exceptionalism, 7, 12, 24, 152; and the fragment, 39; and Fuller, 114, 117, 125; on Goethe, 103–4; and individualism, 56; and intellectual transcendence, 10, 21, 195n5; and Ireland, 45, 199n69; on John Brown, 73; and linguistic self-consciousness, 23; and lyceum network, 32–34; and Mazzini, 117, 209n79; and melting pot, 130–31; Mumford on, 185–86; and national imaginary, 25; on newspapers, 89; on the poet, 152; as public intellectual, 7; and race, 46–48; Santayana on, 171, 173–74; on Thoreau, 84–87. *Works*: "The American Scholar," 7, 19–21; "The Anglo-American," 42; "Boston," 4; "Celebration of Intellect," 1–3; "Circles," 36; "Divinity School Address," 32, 189; "The Editors to the Readers," 93; *English Traits*, 11, 25, 41ff; "Fate," 11; "Fortune of the Republic," 52, 199n81; "Genius," 58; "Intellect," 10; "Lecture on

the Times," 20; "John Brown: Speech at Boston," 12–13; *Nature*, 22, 24, 114; "The Poet," 21; "Powers of Laws of Thought," 38; "The Progress of Culture," 90; "Quotation and Originality," 195n5; "Reforms," 200n15; "The Relation of Intellect to Natural Science," 38; *Representative Men*, 11, 21, 39, 40, 103; "The Scholar," 10, 12; "Self-Reliance," 10, 35, 39, 191; "Speech on Affairs in Kansas," 55; "Thoreau," 84–87; "The Transcendentalist," 20, 25
Emerson, William, 8
Emerson, William Sr., 9
Emersonianism, 12, 53
English, Karen, 107
Enlightenment, 72
Esteve, Mary, 138
exceptionalism, 14, 41, 111, 115, 131, 175, 181; and Emerson, 7, 12, 24; and Fuller, 120; German, 170; New England, 4–5;
exile, 28–29, and Santayana, 161

factionalism, political, 133–34
federalism, 135, 158
Field, Peter S., 7, 8, 10
Fischer, Michael, 189
Fisher, Philip, 36–38
fragment, literary, 39
Franklin, Benjamin, 9
Frothingham, Octavius Brooks, 103
Fugitive Slave Bill (1855), 46, 70
Fukuyama, Francis, 130
Fuller, Margaret, 6, 7, 13–14; and comparativism, 117, 120; and conversation, 97; and cosmopolitanism, 102; as *Dial* editor, 92; and dialogism, 121; and Emerson, 114, 125; and Goethe, 91, 104–6, 206n31; and knowledge, 98; at New York *Tribune*, 89, 116ff; on newspaper publishing, 90–1; and tourism, 116; and translation, 104, 106–7; and transnationalism, 100, 118, 120; and *Weltliteratur*, 108. *Works*: "American Literature, Its Position in the Present Time, and Prospects for the Future," 112, 114–15; autobiographical sketch, 107; "Bettine Brentano and her Friend Günderode," 106; *Conversations with Goethe*, 105–6; "Goethe," 206n34; "Menzel's View of Goethe," 104–5; New York *Tribune* dispatches, 117, 119, 120–25; review of Thomas Arnold, 102; "A Short Essay on Critics," 93, 94–97; *Summer on the Lakes, in 1843*,

107; "Thom's Poems," 101–2; *Woman in the Nineteenth Century*, 107, 122
Fuller, Timothy, 107

Gandhi, Mahatma, 60
Garrison, William Lloyd, 21, 73
Gemme, Paolo, 116
genius, 89
Germany, and Santayana, 170–71; and U.S. relations, 169–70
Giles, Paul, 4, 38, 172
globalization, 111–12
Godkin, E. L., 153
Godwin, Parke, 41
Goethe, Johann Wolfgang von, 91, 111, 170–71, 206n31; reputation in U.S., 103; and *Weltliteratur*, 108–9
Gramsci, Antonio, 71
Greeley, Horace, 89, 204n2
Green, Judith, 143
Grossman, Jay, 130, 132, 133
Guyot, Arnold Henry, 131

Habermas, Jürgen, 214n48
habit, 126, 145–47, 152
Hale, Matthew, 169
Harpers Ferry, 64, 65
Harris, William, 212n16, 214n49
Hartz, Louis, 37, 182
Harvard University, 19, 27, 78–79, 156, 194n27; and elective system, 16, 154–55
Haskell, Thomas, 153
Hawthorne, Nathaniel, 115
Headley, Joel Tyler, 77
Hegel, Georg Wilhelm Friedrich, 151, 170
heterogeneity, 138–39
Higginson, Thomas Wentworth, 33, 57–58
Hill, Geoffrey, 147
Hill, Napoleon, 35
Hillis Miller, J., 109–10, 113
Holmes, Oliver Wendell, 35
Horowitz, Helen Lefkowitz, 16
Horsman, Reginald, 43
Howells, William Dean, 14, 136, 213n34
Hume, David, 145–46
Hutchinson, Anne, 13
Hyde, Lewis, 64

individualism, 35, 36, 37, 56
intellectual: and action, 12, 19–20; and autonomy, 2, 67, 68; and Dreyfus Affair, 26; as elite, 90; and exile, 28–29; as expert,

5, 15; and foreignness, 6; institutional frameworks for, 2, 6, 27, 31, 67, 145, 153–55, 215n72; and the market, 14; as outsider, 3, 28; and professionalism, 89, 153; and transcendence, 69, 72–73, 144; and the university, 7, 215n72; and universalism, 29–30
Italian Revolution (1848–49), 6, 14, 91, 116ff; and U.S. response to, 116

Jackson, Stonewall, 86
Jackson Lears, T. J., 136
Jacoby, Russell, 89
James, Henry, 39, 128, 135, 137, 155–56, 161
James, Henry Sr., 12
James, William, 7, 12; and diversity, 137; and Dreyfus Affair, 26; and Du Bois, 150; on Emerson, 15–16; and habit, 126, 152; and Harvard, 15, 16, 27, 156; and heterogeneity, 138–39; on Hume, 145–46; as intellectual, 140–41, 155; and intellectual institutionalization, 27, 142, 148; on Le Bon, 213n38; and pluralism, 16, 127, 135, 136, 140, 156, 158; and pragmatism, 134, 176; and Roosevelt, 128, 211n5; Santayana on, 175, 176–80; on unity and multiplicity, 141–42; on Whitman, 144–45. *Works*: "Address at the Emerson Centenary in Concord," 15–16; *The Meaning of Truth*, 146; "The Moral Equivalence of War," 217n19; "On a Certain Blindness in Human Beings," 144; "The Ph.D. Octopus," 26–27; "Philosophical Conceptions and Practical Results," 152–53; *A Pluralistic Universe*, 135, 143, 147–48, 151, 158; *Pragmatism: A Series of Lectures*, 142; *Principles of Psychology*, 146–47; "The Social Value of the College Bred," 26; *Some Problems of Philosophy*, 141–42, 145–46; "The True Harvard," 27; *The Varieties of Religious Experience*, 138–40, 144–45
Jarrell, Randall, 3
Jay, John, 128
Jay, Paul, 22
Jefferson, Thomas, 36, 76
Jeffrey, Francis, 103
jeremiad, 70

Kaczynski, Theodore, 67, 201n28
Kadlec, David, 141, 157
Kallen, Horace, 159
Kansas–Nebraska Act (1854), 55
Kaplan, Amy, 136

160; and cosmopolitanism, 17, 160; and democracy, 17, 163–64, 166–67; and egotism, 171; on Emerson, 171, 173–74; and English character, 181; and Europe, 172; and exile, 161; and form, 162–63; and Germany, 170–71; and Harvard, 15, 16; and imperialism, 177–78; and intellectual authority, 166; and liberty, 182–83; and masculinity, 161; and Münsterberg, 170; and nationality, 159–60; on pragmatism, 176-7; on Spain, 178; and taste, 163; and timocracy, 168; and Whitman, 133, 164, 175, 217n31; on William James, 147, 175, 176–80. *Works: Dominations and Powers*, 216n12; *Egotism in German Philosophy*, 169, 170–72; "English Liberty in America," 180–82; "The Genteel Tradition in American Philosophy," 172–73, 175, 176–77, 188; *The Last Puritan*, 7; *The Life of Reason: Or Phases of Human Progress*, 165–66, 168; *My Host the World*, 17; "The Optimism of Ralph Waldo Emerson," 173–74; *Persons and Places*, 161; "The Poetry of Barbarism," 217n31; *Reason in Common Sense*, 171; *Reason in Society*, 166–67; *The Sense of Beauty*, 161–65; *Soliloquies in England and Later Soliloquies*, 168–69; "Spain in America," 218n34; "The Spirit and Ideals of Harvard University," 16, 17; "Young Sammy's First Wild Oats," 218n34

Schlesinger, Arthur, 129–30
Scott, Walter, 123
"Secret Six," 65, 77
Seigfried, Charlene Haddock, 140
Seyhan, Azade, 109
Shakespeare, William, 21
Shils, Edward, 30
Shumway, David, 37
Singer, Irving, 183
Snead, James, 97
Soriso, Carolyn, 46
Stadler, Gustavus, 89
Stearns, George, 77
Stein, Gertrude, 39
Stevens, Wallace, 184
Stowe, William, 123
Sturgis, Howard, 161
Sundquist, Eric, 70

Tamarkin, Elisa, 194n27
terrorism, 63–64, 66–67, 83; and textuality, 200n18

Thom, William, 101–2
Thoreau, Henry David, 7, 12–13, 58, 122; Arendt on, 202n34; Cavell on, 187; and small government, 202n29; and translation, 60–1; and transnationalism, 59. *Works*: "A Plea for Captain John Brown," 62ff; "Resistance to Civil Government," 62, 67, 70; "Slavery in Massachusetts," 70; *Walden*, 58, 61, 70, 85; "Walking," 212n19; *A Week on the Concord and Merrimack Rivers*, 62
timocracy, 168
Tönnies, Ferdinand, 100
Transcendentalism, and the *Dial*, 92; and John Brown, 62; New England, 4, 76, 117, 174
transatlanticism, 10, 38, 78, 110
translatio imperii, 131
translatio studii, 121
translation, 13, 58, 59, 60–61
transnationalism, 4, 7, 14, 38, 42, 59, 100, 111
Trask, Michael, 148
Traubel, Horace, 145
Tuchinsky, Adam-Max, 88
Tufts College, 1–3
Turner, Jack, 62, 69
Tursi, Renee, 146, 147

Unitarianism, 9, 88
universalism, 29–30
universities: and academic disciplines, 153–54; development of in U.S., 153

variety, 131, 134, 143
von Baer, Karl Ernst, 131
von Harnack, Adolf, 169

Ward, Samuel, 89
Warren, James Perrin, 59
Washington, George, 128
Watts, Edward, 41
Weber, Samuel, 60
Weltliteratur, 108–9
West, Cornel, 157
Whicher, Stephen, 85
Whitman, Walt, 17, 82, 111, 132, 138, 144–45, 164, 175, 212n24
Wilson, Eric, 107
Wilson, Rob, 21
Wittgenstein, Ludwig, 189–90
Wolosky, Shira, 217n31
Wordsworth, William, 43, 198n67
Worley, Sam, 72, 78, 80